THE
30
DAY
MBA
IN BUSINESS FINANCE

For many of the topics in the book there are direct links to the **free** teaching resources of the world's best business schools.

There are also links to hundreds of hours of **free** video lectures given by other distinguished Business School professors, from top schools including Cranfield, Wharton, Chicago, Harvard and CEIBS (China Europe International Business School).

From the Yale University School of Management (https://som.yale.edu/about/news/podcasts) you can access podcasts on such topics as the State of Private Equity, Banking, Early Stage Investing and How to Write a Business Plan.

You can download Duke University's top ranking Fuqua School of Business's lecture material on forecasting; a vital aid to anyone preparing financial projections.

Link into Cranfield's School of Management's Research Paper Series and see the latest insights in global supply chain logistics, or watch Harvard's Professor Michael Porter – a leading world proponent of international business strategy methodology – outline his ideas.

You can find a list of all these online resources and more interspersed within the chapters. Visit www.koganpage.com/product/the-30-day-mba-9781398609877.

THE 30 DAY MBA

IN BUSINESS FINANCE

3rd Edition

Your fast track guide to business success

Colin Barrow

KoganPage

Publisher's note

Every possible effort has been made to ensure that the information contained in this book is accurate at the time of going to press, and the publishers and authors cannot accept responsibility for any errors or omissions, however caused. No responsibility for loss or damage occasioned to any person acting, or refraining from action, as a result of the material in this publication can be accepted by the editor, the publisher or the author.

First published in Great Britain and the United States in 2011 by Kogan Page Limited
Second edition 2016
Third edition 2023

Apart from any fair dealing for the purposes of research or private study, or criticism or review, as permitted under the Copyright, Designs and Patents Act 1988, this publication may only be reproduced, stored or transmitted, in any form or by any means, with the prior permission in writing of the publishers, or in the case of reprographic reproduction in accordance with the terms and licences issued by the CLA. Enquiries concerning reproduction outside these terms should be sent to the publishers at the undermentioned addresses:

2nd Floor, 45 Gee Street	8 W 38th Street, Suite 902	4737/23 Ansari Road
London	New York, NY 10018	Daryaganj
EC1V 3RS	USA	New Delhi 110002
United Kingdom		India
www.koganpage.com		

© Colin Barrow 2011, 2016, 2023

The right of Colin Barrow to be identified as the author of this work has been asserted by him in accordance with the Copyright, Designs and Patents Act 1988.

ISBNs
Hardback   9781398610941
Paperback   9781398610927
Ebook   9781398610934

British Library Cataloguing-in-Publication Data

A CIP record for this book is available from the British Library.

Library of Congress Control Number

2023934510

Typeset by Hong Kong FIVE Workshop, Hong Kong
Print production managed by Jellyfish
Printed and bound by CPI Group (UK) Ltd, Croydon CR0 4YY
Kogan Page books are printed on paper from sustainable forests.

CONTENTS

LIST OF FIGURES

LIST OF TABLES

Introduction

- What businesses value Finance MBAs
- Why you need MBA knowledge
- Planning your 30 day learning programme
- Getting to see the world's best professors in action

The companies below have a number of interesting things in common. Although they straddle a disparate range of industries – retail, technology, banking, healthcare and food, you almost certainly know something about all of them, and a lot about some. You probably know McDonald's 'I'm Lovin' It', their slogan since 2003, if for no other reason than you have paid an occasional visit to one of their 34,000 outlets in 118 countries worldwide. The reason these businesses are near universally recognized is in no small part down to their financial prowess. Apple, for example, made $120.47 billion earnings in a single year.

Alphabet (Google)	Marathon Petroleum
Amazon	McDonald's
Apple	Meta (Facebook)
Berkshire Hathaway	Microsoft
Credit Suisse	Nike
ExxonMobil	PepsiCo
General Motors	Procter and Gamble
Goldman Sachs	Visa
IBM	Walmart
Johnson and Johnson	Wells Fargo
JP Morgan Chase	

What you may also suspect is that these businesses are enormously profitable. All these companies are amongst the most profitable in the world (https://companiesmarketcap.com/most-profitable-companies). They are listed in the Kantar BrandZ Top 100 Most Valuable Global Brands (www.kantar.com/campaigns/brandz/global/), which rose 23 per cent for 2022, to reach a total value of nearly $8.7 trillion. This represents the second-greatest annual rise in BrandZ history. What's striking, however, is that the same cannot be said of the global economy as a whole. In April, the International

Monetary Fund revised its projections for 2022 global GDP growth downward to 3.6 per cent.

What may be less well known is that these companies are major MBA recruiters. Amazon and Google, for example, recruit from over 25 business schools each year. Apple, Credit Suisse, Johnson and Johnson, Meta, PepsiCo, Procter and Gamble, and Walmart do the rounds of over a dozen business schools to top up their management talent. According to Sydney Lake, a journalist for Fortune Magazine (17 May 2022), between 2018 and 2020, 426 MBA graduates were hired by Google and 139 by Alphabet. That's on top of the few hundred they already had on their payrolls. Over 100 of the Fortune 500 companies have an MBA for their CEO. Walmart, ExxonMobil, General Motors, JPMorgan Chase, Marathon Petroleum and even Apple, whose founder Steve Jobs famously flunked college, have an MBA at the helm. Tim Cook, Apple's CEO, took his MBA at Duke University's Fuqua School of Business, ranked 5th in the world for its marketing teaching and research. Tracy Britt Cool took her MBA at Harvard before joining Berkshire Hathaway. She chaired four companies under the Berkshire Hathaway umbrella before leaving in 2020 to co-found Kanbrick, a private equity firm – more about private equity and its important role in later chapters.

A brief history of business schools

The claim to being the world's first business school is, like everything else in business, hotly disputed. The honour is usually said to rest with Ecole Spéciale de Commerce et d'Industrie (now ESCP Europe), established in Paris in December 1819, with Jean-Baptiste Say, who coined the word 'entrepreneur', as its first professor of economics. Wharton led the field in the US, founded in 1881 by Joseph Wharton, a self-taught businessman. A miner, he made his fortune through the American Nickel Company and the Bethlehem Steel Corporation, later to become the subject of the earliest business case studies. The school is based in an urban campus at Philadelphia's University of Pennsylvania.

It wasn't until 1900 that Tuck School of Business, part of Dartmouth College, began conferring advanced degrees in management sciences. In 1908 Harvard Business School opened, with a faculty of 15 and some 80 students, and two years later it was offering a Management Masters programme. By 1922 Harvard was running a doctoral programme pioneering research into business methods.

The UK was late into the business school game. The Administrative Staff College at Henley (now Henley Business School), established in 1945 as the civilian equivalent of the Military Staff Colleges, was a business school in all but name. It took a further decade or so before the long-held belief of politicians and business leaders that management was an inherited ability, a view reinforced by the heavy concentration of family run businesses, diminished. Business schools at Manchester (1965), London (1966) and Cranfield (1968) led a field, now swollen substantially.

So should you go to business school?

The best business schools are very good, but in truth that description only applies to a hundred or so schools around the globe. Whether you should pay or forgo salary to a total sum north of £100,000, for a programme that is 75 per cent certain not to be excellent, seems like an easy question. You've already more or less answered that question by reaching page 3 of this book!

One GMAC study listed the top three prospective MBA students' personal and career goals as typically as to:

- remain marketable (competitive);
- develop management knowledge and technical skills;
- improve long-term income and financial stability.

You certainly don't need to spend a fortune in time or money to achieve these goals, a fact tacitly recognized by the London School of Economics and Political Science, a prestigious establishment if ever there was one. Their MBA Essentials Online Certificate Course aims to help you build a toolkit of key strategic, managerial, and leadership skills. It is a ten-week, ten-module online course that when completed leads to a certificate. It looks to be a valuable programme, but it cost £3,250 in 2022 (www.getsmarter.com/products/lse-mba-essentials-online-certificate-course).

There is no aspect of business school teaching and virtually no world-class professor that you can't listen to for free to complement the content of this book. But you do need willpower! If and when you decide that business school is right for you, this book will be a sound preparation for the programme and help you choose the right school. It will also be a worthwhile resource when you start revising for exams.

Using this book

If you decide, as do most students of business, that attending a business school is not the best way for you to acquire an MBA skill set, or perhaps it is not right for you now for reasons of cost, time or convenience, then you can fall back on your own resources. Remember that for every manager or executive with an MBA there are over 200 with no formal business qualification and often with absolutely no knowledge save that acquired in their single personal discipline.

In the following chapters you will get a flavour of how all the top business schools teach, in the areas in which they excel. Download their teaching notes, read up on their latest research and see their faculty teach: a better strategy than just attending one business school – however great.

The schools whose teaching and research I have drawn on for this book are mostly 'triple-accredited' business schools, those that have accreditations from each of the main international accreditation agencies: Association to Advance Collegiate Schools of Business (AACSB), Association of MBAs (AMBA) and European Quality Improvement System (EQUIS). As of September 2022 only 110 business schools were so rated, and in this book you will find material from nearly a quarter of those (see list below). They are all in the top ranks in the world. In the list below, I have put the businesses schools rated in the top ten in the world for *finance* first; however, the rest are no slouches. Cranfield, for example, is ranked 8th in the UK and 44th in the world in the Financial Times Masters in Finance ranking 2022.

Wharton – 1st
Harvard – 2nd
Columbia – 3rd
Chicago (Booth) – 4th
NYU Stern School of
    Business – 5th
London Business
    School – 6th
Cornell (Johnson) –
    7th
INSEAD – 8th
Virginia Darden – 9th
Stanford – 10th
Duke University
    (Fuqua)
University of Texas –
    Austin (McCombs)

Cranfield
Dartmouth College
    (Tuck)
Durham University
HASS (Berkley)
IE Madrid
IESE Business School
IMD
Indiana University
    (Kelley)
London School of
    Economics
Massachusetts
    Institute of
    Technology (MIT)
Northwestern
    University (Kellogg)

Said Business School,
    Oxford
SDA Bocconi
The Open University
University of
    California at
    Berkeley (Hass)
University of Chicago
    (Booth)
University of Michigan
    – Ann Arbor (Ross)
University of Texas –
    Austin (McCombs)
Warwick Business
    School
Yale

Case studies are absolutely at the heart of business school teaching, the point at which theory and practice often collide. I have drawn on the experiences of over sixty of the most interesting businesses to illustrate and emphasize the learning topics.

The MBA in Business Finance, the subject of this book, goes under various titles. Initially the subject started out as a specialization within the general MBA. Edinburgh runs an MBA with a 'Specialism in Finance', as does Wharton, which was first with a specialist finance Master's programme in 1881. The University of Chicago Booth School of Business runs a finance programme with a strong focus on understanding the behaviour of securities, drawn from its Center for Research in Security Prices – the leading provider of historical stock market data. At the LBS its pre-eminent programme is its Master's in Finance, and Cranfield, MIT (Massachusetts

Institute of Technology) and Stanford use that title also. However, at Liverpool and Northeastern Universities, as with many others, the subject goes by the title 'MBA in Finance'. Even the MBAs in the financial arena are being subjected to further specialization. Bangor Business School in North Wales offers an MBA in Islamic Banking and Finance.

What is the content of an MBA in Financial Management and what use will that be to me?

Anyone who wants to play a more rounded role in shaping and implementing the direction of the organization he or she works in but is inhibited by his or her lack of financial and accounting knowledge will find that reading this book will equip him or her to take part in the strategic decision making on an equal footing with MBA graduates, while feeling at ease in the process. It places MBA finance and accounting skills within reach of all professionals in large and small organizations in both the public and private sectors, providing them with a competitive edge over less knowledgeable colleagues.

Business finance comprises a number of disciplinary areas, each with a number of components. The disciplines contain the tools with which you can effectively analyse a business's financial situation, drawing on both internal information relevant to the business and external information on its markets, competitors and general business environment as a prelude to deciding what to do.

The emphasis in this book is on the terms 'concepts' and 'tools'. The business world is full of conflicting theories and ideas on how organizations could or should work, or how they could be made to work better. They come in and out of fashion, get embellished or replaced over time. A good analogy would be the difference between the limited number of tools a carpenter, for example, has in his or her toolbox, and the infinite number of products that could be made from those same tools. The ultimate success of the product the carpenter makes is partly down to his or her skills in using those tools and partly down to the world he or she is operating in at a particular time. A glance in a carpenter's toolbox will reveal an enduring range of common robust implements – screwdrivers, pliers, spanners, smoothing planes, saws and hammers.

In business, for example, there is no such thing as an optimal capital structure, or the right number of new products to bring to market, or whether or not going for an acquisition is a winning strategy. What's best in terms of, say, a debt to equity ratio varies with the type of organization and the prevailing conditions in the money market. That ratio will be different for the same organization at different times and when it is pursuing different strategies. Layering an inherently risky marketing strategy, say diversifying, with a risky financing strategy, using borrowed rather than shareholders' money, creates a potentially more risky situation than any one of those actions in isolation. But whichever of the choices a business makes, the tools used to assess financial and marketing strengths and weaknesses are much the same. It is the concepts and tools to be used in those disciplines that this book explains, and it shows you how to use both individually to comprehensively assess a business situation.

The MBA Business Finance core disciplines

There are a small number of core subject areas that comprise the subject matter of an MBA Business Finance programme. Many business schools eschew some vital elements within these disciplines as they are considered either too practical, un-sexy from a research/career prospective or more skill- or art-oriented than academic. So, for example, some schools assume a high degree of basic accounting knowledge as a prerequisite or simply provide an online learning resource to cover the subject. In some cases there may well be unique content in specialized electives, say on Financial Analysis of Mergers, Acquisitions and Other Complex Corporate Restructurings as taught at the London Business School, or Dealing with Financial Crime on offer at Cass Business School. At Wharton, the top school for Finance, Professor David Wessels 'examines how the world's most valuable companies have created value, and how they have protected their competitive position', whilst the other 80 or so members of the Finance Department's faculty hone in on other special areas of interest. Incidentally, some business schools don't run to that number of professors in total, which goes some way to explaining Wharton's pre-eminence.

The main uses of MBA Business Finance knowledge

Specialist business finance knowledge as covered in this book or in a business school equips the student with a thorough understanding of financial theory and practice and helps him or her master the skills needed to use accounting and finance tools essential to interpreting and influencing financial performance. With these skills you can:

- Gain the financial analysis and strategic perspective you need to interact effectively with top management as a partner in making key business decisions.
- Play a full role in financial planning and control, financial analyses, foreign exchange risk management and capital budgeting.
- Take part effectively in acquisition strategies – buying, selling and joint ventures.

- Understand how businesses are financed and the criteria used by financial institutions when making funding decisions, and play a role in helping a business raise funds.
- Prepare business plans and financial projections.
- Understand how equity markets operate and how businesses can use such markets effectively.

MBA Business Finance knowledge can also open up opportunities for career development and change in a wide variety of areas including business analyst, mergers and acquisitions, investment, banking, trading, investment management, hedge funds, security analysis, institutional sales, security brokerage, capital markets, risk management, the finance function for companies or non-profits as well as regulatory and trade bodies, and investor relations. Even quite dramatic career changes may be possible once you have a sound grasp of this subject area. The LBS quotes the case of a part-time student on its programme who within the three years made the transition from broadcast financial journalism to boutique investment management in the emerging markets fixed income field.

Tracy Britt Cool took her MBA at Harvard, and in a short time moved to chairing four companies under the Berkshire Hathaway umbrella then to co-founding Kanbrick, a private equity firm, in 2020.

How this book is organized and how to use It

Each of the chapters in the book covers the essential elements of each of the core disciplines in a top MBA Business Finance programme. For many of the topics there are web addresses for *free* teaching resources from the world's best business schools. There are also web addresses for hundreds of hours of *free* video lectures given by distinguished business school professors from top schools including LBS, Imperial, Oxford and Aston. You will find the address to download Duke University's top-ranking Fuqua School of Business's lecture material on forecasting, and the link for Cranfield School of Management's Research Paper Series, where you can see the latest insights into business finance.

Depending on your knowledge of basic finance you should plan to spend about two days on each chapter. You should draw up a timetable spread over, say, 12, 24 or 36 weeks. You will need to build in a couple of days for revision before you take your final exams. Some sample exam papers are available online at www.koganpage.com/30DayMBA.

The subject areas within each chapter correspond to what you would find in the syllabus at major business schools in terms of theoretical underpinning and the practical application of that theory that you would pick up from fellow students.

Additional learning resources

At the end of each chapter are two lists of additional resources which, if used, will extend and cement your learning.

Online video courses and lectures

These include topical and relevant classroom or lecture theatre presentations and discussions. With a few exceptions these are free and delivered by faculty members of leading business schools. Some of those from business schools are by way of an entire course of anything up to 20 or so lectures. These can comprise everything you would receive had you attended the class in person, teaching notes, handouts and discussion forums using the latest in peer-to-peer social learning tools. Most of the lectures are available all the time, but some of the full courses run periodically, up to four times a year. Some courses will enable you to earn a Certificate of Achievement, or you can just audit the course. Delivery is usually via a virtual 'classroom' open 24/7 where everyone is accepted.

The online courses are often delivered by one of the main MOOCs (massive open online courses) platforms. These courses are free for everyone, although some courses have a fee for verified certificates but are free to audit. The primary MOOC platforms are:

- **Coursera** (www.coursera.org) Founded at Stanford in 2012, their mission is to 'provide universal access to the world's best education'. They are 'an education platform that partners with top universities and organizations worldwide, to offer courses online for anyone to take, for free'. There are over a hundred universities offering lecture courses including Stanford, IE Business School, Yale, Princeton, Northwestern, Rutgers, Duke, Copenhagen, Tokyo, HEC Paris, Columbia and LMU Munich.

- **EdX** (www.edx.org) Founded by the Massachusetts Institute of Technology and Harvard University in May 2012. Over 400 courses are on offer from universities including: MIT, Harvard, Berkeley, Caltech, Georgetown, the Sorbonne, Peking, IIT Bombay, Rice, Kyoto, Columbia, Australian National and Cornell. EdX's goal is to 'offer the highest quality courses from institutions who share our commitment to excellence in teaching and learning'.

- **MERLOT** (www.merlot.org) Multimedia Educational Resource for Learning and Online Teaching (MERLOT) began in 1997 at the California State University Center for Distributed Learning. Their 4,500 members have posted close on 100,000 free online learning resources.

You can either search within these individual MOOCs or cut to the chase and visit Class Central (www.classcentral.com). They aggregate courses from over 1,000 universities, 50 providers and 600 other institutions to help you find the best free courses on almost any subject, wherever they exist.

Online case studies

The list of case studies at the end of each chapter is an eclectic mixture of business school based presentations, often by entrepreneurs and senior managers of business and other organizations. Others are critiques made by journalists on TV, or by student analysis of business behaviour and performance. The case studies complement those in the text.

Elective chapters

Three elective chapters are also available online at www.koganpage.com/30MBA:

- Business communications, which is on offer at IE Madrid and is a subject extensively researched at Harvard.
- Business planning at Wharton, where one of the world's most famous business planning competitions has been run since 1998.
- Business gurus, which introduces my 'top ten' of key management thinkers that every MBA needs a good working knowledge of, as their theories are regularly deployed in business analysis and decision making.

Tests

There are a number of short tests in the online resources at www.koganpage.com/30MBA where you can check your progress and identify any areas that merit revisiting.

PART ONE
The fundamentals of business finance

Financial statements are like the tip of an iceberg: underneath the visible part are a lot of record-keeping, accounting methods and reporting decisions. The managers of a business, the investors in a business and the lenders to a business need a firm grasp on these accounting reports so they will know how to recognize both the good and bad signals.

Accountants prepare three primary financial statements. The *profit and loss account* (*income statement* in the United States) reports the profit-making activities of the business and how much profit or loss the business made. The *balance sheet* reports the financial situation and position of the business in terms of its assets and liabilities at a point in time and usually the last day of the profit period. The *cash flow statement* reports how much cash was actually realized from profit and other sources of cash, and what the business did with this money. In short, the financial life of a business and its prospects for success or danger of failing are all revealed in its financial statements.

The way in which accounting information is recorded and reported is regulated by statutory bodies and the accounting profession. Auditors, amongst other responsibilities, have a duty to ensure these rules are followed and the accounts represent a *true and fair* picture of the enterprise for the period under consideration. The way in which accounting information is analysed involves the use of a standard range of business tools and ratios that can be applied across all types of venture, so providing some common yardstick.

The final section of this part is concerned with the specific ways in which accounting information can help managers add value to the business by, amongst other things, ensuring profitability is achieved quickly and that all investments are at least planned so as to improve the venture's profitability.

01
Financial business reports

- The bookkeeping process
- Cash flow forecasts and statements
- Calculating profit
- Balancing the books

Accounting is the process of recording and analysing transactions that involve events that can be assigned a monetary value. By definition financial information can only be a partial picture of the performance of an enterprise. People, arguably a business's most valuable asset, don't appear anywhere in the accounts, except for football clubs and the like where people are the subject of a transaction.

Although accounting has become more complex, involving ever more regulations, and has moved from visible records written in books to key strokes in a software program, the purpose is the same; to establish:

- what a business owns by way of assets;
- what a business owes by way of liabilities;
- the profitability, or otherwise, at certain time intervals, and how that profit was achieved.

An MBA in Finance is unlikely to be required to perform the recording side of the accounting process, except in the very smallest of organizations, or if the venture is his or her own. But it is only by knowing how accounts are prepared and the rules governing the categorizing of assets and liabilities (more on this in Chapter 2) that they can gain a good understanding of what the figures really mean. For example, it is not obvious to the uninitiated that a company's shares are classed as a liability and it is extremely unlikely that the assets as recorded will realize anything like the figures shown in the accounts, audited or not. Bear Stearns, an 85-year-old investment bank, was sold for \$2 (£1.25/€1.50) a share to J P Morgan Chase in 2008, roughly a total of \$236 (£151/€177) million for a business that was worth \$20 (£12.5/€15) billion only a few weeks previously. This provides a vivid insight into the gap between reported and realizable figures in the accounting world. Nevertheless, accounting reports do provide a valuable insight into business performance and in any event are a basic requirement for shareholders and regulators alike.

Who uses financial information and why

The aim of all accounting information is to provide the particular user with relevant and timely data to make decisions. Who are these users of accounting information and what decisions do they need to take? Possible users are an extensive group, who require the information to be impartial, accurate and timely. They include:

- *Shareholders* of limited companies will be influenced in their decision to remain investors or to increase/decrease their holding by receiving information about the financial performance and financial position of the company. This usually occurs twice a year in the form of a profit and loss account and a balance sheet relating to the first half-year and, later on, the full year.

- *Owner-managers* of non-incorporated businesses will require the above information but they will also be privy to more detailed and more frequent information about the business's financial affairs.

- *Management* in companies range from director level down to supervisor level. Each person requires accounting information to help him or her in his or her role. Supervisors may be concerned with operating costs for a very small part of the undertaking. Directors need to control the overall performance of the company and make strategic financing and investment decisions. Middle managers need feedback on whether they are meeting their financial targets.

- *Suppliers* need to assess the creditworthiness of potential and existing customers when setting the amount and period of credit allowed. This will partly, if not mainly, be based on the financial history of each customer, so the supplier's accountants will assess the latest profit and loss account and balance sheet. Other data on payment history may be obtained from credit agencies, for example, Dun & Bradstreet, to assist in this decision. Suppliers have been particularly vigilant since Covid-19 and the Russo/Ukraine war disrupted global supply chains.

- *Customers* also need to be reassured, in this case to minimize the risk of their supplies drying up and disrupting their own output. Firms entering into a joint venture will also need mutual reassurance. Similar checks to those outlined above for suppliers will need to be carried out.

- *Employees* and their representatives have a vested interest in the financial health and future prospects of their employer. They rely on an assessment of the published accounts by experts for this.

- *Government* levies tax on the profits earned by businesses and Value Added Tax (or sales tax) on the sales value of most industries. Tax authorities rely on the information provided by companies for these purposes.

- *Competitors* can make some comparisons, for example, sales, profit or asset utilization per employee, from published accounting data in a process known as 'benchmarking'. This may provide clues to areas where performance may be improved particularly if explanations of differences in operating systems can be obtained.

- *Lenders* need to be confident that their capital is safe and that the borrowing company can service the loan or overdraft adequately, so again the financial statements of profit and loss account and balance sheet will be examined from this viewpoint.

- *Partners* need to keep track of business performance in much the same way as shareholders and to ensure appropriate and fair treatment by their fellow partners.

- *Special interest groups* ranging from Friends of the Earth, Sierra Club (environment), National Right to Life (anti-abortion), Common Cause (campaign finance reform) and PETA (ethical treatment of animals), track the accounts of companies operating in their sectors to monitor and comment on their behaviour, usually adversely.

Accounting branches

Different users of accounting information will require different information and use it for different purposes. Accounting can be broken down into three main branches, with some overlap between, particularly in smaller enterprises where in effect all three areas will be the responsibility of a single person or department:

1 financial accounting;
2 management accounting; and
3 financial management.

1. *Financial accounting* is concerned with preparing financial statements summarizing past events, usually in the form of profit and loss accounts and balance sheets. These historic statements are mainly of interest to outside parties such as investors, loan providers and suppliers.

2. *Management accounting* involves assembling much more detailed information about current and future planned events to allow managers to

carry out their roles of planning, control and decision making. Examples of management accounting information are product costs and cost data relevant to a particular decision, say, a choice between make or buy. Also included in management accounting are preparing and monitoring budgeted costs relating to a product, activity or service. Management accounting information is rarely disclosed to outside parties, though bankers and private equity providers often ask for monthly management accounts as a condition of funding.

3. *Financial management* covers all matters concerning raising finance and ensuring it is used in the most efficient way. For example, it would be financially inefficient to raise a long-term loan or sell shares just to finance a short-term increase in sales. It would be the role of financial management to select and use a more cost-effective funding source such as an overdraft. The cost of capital is influenced by both the capital structure adopted and the riskiness of the investments undertaken.

Within these three broad areas of accounting there may be further subsets of accounting relating either to one specific activity, or across the whole spectrum. Examples of these are:

1 treasury;

2 taxation;

3 audit; and

4 forensic.

1. *Treasury* is a finance function usually only found in a very large company or group of companies. For example, managing bank balances to get the maximum interest on positive balances or minimize the payment of interest on negative balances would be a typical treasury task. This might involve lending money overnight on the money markets. Treasury activity would also be concerned with managing exchange risk where financial transactions in foreign currencies are involved.

2. *Taxation* in a small company will be included in the duties of the financial accountant who may need to call on outside professional advice from time to time. Corporation tax on company profits is not straightforward and the system of capital allowances can be complex for some large companies, groups of companies, or multinational companies. The ramifications of VAT or sales tax where it applies, employee tax and other related deductions such as National Insurance and director benefits in kind, often call for the services of a specialist accountant, or team of accountants. Large companies usually use the services of such firms to minimize the pain and maximize the gain from such taxes and allowances.

3. *Audit* is another accounting function mainly found in larger organizations. Internal auditors monitor that accounting procedures, documents and computerized transactions are carried out correctly. This work is additional or complementary to that undertaken by external auditors who take a

broader approach in providing an independent report to shareholders in the annual report.

4. *Forensic* accounting is exclusively working from the outside and looking in. Forensic accountants are described on the ACA website as 'the detectives of the finance world and help investigate fraud and other financial misrepresentation.' Their work is to aid lawyers, insurance companies and their clients to resolve disputes. They have to look beyond the bare numbers and analyse, interpret and summarize complex business and financial issues. Equally important is being able to communicate clearly and succinctly under pressure in a court of law.

Bookkeeping – the way transactions are recorded

The business world, except for the very smallest of one-man-bands, has moved away from single-entry bookkeeping. Even the elegance of the double-entry variety of bookkeeping with its assorted ledgers has been supplanted by the myriad checks and balances inherent in the software programs that now underpin much of the world's accounting records. Nevertheless, an MBA is expected to have some insight into how we arrived at the system of recording financial data used today.

Single-entry bookkeeping

Sometime before 3,000 BC the people of Uruk and other sister-cities of Mesopotamia began to use pictographic tablets of clay to record economic transactions. The script for the tablets evolved from symbols and provides evidence of an ancient financial system that was growing to accommodate the needs of the Uruk economy. The Mesopotamian equivalent of today's bookkeeper was the scribe. His duties were similar, but even more extensive. In addition to writing up the transaction, he ensured that the agreements complied with the detailed code requirements for commercial transactions. Temples, palaces and private firms employed hundreds of scribes, and much as with the accounting profession today it was considered a prestigious profession. In a typical transaction of the time, the parties might seek out the scribe at the gates to the city. They would describe their agreement to the scribe, who would take from his supply a small quantity of specially prepared clay on which to record the transaction.

Governmental bookkeeping in ancient Egypt developed in a fashion similar to the Mesopotamians. The use of papyrus rather than clay tablets allowed more detailed records to be made more easily. Extensive records were kept, particularly for the network of royal storehouses within which the 'in kind' tax payments such as sheep or cattle were kept, as coinage had not yet been developed. Egyptian bookkeepers associated with each storehouse kept meticulous records, which were checked by an elaborate internal verification system. These early accountants had good reason to be honest and accurate because irregularities disclosed by royal audits were punishable by fine, mutilation or death. Although such records were important, ancient Egyptian accounting never progressed beyond simple list-making in its thousands of years of existence. The almost 1 million accounting records in tablet form survive in museum collections around the world.

China, during the Chou Dynasty (1122–221 BC), used bookkeeping chiefly as a means of evaluating the efficiency of governmental programmes and the civil servants who administered them. A level of sophistication was achieved that was not surpassed in China until after the introduction of the double-entry system a thousand years later.

Accounts in ancient Rome evolved from records traditionally kept by the heads of families, where daily entry of household receipts and payments were kept in an *adversaria* or daybook, and monthly postings were made to a cashbook known as a *codex accepti et expensi*.

Up to medieval times this single-entry system of bookkeeping, divided into two general parts, Income and Outgo, with a statement at the end showing the balance due to the lord of the manor, prevailed in England, as elsewhere. Although these accounts were fairly basic they were sufficient to handle the needs of the very simple business structures that prevailed. Businessmen operated for the most part on their own account, or in single venture partnerships that dissolved at the end of a relatively short period of time. This, incidentally, was still the essence of the structure of Lloyd's insurance market into the 21st century. Judging by the uniformity of the way that single-entry bookkeeping was practised it seems fairly certain that a model was worked out, written up and widely adopted.

Double-entry bookkeeping

Until Luca Paccioli wrote what was in essence the world's first accounting book, over 500 years ago, accounting records were maintained in single-entry format: one event merited one record. This meant that errors could only be prevented by a major duplication of effort, for example by having different people making and counting up parallel records. Paccioli, a mathematician who worked for the Doge of Venice, came up with a system of double-entry bookkeeping that required two entries for each transaction, thus providing built-in checks and balances to ensure accuracy. Each transaction requires an entry as a debit and as a credit.

To give an example, selling goods in a double-entry system might result in two separate journal entries – a debit reducing the stock by £250 and a corresponding credit of £250 of new cash in – a double entry (see Table 1.1). The debits in a double-entry system must always equal the credits. If they

Table 1.1 An example of a double-entry ledger

General Journal of Andrew's Bookshop			
Date	Description of entry	Debit	Credit
10th July	Rent expense	£250	
	Cash		£250

don't, you know there is an error somewhere. So, double entry allows you to balance your books, which you can't do with the single-entry method.

Paccioli's genius lay in seeing that the ultimate balancing number in a company's accounts was the profit or loss for the owners of that enterprise. On the not unreasonable assumption that the business shown in Table 1.1 plans to make a profit from selling goods, the figures will look rather different. To keep the numbers simple, let's suppose the goods sold cost £125 (a 50 per cent margin), then the entries would be as follows. Goods in stock go down by £125, while cash goes up by £250. That net change of £125 is balanced by an increase in profits of £125, so the assets and liabilities are kept in balance. In this example, had the goods sold for less than was paid there would have been a loss, which would have reduced the value of the owners' stake in the business by a corresponding amount.

This is all an MBA Business Finance needs to know about bookkeeping; the main part of the knowledge he or she requires is how to interpret the figures once recorded.

Introducing record-keeping

If you find yourself in a small business without a full-time accountant and a less than satisfactory method of keeping accounting records, you may have to devise and implement one yourself. Accounting record systems, however complex, follow a similar model; see Figure 1.1.

All of the elements – sales invoices, purchase invoices and so forth – are in effect ledgers containing a record of the relevant events. A long time ago these actually were ledgers, but today they are entries in an accounting software package.

So that you don't get stuck doing work that is well below an MBA Business Finance's pay grade you need to buy an accounting package and get a bookkeeper to start entering the data and producing the standard business reports – profit and loss, balance sheets and performance comparisons.

Figure 1.1   A simple system of keeping business records

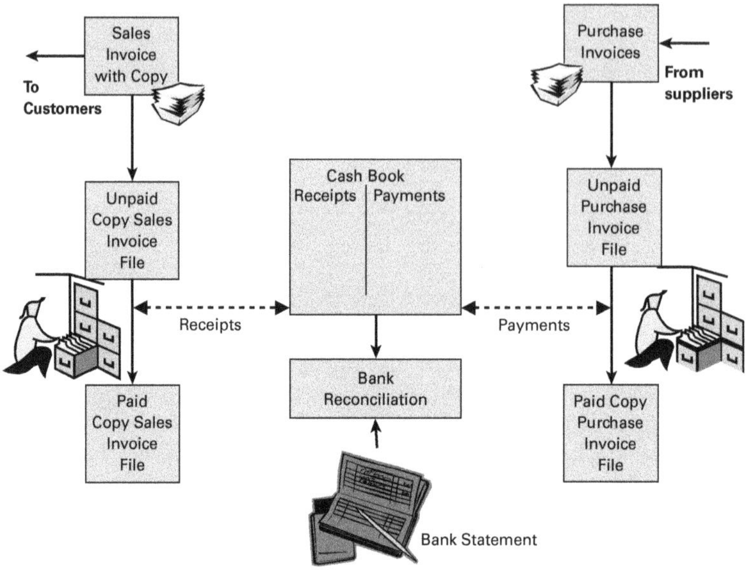

Cash flow

There is a saying in business that profit is vanity and cash flow is sanity. Both are necessary, but in the short term, and often that is all that matters in business as it struggles to get a foothold in the shifting sands of trading, cash flow is life or death. The rules on what constitutes cash are very simple – it has to be just that, or negotiable securities designated as being as good as cash.

Cash flow is looked at in two distinct and important ways: as a projection of future expected cash flows, and as an analysis of where cash came from and went to in an accounting period and the resultant increase or decrease in cash available.

Cash flow forecasts

The future is impossible to predict with great accuracy but it is possible to anticipate likely outcomes and be prepared to deal with events by building in a margin of safety. The starting point for making a projection is to make some assumptions about what you want to achieve and testing those for reasonableness.

Take the situation of High Note, a business being established to sell sheet music, small instruments and music CDs to schools and colleges, which will expect trade credit and members of the public who will pay cash. The owner plans to invest £10,000 and to borrow £10,000 from a bank on a long-term basis. The business will require £11,500 for fixtures and fittings. A further £1,000 will be needed for a computer, software and a printer. That should leave around £7,500 to meet immediate trading expenses such as buying in stock and spending £1,500 on initial advertising. Hopefully customers' payments will start to come in quickly to cover other expenses such as some wages for bookkeeping, administration and fulfilling orders. Sales in the first six months are expected to be £60,000 based on negotiations already in hand, plus some cash sales that always seem to turn up. The rule of thumb in the industry seems to be that stock is marked up by 100 per cent, so £30,000 of bought in goods sell on for £60,000.

On the basis of these assumptions it is possible to make the cash flow forecast set out in Table 1.2. It has been simplified and some elements such as VAT (or sales tax) and tax on profits have been omitted for ease of understanding. The maths in the table is straightforward: the cash receipts from various sources are totalled, as are the payments. Taking one from the other leaves a cash surplus or deficit for the month in question. The bottom row shows the cumulative position. So for example while the business had £2,440 cash left at the end of April, taking the cash deficit of £1,500 in May into account, by the end of May only £950 (£2,450 – £1,500) cash remains.

Overtrading

In the example above the business looks like having insufficient cash, based on the assumptions made. An outsider, a banker perhaps, would look at the figures in August and see that the faster the sales grew the greater the cash flow deficit became. We know, using our crystal ball, that the position will improve from September and that if we can only hang on for a few more months we should eliminate our cash deficit and perhaps even have a surplus. Had we made the cash flow projection at the outset and either raised more money, perhaps by way of an overdraft, spent less on fixtures and fittings, or set a more modest sales goal hence needing less stock and advertising, we would have had a sound business. The figures indicate a business that is trading beyond its financial resources, a condition known as 'overtrading' – anathema to bankers the world over.

Smartsheet have a range of spreadsheet calculators to help you analyse factors that impact your net cash flow and produce projections of future cash flows based on various alternative marketing planning decisions as to profit margins, stock levels and the amount of credit given to customers (www.smartsheet.com/content/cash-flow-forecast-templates).

Statement of cash flows for the year

A cash flow statement summarizes exactly where cash came from and how it was spent during the year. At first glance it seems to draw on a mixture of

Table 1.2 High Note six-month cash flow forecast

Month	April £	May £	June £	July £	Aug £	Sept £	Total £
Receipts							
Sales	4,000	5,000	5,000	7,000	12,000	15,000	
Owner's cash	10,000						
Bank loan	10,000						
Total cash in	24,000	5,000	5,000	7,000	12,000	15,000	48,000
Payments							
Purchases	5,500	2,950	4,220	7,416	9,332	9,690	39,108
Rates, electricity, heat, telephone, internet, etc	1,000	1,000	1,000	1,000	1,000	1,000	
Wages	1,000	1,000	1,000	1,000	1,000	1,000	
Advertising	1,550	1,550	1,550	1,550	1,550	1,550	
Fixtures/fittings	11,500						
Computer, etc	1,000						
Total cash out	21,550	6,500	7,770	10,966	12,882	13,240	
Monthly cash							
Surplus/deficit(−)	2,450	(1,500)	(2,770)	(3,966)	(882)	1,760	
Cumulative cash balance	2,450	950	(1,820)	(5,786)	(6,668)	(4,908)	

transactions included in the profit and loss account and balance sheet for the same period end, but this is not the whole story. Because there is a time lag on many cash transactions, for example tax and dividend payments, the statement is a mixture of some previous year and some current year transactions; the remaining current year transactions go into the following year's cash flow statement during which the cash actually changes hands. Similarly, the realization and accrual conventions relating to sales and purchases respectively result in cash transactions having a different timing to when they were entered in the profit and loss account.

The movement of cash in and out of a businesses can be quite a complicated business. From an MBA's perspective, it is being able to interpret the figures that matters. You can see an illustrated consolidated statement of cash flows at page 11 of this illustrative document from PwC: www.pwc.com/gx/en/services/audit-assurance/assets/pwc-illustrative-condensed-interim-financial-statements-2020.pdf. Some 50 categories of transaction and a dozen pages of technical notes are used to explain how net cash decreased from 33,329 million to 34,427 million over the period. It shouldn't take too long to see the areas that had the greatest effect – the repayment of a loan and the purchase of a new subsidiary. Both of these activities can be seen as healthy ones, so you can be relatively relaxed about the apparent deterioration in the cash position.

The profit and loss account (income statement)

If you look back to the financial situation in High Note, you will see a good example of the difference between cash and profit. The business has sold £60,000 worth of goods that it only paid £30,000 for, so it has a substantial profit margin to play with. While £39,108 has been paid to suppliers only £30,000 of goods at cost have been sold, meaning that £9,108 worth of instruments, sheet music and CDs are still in stock. A similar situation exists with sales. High Note has billed for £60,000 but only been paid for £48,000; the balance is owed by debtors. The bald figure at the end of the cash flow projection showing High Note to be in the red to the tune of £4,908 seems to be missing some important facts.

The difference between profit and cash

Cash is immediate and takes account of nothing else. Profit, however, is a measurement of economic activity that considers other factors that can be assigned a value or cost. The accounting principle that governs profit is known as the 'matching principle', which means that income and expendi-

Table 1.3   Profit and loss account for High Note for the six months, April–September

	£	£
Sales		60,000
Less cost of goods to be sold		30,000
Gross profit		30,000
Less expenses:		
Heat, electric, phone, internet, etc	6,000	
Wages	6,000	
Advertising	9,300	
Total expenses		21,300
Profit before tax, interest and depreciation charges		8,700

ture are matched to the time period in which they occur. (See Chapter 2 where the concepts that govern the treatment of costs and revenue – realization and accruals – are explained in more detail.) So for High Note the profit and loss account for the first six months would be as shown in Table 1.3.

The structure of the profit and loss statement

This account is set out in more detail for a business to make it more useful when it comes to understanding how a business is performing. For example, though the profit shown in our worked example is £8,700 it would in fact be rather lower. As money has been borrowed to finance cash flow there would be interest due, as there would be on the longer-term loan of £10,000. In practice we have four levels of profit:

1 Gross profit is the profit left after all costs related to making what you sell are deducted from income.

2 Operating profit is what's left after you take away the operating expenses from the gross profit.

3 Profit before tax is what is left after deducting any financing costs.

4 Profit after tax is what is left for the owners to spend or reinvest in the business.

For High Note this could look much as set out in Table 1.4. A more substantial business than High Note will have taken on a wide range of commitments. For example, as well as the owner's money, there may be a long-term loan to be serviced (interest and capital repayments); parts of the workshop

Table 1.4   High Note extended profit and loss account

	£s
Sales	60,000
Less the cost of goods to be sold	30,000
Gross profit	30,000
Less operating expenses	21,300
Operating profit	8,700
Less interest on bank loan and overdraft	600
Profit before tax	8,100
Less tax	1,827
Profit after tax	6,723

or offices may be sublet generating 'non-operating income'; and there will certainly be some depreciation expense to deduct. Like any accounting report it should be prepared in the best form for the user, bearing in mind the requirements of the regulatory authorities.

The elements to be included are:

- Sales (and any other revenues from operations).
- Cost of sales (or cost of goods sold).
- Gross profit – the difference between sales and cost of sales.
- Operating expenses – selling, administration, depreciation and other general costs.
- Operating profit – the difference between gross profit and operating expenses.
- Non-operating revenues – other revenues, including interest, rent, etc.
- Non-operating expenses – financial costs and other expenses not directly related to the running of the business.
- Profit before income tax.
- Provision for income tax.
- Net income (or profit or loss).

Profit and loss spreadsheet

Smartsheet have compiled a useful collection of free profit and loss (P&L) templates covering several different industry types and time periods at: www.smartsheet.com/free-profit-and-loss-templates.

The balance sheet

A balance sheet is a snapshot at a moment in time. On the one hand it shows the value of assets (possessions) owned by the business, and on the other it shows who provided the funds with which to finance those assets and to whom the business is ultimately liable.

Assets are of two main types and are classified under the headings of either fixed assets or current assets. *Fixed assets* come in three forms. First there is the hardware or physical things used by the business itself and which are not for sale to customers. Examples of fixed assets include buildings, plant, machinery, vehicles, furniture and fittings. Next come intangible fixed assets, such as goodwill, intellectual property, etc, and these are also shown under the general heading 'fixed assets'. Finally there are investments in other businesses. Other assets in the process of eventually being turned into cash from customers are called *current assets*, and include stocks, work-in-progress, money owed by customers and cash itself:

Total assets = Fixed assets + Current assets

Assets can only be bought with funds provided by the owners or borrowed from someone else, for example, bankers or creditors. Owners provide funds by directly investing in the business (say, when they buy shares issued by the company) or indirectly by allowing the company to retain some of the profits in reserves. These sources of money are known collectively as *liabilities*.

Total liabilities =
Share capital and reserves + Borrowings and other creditors

Borrowed capital can take the form of a long-term loan at a fixed rate of interest or a short-term loan, such as a bank overdraft, usually at a variable rate of interest. All short-term liabilities owed by a business and due for payment within 12 months are referred to as 'creditors falling due within one year', and long-term indebtedness is called 'creditors falling due after one year'.

So far in our High Note example the money spent on 'capital' items such as the £12,500 spent on a computer and fixtures and fittings have been ignored as has the £9,108 worth of sheet music, etc remaining in stock waiting to be sold and the £12,000 owed by customers who have yet to pay up. An assumption has to be made about where the cash deficit will be made up and the most logical short-term source is a bank overdraft.

For High Note at the end of September the balance sheet is set out in Table 1.5.

Table 1.5   High Note balance sheet at 30 September

	£	£
Assets		
Fixed assets		
Fixtures, fitting, equipment	11,500	
Computer	1,000	
Total fixed assets		12,500
Working capital		
Current assets		
Stock	9,108	
Debtors	12,000	
Cash	0	
	21,108	
Less current liabilities (creditors falling due within one year)		
Overdraft	4,908	
Creditors	0	
	4,908	
Net current assets		
[Working capital (CA-CL)]		16,200
Total assets less current liabilities		28,700
Less creditors falling due after one year		
Long-term bank loan		10,000
Net total assets		18,700
Capital and reserves		
Owner's capital introduced	10,000	
Profit retained (from P&L account)	8,700	
Total capital and reserves		18,700

Balance sheet structure

The layout of the balance sheet using UK accounting rules is something of a jumble, with assets and liabilities intermingled. In the United States the balance sheet traditionally separates assets and liabilities and sets the figures out either horizontally or vertically (see Table 1.6).

The most confusing aspect of the US balance sheet structure is that equities, that is the owners' stake in the venture, is lumped in with the liabilities.

Table 1.6   Equivalent balance sheet for a US corporation

Assets (£)		Liabilities (£)	
Current		Current	
Cash	0	Overdraft	4,908
Accounts receivable	12,000	Accs Payable	0
Inventory	9,108	Loans longer than 1 year	10,000
Fixed assets	12,500	*Equity*	
		Owners' capital	10,000
		Retained profit	8,700
Total assets	33,608	Total liabilities and equity	33,608

But when you consider that the accounts are prepared for the company or corporation, which has a separate legal identity from the various owners, this has as sort of pure logic to it. The profit and loss account (income statement) and cash flow layouts are broadly similar.

Other countries have their own variations and attempts are being made to harmonize accounting standards worldwide, with modest success.

Working capital

You will also have noticed in this example that the assets and liabilities have been jumbled together in the middle to net off the current assets and current liabilities and so end up with a figure for the working capital. 'Current' in accounting means within the trading cycle, usually taken to be one year. Stock will be used up and debtors will pay up within the year, and the overdraft, being repayable on demand, also appears as a short-term liability.

There are a number of other items not shown in the working capital section of the example balance sheet that should appear such as liability for tax and VAT (or sales tax) that have not yet been paid and should appear as current liability.

Intangible fixed assets

There are a number of seemingly invisible items that nevertheless have been acquired for a measurable money cost and so have to be accounted for. These are *goodwill*, where the price paid for an asset is above its fair market price. This is fairly common in the case of acquisitions where competition for a company can push prices higher. The other is *intellectual property* such as patents, copyright, designs and logos. These items too are amortized over their working life. So, for example, if a patent is considered to have a 10-year life and cost £1 million to acquire it would be written down in the accounts by £100,000 a year.

Accounting for stock

Deciding on the stock figure to put into a balance sheet is a tricky calculation. Theoretically it is simple; after all you know what you paid for it. The rule that stock should be entered in the balance sheet at cost or market price, whichever is the lower, is also not too difficult to follow. But in the real world a business keeps on buying in stock so it has product to sell and the cost can vary every time a purchase is made.

Take the example of a business selling a breakfast cereal. Four pallets of cereal are bought in from various suppliers at prices of £1,000, £1,020, £1,040 and £1,060 respectively, a total of £4,120. At the end of the period three pallets have been sold, so logically the cost of goods sold in the profit and loss account will show a figure of £3,060 (£1,000 + £1,020 + £1,040). The last pallet costing £1,060 will be the figure to put into the balance sheet, thus ensuring that all £4,120 of total costs are accounted for.

This method of dealing with stock is known as FIFO (First in First Out), for obvious reason. There are two other popular costing methods that have their own merits. LIFO (Last in First Out) is based on the argument that if you are staying in business you will have to keep on replacing stock at the latest (higher) price, so you might just as well get used to that sooner by accounting for it in your profit and loss account. In this case the cost of goods sold would be £3,120 (£1,060 + £1,040 + £1,020), rather than the £3,060 that FIFO produces.

The third popular costing method is the average cost method, which does what it says on the box. In the above example this would produce a cost midway between that obtained by the other two methods; in this example £3,090.

All these methods have their merits, but FIFO usually wins the argument as it accommodates the realities that prices rise steadily and goods move in and out of a business in the order in which they are bought. It would be a very badly run shop that sold its last delivery of cereal before clearing out its existing stocks.

Methods of depreciation

Depreciation is how we show the asset being 'consumed' over its working life. It is simply a bookkeeping record to allow us to allocate some of the cost of an asset to the appropriate time period. The time period will be determined by such factors as how long the working life of the asset is. The principle methods of depreciation used in business are as follows.

The straight-line method

This assumes that the asset will be 'consumed' evenly throughout its life. If, for example, an asset is being bought for £1,200 and sold at the end of five years for £200, the amount of cost we have to write off is £1,000. Using 20 per cent per year so that the whole 100 per cent of cost is allocated we can work out the 'book value' for each year.

The declining balance method

This works in a similar way, but instead of an even depreciation each year we assume the drop will be less. Some assets, motor vehicles for example, will reduce sharply in their first year and less so later on. So while at the end of year one in both these methods of depreciation there is a £200 fall, in year two the picture starts to change. The straight-line method takes a further fall of £200, while the declining balance method reduces by 20 per cent (our agreed depreciation rate) of £800 (the balance of £1,000 minus the £200 depreciation so far), which is £160.

The sum of the digits method

This is more common in the United States than in the UK. While the declining balance method applies a constant percentage to a declining figure, this method applies a progressively smaller percentage to the initial cost. It involves adding up the individual numbers in the expected life span of the asset to arrive at the denominator of a fraction. The numerator is the year number concerned, but in reverse order.

For example, if our computer asset bought for $1,200 had an expected useful life of five years (unlikely) then the denominator in our sum would be 1 + 2 + 3 + 4 + 5 which equals 15. In the first year we would depreciate by 5/15 times the initial purchase price of $1,200, which equals $400. In year two we would depreciate by 4/15 and so on.

These are just three of the most common of many ways of depreciating fixed assets. In choosing which method of depreciation to use, and in practice you may have to use different methods with different types of asset, it is useful to remember what you are trying to do. You are aiming to allocate the *cost* of buying the asset as it should apply to each year of its working life.

Amortization

Amortization is a very similar process to depreciation but it usually refers to spreading the cost of an intangible over its useful life. In some countries the terms 'depreciation' and 'amortization' are interchangeable. Some intangible assets have a precise useful life, patents, for example. Some such as goodwill are not easily assigned a useful life so conventions based on accounting rules are applied. See the video lecture at the end of this chapter for an explanation of amortization and depreciation.

Table 1.7 A package of accounts

Balance sheet at 31 Dec 2010 (£)		P & L for year to 31 Dec 2011 (£)		Balance sheet at 2011 (£)	
Fixed assets	1,000	Sales	10,000	Fixed assets	1,200
Working capital	1,000	less cost of sales	6,000	Working capital	1,400
	2,000	Gross profit	4,000		2,600
		less expenses	3,000		
Financed by		Profit before tax	1,000	Financed by	
Owners' equity	2,000	Tax	400	Owners' equity	2,000
		Profit after tax	600	Reserves	600
					2,600

Balance sheet and other online tools

You can find further guidance on all matters relating to balance sheets and the other accounting reports at Accounting Coach. This was set up by Harold Averkamp, CPA, MBA, 'to utilize the internet for communicating a more clear explanation of accounting concepts to people in all parts of the world and at a low cost' (www.accountingcoach.com/outline). The basic information is free, which may be sufficient to get a good feel for the subject. The Pro version costs £45 ($49) and includes a series of short videos, lecture notes and exams in the main financial topics. The 'Dictionary of Terms' tab on this website will take you to a definition and explanation of most terms in the field.

Package of accounts

The cash flow statement, the profit and loss account and the balance sheet between them constitute a set of accounts, but conventionally two balance sheets, the opening and closing one, are provided to make a 'package'. By including these balance sheets we can see the full picture of what has happened to the owners' investment in the business.

Table 1.7 shows a simplified package of accounts. We can see from these that over the year the business has made £600 of profit after tax, invested that in £200 of additional fixed assets, £400 of working capital such as stock and debtors, balancing that off with the £600 put into reserves from the year's profits.

Online video courses and lectures

Accrual basis of accounting: Khan Academy: youtu.be/NNhyZFHAzaA

Amortization and depreciation: Khan Academy: youtu.be/eKw3Aq0vvbo

Introduction to Financial Accounting: Contents include an introduction to the balance sheet, the income statement, cash flows and working capital assets and how to read an annual report. This course is presented as a combination of lecture videos, quizzes and discussion. The only required maths knowledge is addition, subtraction, multiplication, and division. Delivered four times a year by Wharton's faculty: www.coursera.org/learn/whartonaccounting

Why Finance? A brief history of the young field of financial theory. Professor John Geanakoplos, James Tobin Professor of Economics at Yale University: www.youtube.com/watch?v=vTs2IQ8OefQ

Online video case studies

How we helped IT contractor Ronan Moriarty understand his income. Crunch Accounting: www.youtube.com/watch?v=cCja3dEpsXY

How we're brightening up Greyworld's finances: Crunch Accounting: www.youtube.com/watch?v=9NfghzMKXZQ

02
The rules of the game

- Accounting conventions and principles
- Financial rule makers
- International accounting standards
- Protecting investors

Accounting is certainly not an exact science. Even the most enthusiastic member of the profession would not make that claim. There is considerable scope for interpretation and educated guesswork as all the facts are rarely available when the accounts are drawn up. For example we may not know for certain that a particular customer will actually pay up, yet unless we have firm evidence that they won't, for example if the business is failing, then the value of the money owed will appear in the accounts.

Obviously, if accountants and managers had complete freedom to interpret events as they will, no one inside or outside the business would place any reliance on the figures, so certain ground rules have been laid down by the profession to help get a level of consistency into accounting information.

Fundamental conventions

These are the enduring principles that govern the way in which the accounting profession assembles and presents financial information.

Money measurement

In accounting, a record is kept only of the facts that can be expressed in money terms. For example, the state of the managing director's health and the news that your main competitor is opening up right opposite in a more attractive outlet are important business facts. No accounting record of them is made, however, and they do not show up on the balance sheet, simply because no objective monetary value can be assigned to these facts.

Expressing business facts in money terms has the great advantage of providing a common denominator. Just imagine trying to add computer equipment and vehicles, together with a 4,000 sq m office, and then arriving at a total. You need a common term to be able to carry out the basic arithmetical functions, and to compare one set of accounts with another.

Business entity

The accounts are kept for the business itself, rather than for the owner(s), bankers, or anyone else associated with the firm. The concept states that assets and liabilities are always defined from the business's viewpoint. So, for example, were a business owner to lend his business money it would appear in the accounts as a liability, though in effect he might see it as his own money. Anything done with that money, say buying equipment, would appear in the accounts as an asset of the business. The owner's stake is accounted for only by the increase or decrease in net worth of the enterprise as a whole.

Cost concept

Assets are usually entered into the accounts at the cost on date of purchase. For a variety of reasons, the real 'worth' of an asset will probably change over time. The worth or value of an asset is a subjective estimate that no two people are likely to agree on. This is made even more complex, and artificial, because the assets themselves are usually not for sale.

So in the search for objectivity, the accountants have settled for cost as the figure to record. It does mean that a balance sheet does not show the current worth or value of a business. That is not its intention. Nor does it mean that the 'cost' figure remains unchanged forever. For example, the worth of a motor vehicle costing £6,000 may end up looking like Table 2.1 after two years.

The depreciation is how we show the asset being 'consumed' over its working life. It is simply a bookkeeping record to allow us to allocate some of the cost of an asset to the appropriate time period. (See Chapter 1 for more on depreciation methods.)

The time period will be determined by factors such as the working life of the asset. The tax authorities do not allow depreciation as a business expense, so this figure can't be manipulated to reduce tax liability, for example. A tax relief on the capital expenditure known as 'writing down' is

Table 2.1   Example of the changing 'worth' of an asset

	Year 1	Year 2
Fixed assets	£	£
Vehicle	6,000	6,000
Less cumulative depreciation	1,500	3,000
Net asset	4,500	3,000

allowed, using a formula set by government that varies from time to time depending on current economic goals, for example to stimulate capital expenditure.

Other assets, such as freehold land and buildings, will be re-valued from time to time, and stock will be entered at cost, or market value, whichever is the lower, in line with the principle of conservatism (see later in this chapter).

Other methods for recording assets

While cost at date of purchase is the norm for accounting for assets in conventional enterprises, there are certain types of businesses and certain situations when other methods of recording a monetary figure are used:

- *Market value:* this is usually used when an asset is actually to be sold and there is an established market for that particular type of asset. This could arise when a business or part of a business is to be closed down.

- *Fair value:* this is described as the estimated price at which an asset could be exchanged between knowledgeable but unrelated willing parties who have not and may not actually exchange. This basis is often used in the due diligence process where because of particular synergies a price higher than market value (resulting in goodwill) could reasonably be set.

- *Market to market:* this is where market value is calculated on a daily basis, usually by financial institutions such as banks and stockbrokers. This can result in dramatic changes in value in turbulent market conditions requiring additional assets, including cash, to be found to cover a fall in market price. This approach is blamed for helping to create liquidity 'black holes' by forcing banks to sell assets to meet liquidity targets, which in turn forces prices lower, requiring yet more assets to be sold.

Going concern

Accounting reports always assume that a business will continue trading indefinitely into the future – unless there is good evidence to the contrary. This means that the assets of the business are looked at simply as profit generators and not as being available for sale. Look again at the motor vehicle example above. In year two, the net asset figures in the accounts, prepared on a 'going concern' basis, is £3,000. If we knew that the business was to close down in a few weeks, then we would be more interested in the car's resale value than its 'book' value: the car might fetch only £2,000, which is quite a different figure.

Once a business stops trading, we cannot realistically look at the assets in the same way. They are no longer being used in the business to help generate sales and profits. The most objective figure is what they might realize in the marketplace.

In practice the directors and auditors have to believe a company will be viable for at least the next 12 months otherwise they have an obligation to draw attention to the danger that the company may not be a going concern, History shows that more companies experience going concern difficulties towards the end of a recession. In April 2022 KPMG, one of the big four global accounting firms, refused to sign off the 2021 financial results of German real estate group Adler. The stark statement that 'the auditor has not been able to obtain sufficient appropriate audit evidence to provide a basis for an audit opinion on these annual accounts' forced the company to withhold dividend payments, as the amount of profit could not be confirmed. Suspicion was aroused in 2020 when a whistleblower told regulators that an Austrian property magnate who had presided over Germany's second-largest real estate bankruptcy at the age of 35 was involved with Adler. The general view is that a company has a better chance of survival if it is up-front about liquidity problems rather than letting the market find out about difficulties and, in an atmosphere of mistrust, exaggerate the situation beyond what is warranted by the facts.

Dual aspect

To keep a complete record of any business transaction we need to know both where money came from and what has been done with it. It is not enough simply to say, for example, that a bank has lent a business €1 million; we have to show how that money has been used; for example to buy a property, increase stock levels, or in some other way. You can think of it as the accounting equivalent of Newton's third law: 'For every force there is an equal and opposite reaction.' Dual aspect is the basis of double-entry book-keeping (see Chapter 1).

The realization concept

A particularly prudent sales manager once said that an order was not an order until the customer's cheque had cleared, he or she had consumed the product, had not died as a result and, finally, had shown every indication of wanting to buy again. Most of us know quite different salespeople who can 'anticipate' the most unlikely volume of sales. In accounting, income is usually recognized as having been earned when the goods (or services) are dispatched and the invoice sent out. This has nothing to do with when an order is received, how firm an order is or how likely a customer is to pay up promptly. It is also possible that some of the products dispatched may be returned at some later date – perhaps for quality reasons. This means that income, and consequently profit, can be brought into the business in one period, and have to be removed later on.

Obviously, if these returns can be estimated accurately, then an adjustment can be made to income at the time. So the 'sales income' figure that is seen at the top of a profit and loss account is the value of the goods dispatched and invoiced to customers in the period in question.

The accrual concept

The profit and loss account sets out to 'match' income and expenditure to the appropriate time period. It is only in this way that the profit for the period can be realistically calculated. Suppose, for example, that you are calculating one month's profits when the quarterly telephone bill comes in. The picture might look like Table 2.2.

This is clearly wrong. In the first place, three months' telephone charges have been 'matched' against one month's sales. Equally wrong is charging anything other than January's telephone bill against January's income. Unfortunately, bills such as this are rarely to hand when you want the accounts, so in practice the telephone bill is 'accrued' for. The figure (which may even be absolutely correct if you have a meter) is put in as a provision to meet this liability when it becomes due.

Table 2.2   Example of a badly matched profit and loss account

Profit and loss account for January, year 20XX	
	£
Sales income for January	4,000
Less telephone bill (last quarter)	800
Profit before other expenses	3,200

Accounting conventions

These concepts provide a useful set of ground rules, but they are open to a range of possible interpretations. Over time, a generally accepted approach to how the concepts are applied has been arrived at. This approach hinges on the use of three conventions: conservatism, materiality and consistency.

Conservatism

Accountants are often viewed as merchants of gloom, always prone to taking a pessimistic point of view. The fact that a point of view has to be taken at all is the root of the problem. The convention of conservatism means that, given a choice, the accountant takes the figure that will result in a lower end profit. This might mean, for example, taking the higher of two possible expense figures. Few people are upset if the profit figure at the end of the day is higher than earlier estimates. The converse is never true.

Materiality

A strict interpretation of depreciation (see above) could lead to all sorts of trivial paperwork. For example, pencil sharpeners, staplers and paperclips, all theoretically items of fixed assets, should be depreciated over their working lives. This is obviously a useless exercise and in practice these items are written-off when they are bought.

Clearly, the level of 'materiality' is not the same for all businesses. A multinational may not keep meticulous records of every item of machinery under $1,000. For a small business this may represent all the machinery it has.

Consistency

Even with the help of those concepts and conventions, there is a fair degree of latitude in how you can record and interpret financial information. You should choose the methods that give the fairest picture of how the firm is performing and stick with them. It is very difficult to keep track of events in a business that is always changing its accounting methods. This does not mean that you are stuck with one method forever. Any change, however, is an important step.

The rule makers

The accounting professional bodies, with a little prodding from governments, are responsible for ensuring that accounting reports conform to what are known as Generally Accepted Accounting Practices (GAAP). A new entrant, International Accounting Standards, is challenging that term itself as GAAP rules have been interpreted differently on different continents and indeed largely ignored on others.

The rule book has to be adapted to accommodate changes in the way business is done. For example, international business across frontiers is now the norm, so rules on handling currency and reporting taxable profits in different countries have to be accommodated within a company's accounts in a consistent manner.

Although an MBA isn't usually expected to know all the rules, you should be able to get up to date before any meetings where the subject is likely to come up. You can keep track of changes in company reporting rules on the Institute of Chartered Accountants website (www.icaew.com/technical).

International accounting standards

Having accounting rules and conventions is one thing, but having them accepted and applied in a common manner across business, country borders and time is quite a different matter. Whilst most countries in the advanced economies, particularly those in North America and Europe, apply the rules and where there are differences seek actively to harmonize them, like accounting itself it is far from an exact process. For example on 1 April 2015, Reuters reported that 'The board that sets accounting rules for US public companies proposed on Wednesday a one-year delay in sweeping new rules that would change the way companies recognize revenue, one of the most important numbers in corporate financial statements.' At present there are 'complex, detailed, and disparate revenue recognition requirements for specific transactions and industries' according to the Financial Accounting Standards Board. As a result different industries report the most important single number – the sales revenue achieved in a specific time period – in different and non-comparable ways. That leaves those seeking to understand the accounts to compare apples with pears; fruits to be sure, but very different ones. The delay has shifted the new standard for revenue recognition that was approved back in May 2014 to being implemented for public companies starting in 2018 and for private companies in 2019.

These organizations can help keep MBAs up to date on this subject area:

- The Financial Accounting Standards Board (www.fasb.org) is 'the designated organization in the private sector for establishing standards of financial accounting that govern the preparation of financial reports by nongovernmental organizations' in the United States.
- The IFRS Foundation (www.ifrs.org) is an independent, not-for-profit organization whose mission 'is to develop a single set of high quality, understandable, enforceable and globally accepted International Financial Reporting Standards (IFRS) based upon clearly articulated principles'.

Protecting investors

When confidence in US businesses was rocked badly with a series of high profile financial frauds, Enron and Worldcom for example, the US government introduced the Sarbanes-Oxley Act, known less commonly but better understood as the Public Company Accounting Reforms and Investor Protection Act 2002. The Act's purpose is to close the loopholes opened up by creative accountants who are always devising ways to overstate profits and understate liabilities and so make it easier for shareholders to see how profitable a business really is. The Act doesn't just apply to US companies; any businesses with shares listed on a US stock market that does business in the United States is swept into the net. Check out www.soxlaw.com for the low-down on that Act.

The UK version is the Companies (Audit, Investigations and Community Enterprise) Act. You can read up on the UK rules at www.legislation.gov.uk/ putting the title in the search pane.

CASE STUDY
HP vs Autonomy

In the spring of 2015 the financial press both sides of the Atlantic had headlines on the legal battle between Hewlett Packard and Autonomy, the company it had acquired four years earlier. HP paid its lawyers an $18 million retainer and up to $30 million more in contingency fees, depending on how much money HP is able to recover from Autonomy executives and advisers.

When HP, the Silicon Valley giant founded in 1935 by Bill Hewlett and Dave Packard, electrical engineering graduates from Stanford University, bought Autonomy, founded in 1996 in Cambridge, England, by Dr Mike Lynch and Richard Gaunt, for $11.1 billion (£7.4 billion) it was seen as a great deal – for Autonomy shareholders at least. Autonomy, a pioneer in creating search software that can make sense of complex, unstructured information, was unique in being virtually the only UK technology player operating on a worldwide stage. HP, run by Meg Whitman, a Harvard MBA from the class of 1979, was reported in the Financial Times as having just 'revealed disappointing quarterly earnings along with plans to spin off its personal computer business. It also said it was cancelling its attempt to compete with Apple iPad.' Whitman needed corporate noise to drown out the bad news and Autonomy, although a relative minnow with sales of $870.4 million (£583.4 million) and 1,878 employees to HP's net revenue of $119 billion and 331,800 employees, seemed a good fit. Autonomy was a rising star, having won the Queen's Award for Enterprise and Management Today's 'Britain's Most Admired Companies' award for the software sector, positive messages that HP hadn't seen in the press for a long time. Autonomy's shares rose 79 per cent on the day the bid was announced, a staggering premium for a company whose earnings grew by just six per cent in the first half of the year in question. Whitman had only been HP's CEO since September 2011, the year of the Autonomy acquisition, but she had sector experience from her time on the board of eBay and HP had made some 100 acquisitions over the preceding four decades, albeit none the size of this deal.

The dispute between HP and the directors of Autonomy with whom the deal was struck started on 20 November 2012, when Whitman stunned the business world by declaring that it would take an $8.8 billion write down on its $11.1 billion acquisition of Autonomy with $5 billion of that write down related to accounting irregularities at the UK software group. HP's advisors claim that Autonomy booked phantom sales where no money changed hands, so inflating their sales revenue and as a consequence the value of the company. Sushovan Hussain, Autonomy's former Chief Financial Officer, claims the differences in HP's interpretation of Autonomy's financial status were based only on transatlantic differences in accounting standards.

Online video courses and lectures

Accounting Concepts for Managers, Professor Asokan Anandarajan, New Jersey Institute of Technology School of Management: www.youtube.com/watch?v=N2YyiVAO5Do

Finance Theory I: Professor Andrew Lo, MIT Sloane: www.youtube.com/watch?v=HdHlfiOAJyE

Forming an international management accounting system: The Chartered Institute of Management Accountants, alongside the American Institute of Certified Public Accountants have launched a set of Global Management Accounting Principles to help organizations across the world ensure that they have substantial and uniform management accounting systems: www.youtube.com/watch?v=rKNv2hVCfNU

What are US GAAP and IFRS: Kevin Kimball, Brigham Young University–Hawaii: www.youtube.com/watch?v=qxGbbtroDwg

Online video case studies

Berkshire Hathaway: Warren Buffett talks to MBA students at the Terry College of Business at the University of Georgia: www.youtube.com/watch?v=2a9Lx9J8uSs

Gloucestershire Health and Care NHS Foundation Trust, annual general meeting 2022: www.ghc.nhs.uk/who-we-are/agm

Telefónica's general shareholders meeting: www.telefonica.com/en/communication-room/blog/chairmans-speech-2022-general-shareholders-meeting

Wisconsin Energy's Annual Meeting of Stockholders at Concordia University – Wisconsin, 2 May 2014: www.youtube.com/watch?v=IA-qVwoxFyw

03
Analysing financial reports

- The significance of accounting information
- Using business ratios
- Understanding the limitations of ratios
- Finding competitor accounts
- Improving business performance

In Chapter 1 the important financial statement of profit and loss (income statement), balance sheet and cash flow statement were explained. To recap – the trading performance of a company for a period of time is measured in the profit and loss account by deducting running costs from sales income. A balance sheet sets out the financial position of the company at a particular point in time, usually the end of the accounting period. It lists the assets owned by the company at that date matched by an equal list of the sources of finance. Cash flow measures the movement of money in and out of the organization at the time such events actually occur.

Reading company accounts, with practice, you can get some insight into a company's affairs. Comparing the current year's figure with the previous year's figure can identify changes in some of the key items and give insights into likely causes and remedies. Competitors' accounts can be studied to see their strengths and weaknesses from a financial perspective and perhaps also to give pointers as to how your own business's performance can be improved or modified.

However, just having the accounts of a business is not of much use if you can't analyse and interpret them. The tools for measuring the relationship between various elements of performance to see whether we are getting better or worse are known as ratios; simply put these involve expressing one thing as a proportion of another with a view to gaining an appreciation of what has happened. For example, miles per gallon is a measure of the efficiency of a motor vehicle. If that 'ratio' is 40 mpg in one period and 30 mpg in another it would be a cause for concern and investigation as to what had caused the drop in performance.

Ratios are used to compare performance in one period, say last month or year, with another – this month or year; they can also be used to see how well your business is performing compared with another, say a competitor. You can also use ratios to compare how well you have done against your target or budget. In the financial field the opportunity for calculating ratios is great, for computing useful ratios, not quite so great. Here we will cover the key ratios every business needs to keep track of.

You can see that Table 3.1 is nothing more than a simplified profit and loss account on the left and the assets section of the balance sheet on the right. Any change that increases net profit (more sales, lower expenses, less tax, etc), but does not increase the amount of assets employed (lower stocks, fewer debtors, etc), will increase the return on assets. Conversely, any change that increases capital employed without increasing profits in proportion will reduce the return on assets.

Table 3.1   Factors that affect profit performance

	£			£	£
Sales	100,000	Fixed assets			12,500
– Cost of sales	50,000				
= Gross profit	50,000	Working capital			
– Expenses	33,000	Current assets	23,100		
= Operating profit	17,000	– Current liabilities	6,690 = 16,410		
– Finance charges	8,090	Total net assets			28,910
= Net profit	8,910				

Now let us suppose that events occur to increase sales by £25,000 and profits by £1,000 to £9,910. Superficially that would look like an improved position. But if we then discover that to achieve that extra profit new equipment costing £5,000 and a further £2,500 had to be tied up in working capital (stock and debtors) the picture might not look so attractive. The return being made on assets employed has dropped from 31 per cent (£8,910/28,910 × 100) to 27 per cent (£9,910/[28,910 + 5,000 + 2,500] × 100).

Analysing accounts

The main analytical approach is to examine the relationship of pairs of figures extracted from the accounts. A pair may be taken from the same statement, or one figure from each of the profit and loss account and balance sheet statements. When brought together, the two figures are called ratios. Some financial ratios are meaningful in themselves, but their value mainly lies in their comparison with the equivalent ratio last year, a target ratio, or a competitor's ratio.

Before we can measure and analyse anything about a business's accounts we need some idea of what level or type of performance a business wants to achieve. All businesses have three fundamental objectives in common which allow us to see how well (or otherwise) they are doing.

Making a satisfactory return on investment

The first of these objectives is to make a satisfactory return (profit) on the money invested in the business. It is hard to think of a sound argument against this aim. To be satisfactory the return must meet four criteria:

1 It must give a fair return to shareholders, bearing in mind the risk they are taking. If the venture is highly speculative and the profits are less than bank interest rates, your shareholders (yourself included) will not be happy.

2 You must make enough profit to allow the company to grow. If a business wants to expand sales it will need more working capital and eventually more space or equipment. The safest and surest source of new money for this is internally generated profits, retained in the business: reserves. (A business has three sources of new money: share capital or the owner's money; loan capital, put up by banks, etc; and retained profits, generated by the business.)

3 The return must be good enough to attract new investors or lenders. If investors can get a greater return on their money in some other comparable business, then that is where they will put it.

4 The return must provide enough reserves to keep the real capital intact. This means that you must recognize the impact inflation has on the business. A business retaining enough profits each year to make a 3 per cent growth is actually contracting by 1 per cent if inflation is running at 4 per cent.

Maintaining a sound financial position

As well as making a satisfactory return, investors, creditors and employees expect the business to be protected from unnecessary risks. Clearly, all businesses are exposed to market risks: competitors, new products and price changes are all part of a healthy commercial environment. The sorts of unnecessary risk that investors and lenders are particularly concerned about are high financial risks, such as overtrading.

Cash flow problems are not the only threat to a business's financial position. Heavy borrowing can bring a big interest burden to a small business, especially when interest rates rise unexpectedly. This may be acceptable when sales and profits are good; however, when times are bad, bankers, unlike shareholders, cannot be asked to tighten their belts – they expect to be paid all the time. So the position audit is not just about profitability, but about survival capabilities and the practice of sound financial disciplines.

Achieving growth

Making profit and surviving are insufficient achievements in themselves to satisfy shareholders, directors or ambitious MBAs – they want the business to grow too. But they do not just want the number of people they employ to increase or the sales turnover to rise, however nice that may be. They want the firm to become more efficient, to gain economies of scale and to improve the quality and amount of profits.

Accounting ratios

Ratios used in analysing company accounts are clustered under five headings and are usually referred to as 'tests':

1 tests of profitability;
2 tests of liquidity;
3 tests of solvency;
4 tests of growth; and
5 market tests.

Tests of profitability

There are six ratios generally used to measure profit performance. The first four profit ratios are arrived at using only the profit and loss account and the other two use information from both that account and the balance sheet.

Gross profit

This is calculated by dividing the gross profit by sales and multiplying by 100. Using the example of High Note from Chapter 1 (see Table 3.2), the

Table 3.2   High Note extended profit and loss account

	£
Sales	60,000
Less the cost of goods to be sold	30,000
Gross profit	30,000
Less operating expenses	21,300
Operating profit	8,700
Less interest on bank loan and overdraft	600
Profit before tax	8,100
Less tax	1,827
Profit after tax	6,723

sum is £30,000/£60,000 × 100 = 50%. This is a measure of the value we are adding to the bought in materials and services we need to 'make' our product or service; the higher the figure the better.

Operating profit

This is calculated by dividing the operating profit by sales and multiplying by 100. In this example the sum is £8,700/£60,000 × 100 = 14.5%. This is a measure of how efficiently we are running the business, before taking account of financing costs and tax. These are excluded as interest and tax rates change periodically and are outside our direct control. Excluding them makes it easier to compare one period with another or with another business. Once again the rule here is the higher the figure the better.

Net profit before and after tax

Dividing the net profit before and after tax by the sales and multiplying by 100 calculates these next two ratios. In this example the sums are £8,100/£60,000 × 100 = 13.5% and £6,723/£60,000 × 100 = 11.21%. This is a measure of how efficiently we are running the business, after taking account of financing costs and tax. The last figure shows how successful we are at creating additional money to either invest back in the business or distribute to the owner(s) as drawings or dividends. Once again the rule here is the higher the figure the better.

Return on equity

This ratio is usually expressed as a percentage in the way we might think of the return on any personal financial investment. Taking the owners' viewpoint, their concern is with the profit earned for them relative to the amount of funds they have invested in the business. The relevant profit here is *after* interest, tax (and any preference dividends) have been deducted. This is expressed as a percentage of the equity that comprises ordinary share capital and reserves. So in this example the sum is: return on equity = £6,723/£18,700 × 100 = 36%.

Return on capital employed (also known as 'return on assets')

This takes a wider view of company performance than return on equity by expressing profit before interest, tax and dividend deductions as a percentage of the total capital employed, irrespective of whether this capital is borrowed or provided by the owners.

Capital employed is defined as share capital plus reserves plus long-term borrowings. Where, say, a bank overdraft is included in current liabilities every year and in effect becomes a source of capital, this may be regarded as part of capital employed. If the bank overdraft varies considerably from year to year, a more reliable ratio could be calculated by averaging the start- and end-year figures. There is no one precise definition used by companies for capital employed. In High Note's balance sheet (see Table 3.3) the sum is: return on capital employed = £8,700/£18,700 + £10,000 × 100 = 30%.

EBITDA (Earnings before interest, tax, depreciation and amortization)

This measure of a company's operating efficiency is the one favoured by acquisitive firms as it strips out extraneous costs that may not continue post acquisition, or if they do continue they may not be of a similar proportion. Factors such as:

- Financing costs: Interest rates, for example, may not be the same for both parties to an acquisition and in the case of a cash or share based transaction there may be no residual debt post the event for interest to be paid on.

- Accounting practices: Such items as depreciation and amortization may be different if, for example, some assets were to be eliminated should the acquiring business not require them or have different accounting procedures.

- Tax: If the acquiring company operates in a country where tax rates are lower or higher than the business to be acquired it makes sense to remove them from consideration. This is particularly important where, as is typically the case, the acquiring company has more than one acquisition target in mind. If one of those targets operates in a country with a high tax rate they will appear less attractive as their net profits will appear lower, a factor that may not be relevant after the acquisition has been concluded.

You can see more on the treatment of this subject in Chapter 10.

Table 3.3   High Note balance sheet at 30 September

	£	£
Assets		
Fixed assets		
Fixtures, fitting, equipment	11,500	
Computer	1,000	
Total fixed assets		12,500
Working capital		
Current assets		
Stock	9,108	
Debtors	12,000	
Cash	0	
	21,108	
Less current liabilities (creditors falling due within one year)		
Overdraft	4,908	
Creditors	0	
	4,908	
Net current assets		
[Working capital (CA-CL)]		16,200
Total assets less current liabilities		28,700
Less creditors falling due after one year		
Long-term bank loan		10,000
Net total assets		18,700
Capital and reserves		
Owner's capital introduced	10,000	
Profit retained (from P&L account)	8,700	
Total capital and reserves		18,700

Tests of liquidity

In order to survive companies must also watch their liquidity position, by which is meant keeping enough short-term assets to pay short-term debts. Companies go out of business compulsorily when they fail to pay money due to employees, bankers or suppliers.

The liquid money tied up in day-to-day activities is known as working capital, the sum of which is arrived at by subtracting the current liabilities from the current assets. In the case of High Note we have £21,108 in current assets and £4,908 in current liabilities, so the working capital is £16,200.

Current ratio

As a figure the working capital doesn't tell us much. It is rather as if you knew your car had used 20 gallons of petrol but had no idea how far you had travelled. It would be more helpful to know how much larger the current assets are than the current liabilities. That would give us some idea whether the funds would be available to pay bills for stock, the tax liability and any other short-term liabilities that may arise. The current ratio, which is arrived at by dividing the current assets by the current liabilities, is the measure used. For High Note this is £21,108/£4,908 = 4.30. The convention is to express this as 4.30:1 and the aim is to have a ratio of between 1.5:1 and 2:1. Any lower and bills can't be met easily and much higher and money is being tied up unnecessarily.

Quick ratio (acid test)

This is a belt and braces ratio used to ensure a business has sufficient ready cash or near-cash to meet all its current liabilities. Items such as stock are stripped out as although these are assets the money involved is not immediately available to pay bills. In effect the only liquid assets a business has are cash, debtors and any short-term investment such as bank deposits or government securities. For High Note this ratio is £12,000/£4,908 = 2.44:1. The ratio should be greater than 1:1 for a business to be sufficiently liquid.

Average collection period

We can see that High Note's current ratio is high, which is an indication that some elements of working capital are being used inefficiently. The business has £12,000 owed by customers on sales of £60,000 over a six-month period. The average period it takes High Note to collect money owed is calculated by dividing the sales made on credit by the money owed (debtors) and multiplying it by the time period, in days; in this case the sum is as follows: £12,000/£60,000 × 182.5 = 36.5 days.

If the credit terms are cash with order or seven days, then something is going seriously wrong. If it is net 30 days then it is probably about right. In this example it has been assumed that all the sales were made on credit.

Average payment period

This ratio shows how long a company is taking on average to pay its suppliers. The calculation is as for average collection period, but substituting creditors for debtors and purchase for sales.

Days stock held

High Note is carrying £9,108 stock of sheet music, CDs, etc and over the period it sold £30,000 of stock at cost. (The cost of sales is £30,000 to support £60,000 of invoiced sales as the mark up in this case is 100 per cent.) Using a similar sum as with average collection period we can calculate that the stock being held is sufficient to support 55.41 days sales (£9,108/£10,000 × 182.5). If High Note's suppliers can make weekly deliveries then this is almost certainly too high a stock figure to hold. Cutting stock back from nearly eight weeks (55.41 days) to one week (7 days) would trim 48.41 days or £7,957.38 worth of stock out of working capital. This in turn would bring the current ratio down to 2.68:1

Circulation of working capital

This is a measure used to evaluate the overall efficiency with which working capital is being used. That is the sales divided by the working capital (current assets – current liabilities). In this example that sum is: £60,000/£16,420 = 3.65 times. In other words we are turning over the working capital over three and a half times each year. There are no hard and fast rules as to what is an acceptable ratio. Clearly the more times working capital is turned over, stock sold for example, the more chance a business has to make a profit on that activity.

Tests of solvency

These measures see how a company is managing its long-term liabilities. There are two principal ratios used here: gearing and interest cover.

Gearing/Leverage

This measures as a percentage the proportion of all borrowing, including long-term loans and bank overdrafts, to either the total of shareholders funds – share capital and all reserves. The gearing ratio is sometimes also known as the *debt/equity ratio*. For High Note this is: (£4,908 + £10,000)/£18,800 = £14,908/£18,800 = 0.79: 1. In other words, for every £ the shareholders have invested in High Note they have borrowed a further 79p. This ratio is usually not expected to exceed 1:1 for long periods.

(NB: 'Leverage' is a term preferred in North America.)

Interest cover

This is a measure of the proportion of profit taken up by interest payments and can be found by dividing the annual interest payment into the annual profit before interest, tax and dividend payments. The greater the number, the less vulnerable the company will be to any setback in profits, or rise in interest rates on variable loans. The smaller the number, the more risk that level of borrowing represents to the company. A figure of between two and five times would be considered acceptable.

Tests of growth

These are arrived at by comparing one year with another, usually for elements of the profit and loss account such as sales and profit. So, for example if next year High Note achieved sales of £100,000 and operating profits of £16,000 the growth ratios would be 67 per cent, that is £40,000 of extra sales as a proportion of the first year's sales of £60,000; and 84 per cent, that is £7,300 of extra operating profit as a percentage of the first year's operating profit of £8,700.

Some additional information can be gleaned from these two ratios. In this example we can see that profits are growing faster than sales, which indicates a healthier trend than if the situation were reversed.

Market tests

This is the name given to stock market measures of performance. The key ratios here are:

1 Earnings per share = net profit/shares outstanding.
2 The after-tax profit made by a company divided by the number of ordinary shares it has issued.
3 Price earnings ratio = market price per share/earnings per share.
4 The market price of an ordinary share divided by the earnings per share.

The PE Ratio expresses the market value placed on the expectation of future earnings, ie the number of years required to earn the price paid for the shares out of profits at the current rate:

$$\text{Yield} = \frac{\text{Dividends per Share}}{\text{Price per Share}}$$

The percentage return a shareholder gets on the 'opportunity' or current value of their investment:

$$\text{Dividend Cover} = \frac{\text{Net Income}}{\text{Dividend}}$$

The number of times the profit exceeds the dividend, the higher the ratio, the more retained profit to finance future growth.

Other ratios

There are a very large number of other ratios that businesses use for measuring aspects of their performance such as:

- Sales per $/£/€ invested in fixed assets – a measure of the use of those fixed assets.
- Sales per employee – showing if your headcount is exceeding your sales growth.
- Sales per manager, per support staff, etc – showing the effectiveness of overhead spending.

Table 3.4 shows some of the measures that Tesco, the leading UK retail chain, sees as important. It operates a balanced scorecard approach to managing the business that is known internally within the group as its 'Steering Wheel'. This is intended to unite resources and focuses the efforts of its staff on operations, financial performance and the delivery of customer metrics. Its philosophy is that if it looks after customers well and operates efficiently and effectively then the shareholders' interests will always be best served by the inevitable outputs of those – growth in sales, profits and returns. Table 3.4 shows some of the ratios that Tesco viewed as key.

Combined ratios

No one would use a single ratio to decide whether one vehicle was a better or worse buy than another. MPG, MPH, annual depreciation percentage and residual value proportion are just a handful of the ratios that would need to be reviewed. So it is with a business. A combination of ratios can be used to form an opinion on the financial state of affairs at any one time.

Table 3.4   Tesco's 'Steering Wheel' ratios

	2009	2008
Sales growth		
Change in Group sales over the year (including Value Added Tax)	15.1%	11.1%
UK sales growth	9.5%	6.7%
International sales growth	30.6%	25.3%
International sales growth (at constant exchange rates)	13.6%	22.5%
Retailing services sales growth	11%	–
Profit before tax	£2,954m	£2,803m
Underlying profit before tax	£3,128m	£2,846m
Trading margin		
UK trading margin	6.2%	5.9%
International trading margin (excluding the United States)	5.3%	5.6%
UK Market Share		
Grocery market share	22.2%	21.8%
Non-food market share	8.8%	8.5%
Employee retention	87%	84%
Reduction in CO_2 emissions		
UK	13.3%	3.8%
The Group	12.6%	3.8%
Reduction in CO_2 emissions, new stores	20.9%	11.7%

SOURCE: www.thesmehub.com.

The best known of these combination ratios is the Altman Z-Score (www.creditguru.com/CalcAltZ.shtml) which uses a combined set of five financial ratios derived from eight variables from a company's financial statements linked to some statistical techniques to predict a company's probability of failure. Entering the figures into the onscreen template at this website produces a score and an explanatory narrative giving a view on the business's financial strengths and weaknesses.

Some problems in using ratios

Finding the information to calculate business ratios is often not the major problem. Being sure of what the ratios are really telling you almost always is. The most common problems lie in the four following areas.

Which way is right?

There is a natural feeling with financial ratios to think that high figures are good ones, and an upward trend represents the right direction. This theory is, to some extent, encouraged by the personal feeling of wealth that having a lot of cash engenders.

Unfortunately, there is no general rule on which way is right for financial ratios. In some cases a high figure is good; in others a low figure is best. Indeed, there are even circumstances in which ratios of the same value are not as good as each other. Look at the two working capital statements in Table 3.5.

Table 3.5 Difficult comparisons

Current assets	1		2	
	£	£	£	£
Stock	10,000		22,990	
Debtors	13,000		100	
Cash	100	23,100	10	23,100
Less current liabilities				
Overdraft	5,000		90	
Creditors	1,690	6,690	6,600	6,690
Working capital		16,410		16,410
Current ratio		3.4:1		3.4:1

The amount of working capital in each example is the same (£16,410) as are the current assets and current liabilities, at £23,100 and £6,690 respectively. It follows that any ratio using these factors would also be the same. For example, the current ratios in these two examples are both identical, 3.4:1, but in the first case there is a reasonable chance that some cash will come in from debtors, certainly enough to meet the modest creditor position. In the second example there is no possibility of useful amounts of cash coming in from trading, with debtors at only £100, while creditors at the relatively substantial figure of £6,600 will pose a real threat to financial stability.

So, in this case the current ratios are identical but the situations being compared are not. In fact, as a general rule, a higher working capital ratio is regarded as a move in the wrong direction. The more money a business has tied up in working capital the more difficult it is to make a satisfactory return on capital employed, simply because the larger the denominator the lower the return on capital employed.

In some cases the right direction is more obvious. A high return on capital employed is usually better than a low one, but even this can be a danger signal, warning that higher risks are being taken. And not all high profit ratios are good: sometimes a higher profit margin can lead to reduced sales volume and so lead to a lower ROCE (return on capital employed).

In general, business performance as measured by ratios is best thought of as lying within a range, liquidity (current ratio), for example, staying between 1.2:1 and 1.8:1. A change in either direction represents a cause for concern.

Accounting for inflation

Financial ratios all use dollars, pounds or some other currency as the basis for comparison: historical currency at that. That would not be so bad if all these pounds and dollars were from the same date in the past, but that is not so. Comparing one year with another from three or four years ago may not be very meaningful unless we account for the change in the value of the currency concerned.

One way of overcoming this problem is to adjust for inflation, perhaps using an index, such as that for consumer prices. Such indices usually take 100 as their base at some time in the past, for example, 2000. Then an index value for each subsequent year is produced showing the relative movement in the item being indexed.

Apples and pears

There are particular problems in trying to compare one business's ratios with another. A small new business can achieve quite startling sales growth ratios in the early months and years. Expanding from £10,000 sales in the first six months to £50,000 in the second would not be unusual. To expect a mature business to achieve the same growth would be unrealistic. For Tesco to grow from sales of £10 billion to £50 billion would imply wiping out every other supermarket chain. So some care must be taken to make sure that like is being compared with like, and allowances made for differing circumstances in the businesses being compared (or if the same business, the trading/economic environment of the years being compared).

It is also important to check that one business's idea of an account category, say current assets, is the same as the one you want to compare it with.

The concepts and principles used to prepare accounts leave some scope for differences.

Seasonal factors

Many of the ratios that we have looked at make use of information in the balance sheet. Balance sheets are prepared at one moment in time, and reflect the position at that moment; they may not represent the average situation. For example, seasonal factors can cause a business's sales to be particularly high once or twice a year, as with fashion retailers for example. A balance sheet prepared just before one of these seasonal upturns might show very high stocks, bought in specially to meet this demand. Conversely, a look at the balance just after the upturn might show very high cash and low stocks. If either of those stock figures were to be treated as an average it would give a false picture.

Getting company accounts

It will be very useful to look at other comparable businesses to see their ratios as a yardstick against which to compare your own business's performance. For publicly quoted and larger business whose accounts are audited this should not be too difficult; for smaller private companies the position is not quite so simple. In many regions small businesses need only file abbreviated accounts that can conceal more about profit performance than they reveal. Though net profit before and after tax is usually shown irrespective of the size of the business, gross and operating profit details are not required. A further complication is that 'small' has different definitions in different geographic areas and for different industries. In the United States, for example, an agricultural business with $750,000 (£500,000) in average annual sales would be considered small, but a firm in general building and construction would still be 'small' with $36.5 million (£24 million) in average annual sales. Only public companies listed on a stock market and larger companies have to provide full financial statements. Despite this it is still possible to glean some valuable information on financial performance using the following sources.

These two links will help you locate the financial accounts of companies in most countries:

- Kyckr (https://app.kyckr.com): Provides access to over 180 corporate registries and 170+ million legal entities across 120 countries. Charges start from around €5 for the accounts for a single year.
- Gov.UK (www.gov.uk/get-information-about-a-company): Here you can get some details about all UK a companies at no cost, including:

- company information, for example registered address and date of incorporation;
- current and resigned officers;
- document images;
- mortgage charge data;
- previous company names;
- insolvency information.

You can also set up free email alerts to tell you when a company updates its details.

Example of the accounting information that is readily available on most limited and all public companies are shown in the tables that follow. Table 3.6 shows part of the accounts for 2012 to 2014 on an annual basis and for the final year on a quarter by quarter basis for Google Inc. The final figures are also designated as 'unaudited,' which means they could change if the auditors take a different view on some items from the company's accountants. (I cover more on the role of auditors in Chapter 9).

From Google's accounts you can see websites account for only the second largest portion of the company's revenues and that is still growing at a double digit rate. Advertising is Google's biggest earner. Despite all the press comment on Google Glass, smart phones and its suite of productivity applications, including spreadsheet, word-processing, and photo-editing software, those products account for just a couple of per cent of the business. Looking down the figures raises as many questions as answers. For example just what has cost the company nearly \$2 billion in discontinued operations over the period? That question and dozens more are answered in 'Notes' to the accounts. I cover these in Chapter 9.

The figures for Tesco (Table 3.7), the largest UK grocery retailer and still number 5 in the world despite its fall from grace in 2014, show a business recovering fast from the profit collapse in 2013. By 2022 Tesco had more than recovered its crown, showing annual sales £54.8 billion and profit £2.825 billion (www.tescoplc.com/investors/reports-results-and-presentations/annual-report-2022).

Using financial data to improve performance

A priority task for any MBA will be to assist managers in improving business performance. This is an area in which the MBA will be best able to demonstrate the value of his or her skills and so build allies in the organization. The most successful businesses, when it comes to becoming more profitable (the acid test of business improvement), concentrate their efforts

Table 3.6 Google Inc company accounts

Revenues	Full Year			2014			
	2012	2013	2014 (unaudited)	Q1 (unaudited)	Q2 (unaudited)	Q3 (unaudited)	Q4 (unaudited)
Google Websites	$31,221	$37,422	$45,085	$10,469	$10,935	$11,252	$12,429
Y/Y Growth Rate	19%	20%	20%	21%	23%	20%	18%
Q/Q Growth Rate	NA	NA	NA	-1%	4%	3%	10%
Google Network Members' Websites	$12,465	$13,125	$13,971	$3,397	$3,424	$3,430	$3,720
Y/Y Growth Rate	20%	5%	6%	4%	7%	9%	6%
Q/Q Growth Rate	NA	NA	NA	-4%	1%	0%	8%
Total Advertising Revenues	$43,686	$50,547	$59,056	$13,866	$14,359	$14,682	$16,149
Y/Y Growth Rate	20%	16%	17%	17%	19%	17%	15%
Q/Q Growth Rate	NA	NA	NA	-1%	4%	2%	10%
Other Revenues	$2,354	$4,972	$6,945	$1,554	$1,596	$1,841	$1,954
Y/Y Growth Rate	71%	111%	40%	48%	53%	50%	19%
Q/Q Growth Rate	NA	NA	NA	-6%	3%	15%	6%
Total Revenues	$46,039	$55,519	$66,001	$15,420	$15,955	$16,523	$18,103
Y/Y Growth Rate	21%	21%	19%	19%	22%	20%	15%

Table 3.6 *continued*

Costs	Full Year			2014			
	2012	2013	2014 (unaudited)	Q1 (unaudited)	Q2 (unaudited)	Q3 (unaudited)	Q4 (unaudited)
Cost of Revenues	$17,176	$21,993	$25,691	$5,961	$6,114	$6,695	$6,921
As a % of Revenues	37%	40%	39%	39%	38%	40%	38%
Traffic Acquisition Cost	$10,956	$12,258	$13,496	$3,232	$3,293	$3,348	$3,623
As % of Revenues	24%	22%	20%	21%	20%	20%	20%
Other Cost of Revenues*	$6,220	$9,735	$12,195	$2,729	$2,821	$3,347	$3,298
As % of Revenues	14%	18%	18%	18%	18%	20%	18%
Research & Development*	$6,083	$7,137	$9,832	$2,126	$2,238	$2,655	$2,813
As % of Revenues	13%	13%	15%	14%	14%	16%	16%
Sales & Marketing*	$5,465	$6,554	$8,131	$1,729	$1,941	$2,084	$2,377
As % of Revenues	12%	12%	12%	11%	12%	13%	13%
General & Administrative*	$3,481	$4,432	$5,851	$1,489	$1,404	$1,365	$1,593
As % of Revenues	8%	8%	9%	9%	9%	8%	9%
Total Costs & Expenses*	$32,205	$40,116	$49,505	$11,305	$11,697	$12,799	$13,704

Profitability	2012	2013	2014	Q1	Q2	Q3	Q4
Income from Operations	$13,834	$15,403	$16,496	$4,115	$4,258	$3,724	$4,399
As % of Revenues	30%	28%	25%	27%	27%	23%	24%
Net income from continuing operations	$11,553	$13,347	$13,928	$3,650	$3,490	$2,998	$3,790
As % of Revenues	25%	24%	21%	24%	22%	18%	21%
Net (loss) income from discontinued operations	($816)	($427)	$516	($198)	($68)	($185)	$967
Net Income	$10,737	$12,920	$14,444	$3,452	$3,422	$2,813	$4,757

SOURCE: https://abc.xyz/investor/

Table 3.7   Tesco plc profit and loss account

	52 weeks 2014 £m	52 weeks 2013 £m
Continuing operations		
Revenue	63,557	63,406
Cost of sales	(59,547)	(59,252)
Gross profit	4,010	4,154
Administrative expenses	(1,657)	(1,482)
Profits/losses arising on property-related items	278	(290)
Operating profit	2,631	2,382
Share of post-tax profits of joint ventures and associates	60	72
Finance income	132	120
Finance costs	(564)	(517)
Profit before tax	2,259	2,057
Taxation	1,912	1,528
Discontinued operations		
Loss for the year from discontinued operations	(942)	(1,504)
Profit for the year	970	24

SOURCE: www.tescoplc.com/files/pdf/reports/ar14/download_annual_report.pdf

in three areas: optimizing resources, maintaining or improving profit margins and of course building up sales revenue. It is this last strategy that draws the most attention, but not pursuing the other two may lead only to unprofitable growth, so leaving a business more vulnerable as it gets bigger. All three of these generic growth strategies are to a greater or lesser extent intertwined, so you should look on this categorization process more as an aide-memoire rather than a rigid structure.

Put simply you can see that any action that tends to increase profits while either not increasing or actually reducing the resources employed to gener-

Table 3.8 High Note's profit and loss account and balance sheet

Profit and loss account		Balance sheet		
	£		£	£
Sales	60,000	Fixed assets		
Less the cost of goods to be sold (materials, labour, etc)	30,000	Garage conversion, etc		11,500
		Computer		1,000
Gross profit	30,000	Total fixed assets		12,500
Less operating expenses (rent, utilities, admin, etc)	21,300			
Operating profit	8,700	Working capital		
Less interest due to bank	600	Current assets		
Profit before tax	8,100	Stock	9,108	
Less tax	1,377	Debtors	12,000	
Profit after tax	6,723	Cash	0	
(11.21%)			21,108	
		Less		
		Current liabilities		
		Overdraft	4,908	
		Creditors	0	
			4,908	
		Working capital (CA–CL)		16,200
		Total assets		28,700

ate those profits produces healthy growth. Using the summarized financial statements for High Note shown in Table 3.8 we can see the effect of various growth strategies. If we can increase sales, say, by £10,000 while maintaining the profit margin at 11.21 per cent we will have grown profits by £1,121. So both sales and profits will have grown by 17 per cent. If that can also be done without needing any more working space or money tied up in stocks, so much the better. Our return on capital will also improve. Contrast that with a strategy that grows sales while costs rise disproportionately and more assets are employed to achieve that growth, and an unhealthy growth pattern will emerge.

Optimizing resources

The first and in some ways the simplest way to grow profits is to get more of what you sell ready for market using fewer resources. This strategy improves profit margins while either reducing the actual amount of money needed to run the business, or allows you to grow without recourse to additional financing. Both are desirable outcomes as it leaves you with a more secure venture as well as a bigger one.

Reviewing working methods

The richest source of opportunities to optimize comes from finding ways to work smarter rather than harder. Finding out about better ways to work can be difficult for a small firm where the founder has few senior employees to learn from – one of the benefits big businesses get by virtue of continuously recruiting new people. Owner-managers can compensate by getting out themselves and seeing what is going on in their industry. Below are some ways you can keep abreast of the latest developments in your field.

Read widely both the magazines that relate to your industry and those of neighbouring topics. In particular read magazines and articles published in the area that is at the leading edge of your business world: Silicon Valley for the internet, Germany for the motor industry, Japan for cameras and photography. Keep track of your competitor's financial performance using the sources described earlier in this chapter and set up Google Alerts (www.google.co.uk/alerts) to flag up news on topics of interest such as new product launches, reporting performance or changes in senior management.

Attend exhibitions, conferences and seminars where you are likely to meet and hear movers and shakers in your industry. All Conferences.com (www.allconferences.com) is a directory focusing on conferences, conventions, trade shows, exhibitions and workshops that can be searched by category, key word, date and venue as well as by title.

Control working capital

The main levers for getting quick wins when it comes to improving performance lie in the working capital area. If sales and profit growth can be achieved using the same proportion of working capital or less then a healthy growth is being achieved.

Debtor control

If you are selling on credit and take 90 days to collect your money from customers, which is by no means uncommon, then you are tying up an extra £150,000 cash for every £1 million of sales, compared to a firm getting its money in 35 days. Even quite small firms, say with a turnover of around £3 million a year, could eliminate the whole value of their overdraft by taking simple measures to improve in this respect. Looking at it another way, getting paid a week earlier would free up nearly £60,000 of lifesaving cash in such a venture.

A very small amount of extra effort put in here can pay great dividends and it's important to remember the less cash needed to finance the business the more profitable that business will be. Here are some things you can do to get paid faster.

If you sell on credit set out your terms of trade clearly on your invoices. Unless customers know when you expect to be paid, they will pay when it suits them. Find out when your biggest customers have their monthly cheque run and make sure your bills reach them in time. Send out statements promptly to chase up late payers, and always follow up with a phone call. Always take trade references when giving credit and look at their accounts to see how sound they are.

Normally the rule is to take credit from your suppliers up to the maximum time allowed. But sometimes it may make good business sense to pay up promptly. While this may sound insane, sometimes suppliers with cash flow difficulties of their own offer what amounts to excessively high rates of interest for settling up promptly.

If a supplier offers 2 per cent to pay up in seven days rather than the 40 days they would usually take, what is on offer is in effect a 22.65 per cent equivalent interest. (Follow the steps below to work out if prompt payment is a good investment.) So if that figure is higher than the return you are making in the business, and your cash flow can stand the pain, paying promptly may be a better way to grow profits than many other options, particularly during a recession. You can use the same arithmetic to work out what you can afford to pay out to get your money in earlier; see Table 3.9.

Table 3.9 Evaluating a discount offer

Step 1	Agree discount	2%
Step 2	100 – discount on offer	98%
Step 3	Divide step 1 by step 2	0.02048
Step 4	Normal payment period in days	40
Step 5	Payment period to get discount	7
Step 6	Step 4 minus step 5	33
Step 7	365 divided by step 6	11.06061
Step 8	Step 7 × step 3 × 100	22.65%

Inventory management

High inventory levels are popular with marketing departments as having them makes satisfying customers an easier task; they are less popular with production departments, which have to carry inventory costs in their budgets. Finance departments insist on having the lowest possible stock levels, as high stock pushes working capital levels up and return on investment down. This tussle between departments is a strategic issue that has to be resolved by top management. The birth of Waterstone's, the bookshop business founded by Tim Waterstone, fortuitously a marketing visionary, qualified accountant and the company's managing director, provides an interesting illustration of the dimension of the stock control issue. Up until the advent of Waterstone's the convention had been to store books spine out on shelves, in alphabetical order, under major subject headings – computing, sport, travel, etc. This had the added advantage of making it easy to see what books needed reordering and stock counts were a simple process. Waterstone, however, knew that 'browsers', the majority (60 per cent, according to his research) of people who go into bookshops to look around, had no idea what book they wanted, so didn't know where to start looking. His differentiating strategy was, as well as following the conventional model of having books on shelves, scattering the books in piles around the store using a variety of methods: new books in one pile, special offers in another. Sales and profits soared sufficiently to more than compensate for the near doubling of book stock.

Inventory categories

There are three different categories of inventory that a business needs to have and keep track of:

1 *Finished goods:* these are products ready to ship out to customers. For Apple these would be computers, iPods and so forth, for General Motors vehicles and for a baker loaves of bread.

2 *Work in progress (WIP):* these are products in the process of being completed. They have used up some raw materials and had workers paid to start the manufacturing process, so the cost will reflect those inputs. For General Motors WIP would include vehicles awaiting paint or a pre-delivery inspection.

3 *Raw materials:* These are the basic materials from which the end product is made. For General Motors this would include metal and paint, but it could also include a complete bought-in engine for the vehicles in which it uses third-party power units.

Economic order quantity (EOQ)

Businesses have to carry a certain minimum amount of stock to ensure the production pipeline works efficiently and likely demand is met. So the costs associated with ordering large quantities infrequently and so reducing the order cost but increasing the cost of holding stock has to be balanced with placing frequent orders, so pushing up the costs of placing orders but reducing stock-holding costs. EOQ is basically an accounting formula that calculates the point at which the combination of order costs and inventory carrying costs are the least, so arriving at the most cost effective quantity to order. The formula for EOQ is:

$$\text{Economic Order Quantity} = \frac{\sqrt{(2 \times R \times O)}}{C}$$

where: R = Annual demand in units; O = Cost of placing an order; C = Cost of carrying a unit of inventory for the year.

InventoryOps.com, a website created and run by Dave Piasecki to support his book *Inventory Accuracy: People, processes, & technology* (2003, Ops Publishing), provides a useful starting point in your quest for information on all aspects of inventory management and warehouse operations. You will find a full explanation of how to use EOQ at: www.inventoryops. com/articles/optomizing-eoq.html.

Improving profit margins

Over time costs tend to creep ahead of the value you are getting for the money spent. The rises happen steadily, often nearly invisibly and in increments sometimes apparently insignificant in themselves. For example, employees expect an annual pay review, which usually means a pay rise not necessarily related to any improvement in performance; suppliers regularly increase prices; the cost of utilities and government taxes consistently rise faster than inflation. Unless you are getting more sales as a result of these cost rises, profits will shrink. There are four courses of action we can take to improve margins.

1. Charge more

It is never easy raising prices but it can, if done selectively, be a path to healthy growth. First, let's examine the potential rewards and risks. Using High Note as our working model, assume its £60,000 of sales come from 60 customers all buying £1,000 worth of goods and services from us, at 50 per cent gross profit margin. If by raising our prices by 10 per cent we lost no customers then our profit would rise by £6,000, all of which would drop to the bottom line, before tax, as there are no additional costs involved; almost doubling our profit before tax.

What would happen if we lost six customers (10 per cent) as a result of the price rise? Now we would only have 54 customers paying £1,100 each, or £59,400. That's only £600 less than before and there are other benefits that have not been shown. Putting the pressure on price rather than volume means carrying less stock, having fewer bills to chase, using less capital and wearing out equipment less quickly. That is not to imply that putting up prices is an easy task, but it may not be much harder than finding new customers, and it is nearly always more profitable. When raising prices try to offer some extra value in return in terms of improved service or extra features.

These sums depend on your level of gross profit. The lower your gross profit the less business you can afford to lose for any given price rise. Charley Kyd, who earned his MBA from the Michael G Foster School of Business at the University of Washington, has a series of Excel spreadsheets and explanations on the effect of prices and margins on overall profitability at https://exceluser.com/2451/should-you-raise-prices-should-you-lower-them/.

2. Change product/service mix

If you sell more than one product or service, or are planning to introduce new ones as part of your growth strategy, analyse costs so that energies are focused on those with the highest profit margin. Very few owner-managers have any true idea as to which products or services generate the most profit, so collecting that data has to be the first step. (If you are a little rusty on costing, read Chapter 4 first.)

Look at the example in Table 3.10. This business makes three products. Product C is bulky, complicated and a comparatively slow seller. It uses all the same sort of equipment, storage space and sales efforts as products A and B, only more so. When fixed costs are allocated across the range it draws the greatest share.

Table 3.10   Product profitability (1)

	A £	B £	C £	Total £
Sales	30,000	50,000	20,000	100,000
Variable costs	20,000	30,000	10,000	60,000
Allocated fixed costs	4,500	9,000	11,500	25,000
Total costs	24,500	39,000	21,500	85,000
Operating profit	5,500	11,000	(1,500)	15,000

These figures seem to show that product C is losing money and should be eliminated. Doing so will produce the situation shown in Table 3.11.

Table 3.11   Product profitability (2)

	A £	B £	Total £
Sales	30,000	50,000	80,000
Variable costs	20,000	30,000	50,000
New allocated fixed costs	8,333	16,667	25,000
Total costs	28,333	46,667	75,000
Operating profit	1,667	3,333	5,000

Fixed costs will not change just because we have dropped a product; our property and any other element of fixed costs will still need to be covered. So dropping the 'unprofitable' C product has actually resulted in less profit than before. This full costing system has given the wrong signal as it ignores any contribution (the difference between selling price and variable costs) that product C makes.

If we allocate fixed costs by reference to the amount of contribution a product makes we will end up with a very different calculation; see Table 3.12.

Table 3.12   Fixed costs allocated by contribution level

		Contribution £	%	Fixed cost allocated £
Product	A	10,000	25	6,250
	B	20,000	50	12,500
	C	10,000	25	6,250
Total		40,000	100	25,000

Recasting the profit and loss account using the contribution each product makes rather than full costing reveals a quite different profit picture; see Table 3.13.

Table 3.13   Product profitability using contribution

	A		B		C		Total
	£	%	£	%	£	%	£
Sales	30,000		50,000		20,000		100,000
Marginal costs	20,000		30,000		10,000		60,000
Contribution	10,000	33	20,000	40	10,000	50	40,000
Fixed costs	6,250		12,500		6,250		25,000
Product profit	3,750	13	7,500	15	3,750	19	15,000

Given that we can't eliminate many fixed costs in a home-based business, contribution as a basis for allocating fixed costs give a more useful signal as to where to concentrate efforts. Far from eliminating product C, all things being equal we should try to sell more.

3. Buy less

The challenge here is to strip out waste or find ways to step up yield. When you are working on your own this will probably not be a fertile field; once you have employees, however dedicated, the problems start. The classic question when people want to buy something is to ask, 'If it were your money would you spend it this way?' One entrepreneur who has built his company to a £3 million business from a standing start five years earlier formed his 20 employees into what he called 'Smart Circles'. He challenged them to find ways the firm could do things faster, better and at a lower cost. In year one he doubled profits and within five years his business was valued at £10 million.

4. Reducing the tax take

Tax on profits is often a business's biggest single expense, slicing anything from 20 to 40 per cent off the bottom line. All money that goes in taxes can be consider a waste as far as a business is concerned, as unlike individuals who may see something of value for their tax a business gets little back. So the rule here is to minimize tax within the law. In April 2021 the Institute on Taxation and Economics reported that 55 profitable corporations would have paid a collective total of $8.5 billion for the year, had they paid that rate on their 2020 income. Instead, they received $3.5 billion in tax rebates (https://itep.org/55-profitable-corporations-zero-corporate-tax). Tax Watch reported that eight large tech companies in the UK made an estimated £9.6 billion in profit from sales to UK customers in 2019 and should have paid £1.8 billion in tax. However, they actually only paid £297 million (www.

taxwatchuk.org/tech_companies_2019_update). Getting taxes down, legally, is a job for your treasury department, if you have one. If not get specialist tax advice, but as an MBA you should be able to act as the catalyst to ensure this area is reviewed frequently (see also Chapter 9).

Online video courses and lectures

Accounting Coach: Using notes, quizzes, question and answer sessions this site provides a clear explanation of financial ratios and financial statement analysis. Business forms for computing 24 popular financial ratios are included in AccountingCoach PRO which costs £45 ($49): www.accountingcoach.com/financial-ratios/explanation

Corporate Finance Essentials: Prof Javier Estrada of IESE Business School offers this course each year. It consists of six sessions requiring no previous knowledge or preparation. Each session will consist of a video lecture of around 45–60 minutes and one or two recommended readings: www.coursera.org/learn/corporate-finance-essentials

The Khan Academy has a comprehensive range of video lectures and exercises on accounting matters at: www.khanacademy.org/economics-finance-domain/core-finance/accounting-and-financial-stateme

Financial forecasting and reporting. These two section are particularly relevant: 'Financial ratio analyses and forecasting techniques' and 'Understanding corporate financial statements'. Delivered by the University of Colorado, Boulder: www.coursera.org/learn/financial-forecasting-and-reporting

Lies My Finance Professor Told Me. Andrew W Lo, Charles E and Susan T Harris Professor; Director, Laboratory for Financial Engineering at the MIT Finance Forum: www.youtube.com/watch?v=sUdUuvbSDiM&t=78s

Financial acumen for non-financial managers, Wharton School at the University of Pennsylvania. Confusingly when you click on the link you see 'finance-healthcare-managers'. Don't be put off, as most of the material is based around a large US multinational consumer goods company: www.coursera.org/learn/finance-healthcare-managers

Online video case studies

Amazon, Apple and Netflix: Accounts analysed by students and reviewed by Professor Clyde Warden at NCHU (National Chung Hsing University), Taiwan: www.youtube.com/watch?v=FtPBgzQp9q4

Capita, 2022 full and half-year financial information, financial results statements, investor presentations, webcasts and annual reports for the last ten years: www.capita.com/investors/results-reports-and-presentations

Case Studies in Finance: Robert F Bruner (Dean of the University of Virginia Darden School of Business), Kenneth M Eades and Michael J Schill (Professors of Business Administration at the Darden School) discuss how the topics in finance are taught effectively through the case method: www.youtube.com/watch?v=3zqAFnF2PN0

Mighty River Power: Doug Heffernan, Chief Executive delivers 'Financial Results–Analyst Presentation': www.youtube.com/watch?v=EzNPBvSyYUI

Shell: Ben van Beurden, Chief Executive Officer, comments on the second quarter 2022: www.youtube.com/watch?v=KchTJqjfXLU

04
Finance as a value creator

- Breaking even, where value begins
- Realizing profit goals
- Profit maximization vs shareholder value
- Putting a cost on capital
- Assessing future profitability

Financial management is not just about historical data and esoteric arguments about the valuation of assets and liabilities. The most useful application of financial tools, from an MBA's perspective, are some powerful but simple techniques to help managers make better decisions now and have a more accurate picture of the likely outcomes, from a financial perspective at least, of future performance. These tools are simple and certainly not new – for example articles assessing the use of break-even analysis had started to appear by 1962 (*Break-Even Analysis: Its uses and misuses*, Howard F Stettler, 1962, American Accounting Association). But most managers have never heard of these tools and those very few that have don't know how to use them. This gives MBAs a powerful edge and allows them to muscle into decisions that are normally the prerogative of those several pay grades higher.

Three further factors work to the MBA's advantage when it comes to appreciating the interplay between financial performance and value. In the first instance profit alone is far less important than accountants would like to have you believe: the steady rise in Amazon's share price, while racking up accelerating losses, is sufficient to prove that point. They lost nearly $3 billion in their first seven years of trading, before turning their first quarterly profit in 2002 – a modest $5 million. On 29 January 2015, Greg Besinger, in the *Wall Street Journal*, reported on Amazon's results that: 'Amazon typically has satisfied investors with rapidly-growing sales and investments, even at the expense of profits' going on to note that even when reporting its largest loss since 2000 '… shares rose sharply in after-hours trading, at one point up 14 per cent.'

The logic behind the shareholders' euphoria was that sales reached $89 billion, whilst conveniently overlooking the fact that operating expenses at $88.8 billion were a fifth higher. So the MBA can bring his or her wider skills to bear, while fully understanding the part finance plays, to get a more rounded picture of what drives value.

The second factor that an MBA needs to keep in mind is that management below the very top matters very little in the eyes of those who assess value, but financial results do. In a study by DDI, a talent management company, of 50 financial analysts only eight said that leadership accounted for over 25 per cent of the criteria they used in assigning value to a company's shares. Financial elements accounted for the remaining 75 per cent. Some 84 per cent rated consistent growth in turnover a most important factor, while 94 per cent ranked the experience of the person at the very top as key. The Tesla case study that follows seems to support these findings.

Third, it is quite possible for a business that is very profitable in one period to be completely worthless in a matter of months or even days. If you think this an unlikely scenario, look back to Lehman Brothers, the 158-year-old bank that failed in September 2008. It was listed as 37th in the Fortune 500 in 2008, up from 47th the preceding year. Its last accounts showed $4,192 million profits, up 4.6 per cent on the year before. Its 'stock in trade' was investment advice, which became worthless as its business model imploded. The MBA should be aware that the wheel is always in spin and yesterday's accounts are just that: yesterday's story.

CASE STUDY
Tesla

The first successful electric car made in the United States is generally attributed to William Morrison, a chemist from Des Moines, Iowa. Around 1890 his six-passenger vehicle, in reality an electrified wagon, hit a top speed of 14 miles per hour. Within a decade, electric cars accounted for a third of all vehicles on the road. Henry Ford's mass-produced Model T effectively killed off electric cars. His Model T cost $650 in 1912, while an electric roadster sold for $1,750.

It was not until nearly a century later that the electric car began its revival. In 2003 Martin Eberhard and Marc Tarpenning founded Tesla. A year later Elon Musk, who co-founded PayPal, bought into the business, pumping in $6.5 million. By 2008 he was the largest shareholder and CEO. Aside from PayPal, Musk already had a string of ventures under his belt. In 1995, alongside his younger brother Kimbal, Musk co-founded Zip2, a web software company helping newspapers to create online city guides. In 1999 Zip2 was sold to Compaq Computer Corp. for $341 million, a decent return on the $15 million Musk had staked. With the money from Zip2 Musk started X.com, later merging that with Confinity, a money transfer business. And so PayPal was born.

Tesla's founders had as their goal to produce a powerful, beautiful electric car with zero emissions. The company opened a 5.3 million square-feet factory, previously owned by Toyota and General Motors, and launched its first car, the Roadster. With the acceleration of a sports car, the Roadster quickly gathered a following, one that was confined to the affluent as it cost over $100,000. Its range was a modest 250 miles and it took up to 48 hours to charge on a standard home outlet. Tesla didn't even have sufficient funds to make the limited number of cars on order. In 2008 Daimler AG bought a 10 per cent stake in Tesla for $50 million and the US Department of Energy provided a $465 million loan. This gave them the breathing space to build up sufficient credibility to take the company public in 2010 and raise $226 million.

But it wasn't until 2020 that the company first started to make a profit That year they made $720 million, which sounds fine until you stack it against the turnover – $31.5 billion. Nevertheless, shareholders had good reason to be satisfied. They had seen a hundred fold return on their investment (Figure 4.1).

Figure 4.1   Tesla finally turns a profit in 2020

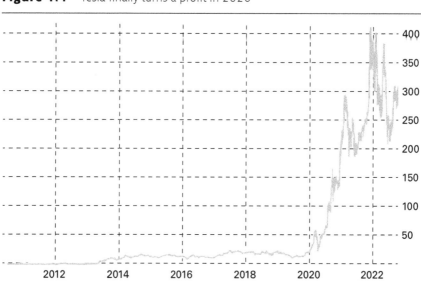

SOURCE: Macrotrends, www.macrotrends.net/stocks/charts/TSLA/tesla/stock-price-history

Cost, volume, pricing and profit decisions

Working out the cost of making a product or delivering a service and consequently how much to charge doesn't seem too complicated. At first glance the problem is simple. You just add up all the costs and charge a bit more. The more you charge above your costs, provided the customers will keep on buying, the more profit you make. Unfortunately, as soon as you start to do the sums the problem gets a little more complex. For a start, not all costs have the same characteristics. Some costs, for example, do not change however much you sell. If you are running a shop, the rent and rates are relatively constant figures, completely independent of the volume of your sales. On the other hand, the cost of the products sold from the shop is completely dependent on volume. The more you sell, the more it costs you to buy in stock.

	€
Rent and rates for shop	2,500
Cost of 1,000 units of volume of product	1,000
Total costs	3,500

You can't really add up those two types of costs until you have made an assumption about volume – how much you plan to sell. Look at the simple example above. Until we decide to buy, and we hope sell, 1,000 units of our product, we cannot total the costs. With the volume hypothesized we can arrive at a cost per unit of product of:

$$\text{Total costs} \div \text{Number of units} = €3,500 \div 1,000 = €3.50$$

Now, provided we sell out all the above at €3.50, we shall always be profitable. But will we? Suppose we do not sell all the 1,000 units, what then? With a selling price of €4.50 we could, in theory, make a profit of €1,000 if we sell all 1,000 units. That is a total sales revenue of €4,500, minus total costs of €3,500. But if we only sell 500 units, our total revenue drops to €2,250 and we actually lose €1,250 (total revenue €2,250 – total costs €3,500). So at one level of sales a selling price of €4.50 is satisfactory, and at another it is a disaster. This very simple example shows that all those decisions are intertwined. Costs, sales volume, selling prices and profits are all linked together. A decision taken in any one of these areas has an impact on the others. To understand the relationship between these factors, we need a picture or model of how they link up. Before we can build this model, we need some more information on each of the component parts of cost.

The components of cost

Understanding the behaviour of costs as the trading patterns in a business change is of vital importance to decision makers. It is this 'dynamic' nature in every business that makes good costing decisions the key to survival and provides the MBA with a wealth of opportunities to demonstrate his or her skill and knowledge.

The last example showed that if the situation was static and predictable, a profit was certain, but if any one component in the equation was not a certainty (in that example it was volume), then the situation was quite different. To see how costs behave under changing conditions we first have to identify the different types of cost.

Fixed costs

Fixed costs are costs that happen, by and large, whatever the level of activity. For example, the cost of buying a car is the same whether it is driven 100 miles a year or 20,000 miles. The same is also true of the road tax, insurance and any extras, such as a stereo system or navigator.

In a business, as well as the cost of buying cars, there are other fixed costs such as plant, equipment, computers, desks and answering machines. But certain less tangible items can also be fixed costs, for example rent, rates, insurance and so on, which are usually set quite independent of how successful or otherwise a business is.

Costs such as most of those mentioned above are fixed irrespective of the timescale under consideration. Other costs, such as those of employing people, while theoretically variable in the short term, in practice are fixed. In other words, if sales demand goes down and a business needs fewer people, the costs cannot be shed for several weeks (notice, holiday pay, redundancy, etc). Also, if the people involved are highly skilled or expensive to recruit and train (or in some other way particularly valuable) and the downturn looks a short one, it may not be cost-effective to reduce those short-run costs in line with falling demand. So viewed over a period of weeks and months, labour is a fixed cost. Over a longer period it may not be fixed. We could draw a simple chart showing how fixed costs behave as the 'dynamic' volume changes. The first phase of our cost model is shown in Figure 4.2. This shows a static level of fixed costs over a particular range of output. To return to the previous example, this could show the fixed cost, rent and rates for a shop to be constant over a wide range of sales levels. Once the shop owner has reached a satisfactory sales and profit level in one shop, he or she may decide to rent another one, in which case the fixed costs will 'step up'. This can be shown in the variation on the fixed cost model in Figure 4.3.

Variable costs

These are costs that change in line with output. Raw materials for production, packaging materials, bonuses, piece rates, sales commission and

Figure 4.2   Cost model 1: showing fixed costs

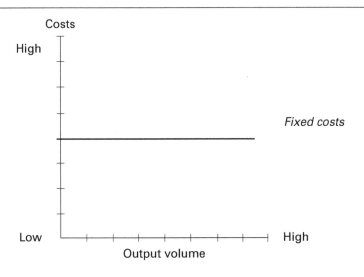

Figure 4.3   Variation on cost model 1: showing a 'step up' in fixed costs

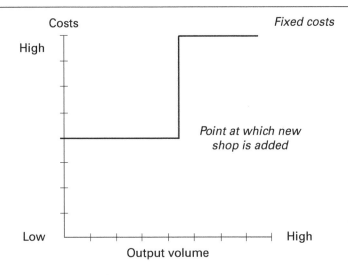

postage are some examples. The important characteristic of a variable cost is that it rises or falls in direct proportion to any growth or decline in output volumes. We can now draw a chart showing how variable costs behave as volume changes. The second phase of our cost model will look like Figure 4.4.

There is a popular misconception that defines fixed costs as those costs that are predictable, and variable costs as those that are subject to change at any moment. The definitions already given are the only valid ones for costing purposes.

Figure 4.4   Cost model 2: showing behaviour of variable costs as volume changes

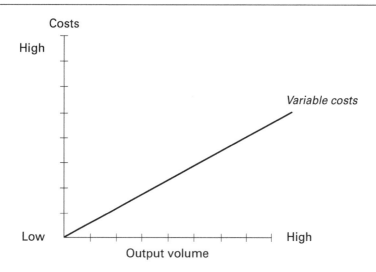

Semi-variable costs

Unfortunately not all costs fit easily into either the fixed or variable category. Some costs have both a fixed and a variable element. For example, a mobile phone has a monthly rental cost that is fixed, and a cost per unit consumed over and above a set usage rate, which is variable. In this particular example low-usage consumers can be seriously penalized. If only a few calls are made each month, their total cost per call (fixed rental + cost per unit ÷ number of calls) can be relatively high. Other examples of this dual-component cost are photocopier rentals, electricity and gas.

These semi-variable costs must be split into their fixed and variable elements. For most small businesses this will be a fairly simple process; nevertheless it is essential to do it accurately or else much of the purpose and benefits of this method of cost analysis will be wasted.

Break-even analysis

Bringing both fixed and variable costs together we can build a costing model that shows how total costs behave for different levels of output; see Figure 4.5.

Any company capturing a sizeable market share will have an implied cost advantage over any competitor with a smaller market share. That cost advantage can be used to make more profit, lower prices and compete for an even greater share of the market or invest in making the product better and so steal a march on competitors. By starting the variable costs from the plateau of the fixed costs, we can produce a line showing the total costs.

Figure 4.5   Cost model showing total costs and fixed costs

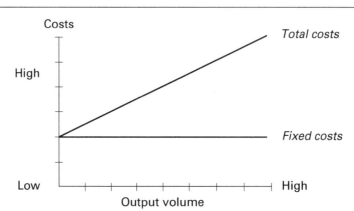

Taking vertical and horizontal lines from any point in the total cost line will give the total costs for any chosen output volume. This is an essential feature of the costing model that lets us see how costs change with different output volumes: in other words, accommodating the dynamic nature of a business. It is to be hoped that we are not simply producing things and creating costs: we are also selling things and creating income. So a further line can be added to the model to show sales revenue as it comes in. To help bring the model to life, let's add some figures, for illustration purposes only.

Figure 4.6 shows the break-even point (BEP). Perhaps the most important single calculation in the whole costing exercise is to find the point at which real profits start to be made. The point where the sales revenue line crosses the total costs line is the break-even point. It is only after that point has been reached that a business can start to make a profit. We can work this out by drawing a graph or by using a simple formula. The advantage of using the formula as well as a graph is that you can experiment by quickly changing the values of some of the elements in the model.

The equation for the BEP is:

$$\frac{\text{Fixed costs}}{\text{Unit selling price} - \text{Variable costs per unit}}$$

This is quite logical. Before you can reach profits you must pay for the variable costs. This is done by deducting those costs from the unit selling price. What is left (usually called the 'unit contribution') is available to meet the fixed costs. Once enough units have been sold to meet these fixed costs, the BEP has been reached. Let's try the sum out, given the following information shown on the break-even chart:

Fixed costs = £10,000
Selling price = £5 per unit
Variable cost = £3 per unit
So BEP = 5,000 units (£5 − £3 = £2)

Figure 4.6   Cost model showing a break-even point

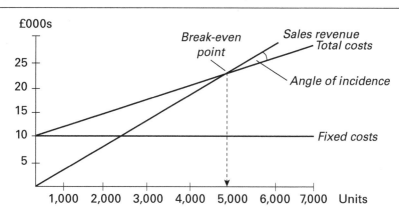

Now we can see that 5,000 units must be sold at £5 each before we can start to make a profit. We can also see that if 7,000 is our maximum output we have only 2,000 units available to make our required profit target. Obviously, the more units we have available for sale (ie the maximum output that can realistically be sold) after our break-even point, the better. The relationship between total sales and the break-even point is called the margin of safety.

Margin of safety

This is usually expressed as a percentage and can be calculated as shown in Table 4.1. Clearly, the lower this percentage, the lower the business's capacity for generating profits. A low margin of safety might signal the need to rethink fixed costs, selling price or the maximum output of the business. The angle formed at the BEP between the sales revenue line and the total costs line is called the 'angle of incidence'. The size of the angle shows the rate at which profit is made after the break-even point. A large angle means a high rate of profit per unit sold after the BEP.

Table 4.1   Calculating a margin of safety

	£	
Total sales	35,000	(7,000 units × £5 selling price)
Minus break-even point	25,000	(5,000 units × £5 selling price)
Margin of safety	10,000	
Margin of safety as a percentage of sales	29%	(10,000 ÷ 35,000)

Meeting profit objectives

By adding in the final element, desired profits, we can have a comprehensive model to help us with costing and pricing decisions. Supposing in the previous example we knew that we had to make £10,000 profit to achieve a satisfactory return on the capital invested in the business, we could amend our BEP formula to take account of this objective:

$$\text{BEPP (break-even profit point)} = \frac{\text{Fixed costs} + \text{Profit objective}}{\text{Unit selling price} - \text{Variable costs per unit}}$$

Putting some figures from our last example into this equation, and choosing £10,000 as our profit objective, we can see how it works. Unfortunately, without further investment in fixed costs, the maximum output in our example is only 7,000 units, so unless we change something the profit objective will not be met.

$$\frac{£10,000 + £10,000}{£5 - £3} = \frac{£20,000}{2}$$
$$\text{BEPP} = 10,000 \text{ units}$$

The great strength of this model is that each element can be changed in turn, on an experimental basis, to arrive at a satisfactory and achievable result. Let us return to this example. We could start our experimenting by seeing what the selling price would have to be to meet our profit objective. In this case we leave the selling price as the unknown, but we have to decide the BEP in advance (you cannot solve a single equation with more than one unknown). It would not be unreasonable to say that we would be prepared to sell our total output to meet the profit objective. So the equation now works out as follows:

$$\frac{20,000}{7,000} = £ \text{ Unit selling price} - £3$$

Moving the unknown over to the left-hand side of the equation we get:

$$£ \text{ Unit selling price} = £3 + 2.86 = £5.86$$

We now know that with a maximum capacity of 7,000 units and a profit objective of £10,000, we have to sell at £5.86 per unit. Now if the market will stand that price, then this is a satisfactory result. If it will not, then we are back to experimenting with the other variables. We must find ways of decreasing the fixed or variable costs, or increasing the output of the plant, by an amount sufficient to meet our profit objective.

Negotiating special deals

Managers are frequently laid open to the temptation of taking a particularly big order at a 'cut-throat' price and it is the MBA's role to make sure that however attractive the proposition may look at first glance, certain conditions are met before the order can be safely accepted. Let us look at an example – a slight variation on the last one. Your company has a maximum output of 10,000 units, without any major investment in fixed costs. At present you are just not prepared to invest more money until the business has proved itself. The background information is:

Maximum output	10,000 units
Output to meet profit objective	7,000 units
Selling price	£5.86
Fixed costs	£10,000
Unit variable cost	£3.00
Profitability objective	£10,000

The break-even chart will look like Figure 4.7.

The managers you are advising are fairly confident that they can sell 7,000 units at £5.86 each, but that still leaves 3,000 units unsold – should they decide to produce them. Out of the blue an enquiry comes in for about 3,000 units, but a strong hint is given that nothing less than a 33 per cent discount will clinch the deal. What should you recommend? Using the costing information assembled so far, you can show the present breakdown of costs and arrive at your selling price:

Figure 4.7   Break-even chart for special deals

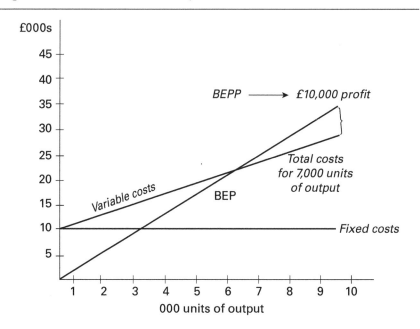

Unit cost breakdown	£3.00
Variable costs	£1.43 (£10,000 fixed costs ÷ 7,000 units)
Contribution to fixed costs	
Contribution to meet profit objective	£1.43 (£10,000 profit objective ÷ 7,000 units)
Selling price	£5.86

As all fixed costs are met on the 7,000 units sold (or to be sold), the remaining units can be sold at a price that covers both variable costs and the profitability contribution, so you can negotiate at the same level of profitability, down to £4.43, just under 25 per cent off the current selling price. However, any selling price above the £3.00 variable cost will generate extra profits, but these sales will be at the expense of your profit margin. A lower profit margin in itself is not necessarily a bad thing if it results in a higher return on capital employed, but first you must do the sums. There is a great danger with negotiating orders at marginal costs, as these costs are called, in that you do not achieve your break-even point and so perpetuate losses.

Dealing with multiple products and services

The examples used to illustrate the break-even profit point model were of necessity simple. Few if any businesses sell only one product or service, so a more general equation may be more useful to deal with real world situations.

In such a business, to calculate your break-even point you must first establish your gross profit. This is calculated by deducting the money paid out to suppliers from the money received from customers. (Look back to Chapter 3 for more on this subject.) For example, if you are aiming for a 40 per cent gross profit, expressed in decimals as 0.4, your fixed costs are £10,000 and your overall profit objective is £4,000, then the sum will be as follows:

$$\text{BEPP} = \frac{£10,000 + £4,000}{0.4} = \frac{£14,000}{0.4} = £35,000$$

So, to reach the target you must achieve a £35,000 turnover. (You can check this out for yourself: look back to the previous example where the BEPP was 7,000 units, and the selling price was £5 each. Multiplying those figures gives a turnover of £35,000. The gross profit in that example was 2/5, or 40 per cent, also.)

Overheads – a final word on costs

An overhead is any regular cost that can't be directly attributed to 'producing' a product or service. The emphasis is on the word 'directly' and overheads are often referred to as indirect costs. So, for instance, the rent, utility costs and staff wages of a grocery store are overhead costs as they can't readily be allocated to any particular product on sale. The cost of buying in stock is directly related to the volume of product sold, so is not an overhead.

The overhead rate ratio compares expenses to sales during a period. Say your overheads during the period were £8,000 and sales were £32,000 then your overhead rate would be 25 per cent (£8,000 / £32,000 X 100). Although overheads are generally viewed negatively, they are essential. It would be hard to sell a can of beans (a direct cost) without staff (an indirect cost or overhead). This is where ratios help. So if in the example above your overhead ratio for the previous year was 30 per cent then you are getting more efficient. If the average overhead ratio for your industry is 20 per cent then you have room for improvement. Overhead costs can be fixed, variable or a mix of both.

Getting help with break-even

You have quite a few options to get help with making breakeven calculations. TemplateLab provide a handy quick overview of breakeven analysis as well as a number of free spreadsheets at: https://templatelab.com/breakeven-analysis. Once you have brushed up your knowledge here you can take a test and see if there are areas you should revisit: www.tutor2u.net/business/reference/breakeven-basics-revision-quiz.

Profit maximization vs shareholder value

Operating managers are focused firmly on the bottom line and usually their rewards and promotion prospects are directly influenced by their ability to maximize profits. Shareholders, on the other hand, and this usually includes the board of directors and a handful of other senior staff whom an MBA could be wise to cultivate, have a different but related goal. They as the owners of the business want to maximize the value of the business, a sum derived by multiplying the number of shares issued by the market price of those shares.

While a business clearly needs money to operate and grow it doesn't all have to come from shareholders who expect to enjoy all the future increase in value, but could be provided by banks, for example, which have much lower expectations for their share in any additional value. They are usually satisfied with a set level of interest and their capital returned intact. (This subject, known as gearing or leverage, is covered more fully in Chapter 10.)

The factors that influence share price go way beyond a simple measure of the amount of profit. First, the efficiency with which that profit was made will weigh heavily on shareholders' minds, so the return on capital and profit margins will count too. Think about which business you would rather have a stake in: one that employed £100 million to make £20 million profit, or one that employed £50 million to make £19 million profit. Cash generation is also a vital factor in value. Profit is an accounting estimate of value, which can be adversely affected by all manner of factors. It's not until profit is turned into cash that shareholders have any real certainty as to the value of their stake. So for otherwise identical ventures, the one that generates the most cash the fastest is likely to be the more valuable in the eyes of the stock market. Factors such as the ability to innovate – Apple for example – or that have global reach and appeal – McDonald's or Coca Cola – will also keep relative value high.

Value-based management

The value-based management (VBM) model is the management approach that goes a stage beyond objectives and introduces the idea that organizations are run consistently for long-term shareholder value. That doesn't mean ignoring other stakeholder groups. The three guiding principles of VBM are:

- Creating value: actively seeking ways to increase or generate maximum long-term value.
- Managing for value: colleagues, customers, community and shareholders.
- Measuring value: validating that long-term, real value has been created by using appropriate financial techniques such as discounted cash flow (see later in this chapter, 'Future investment decisions').

The cost of capital

A business needs to keep track of how much it is paying for the capital it uses, as that is the threshold that has to be passed before value is being added to the business. It is also the minimum hurdle rate for any investment it may make. It also needs to be aware that if new money being raised is more costly than that already in the business, it will only be profitable if it raises the hurdle rate for new projects accordingly.

Cost of debt

This can be very straightforward. If a company takes out a bank loan at a fixed rate of interest of say, 8 per cent, then this is the cost before any tax relief. Taking tax relief at 40 per cent into account then the net cost of debt comes down to 4.8 per cent. In the case of a public offer for bonds or debentures, the rate of interest that has to be paid on new loans to get them taken up by investors at par can be regarded as the cost of borrowed capital.

Cost of equity

Put simply, the cost of equity is the return shareholders expect the company to earn on their money. It is their estimation, often not scientifically calculated, of the rate of return that will be obtained both from future dividends and an increased share value.

Dividend valuation model

One approach to finding the cost of equity is to take the current gross dividend yield for a company and add the expected annual growth.

For example, XYZ plc has forecast payment of a gross equivalent dividend of 10 cents on each ordinary share in the coming year. The company's shares are quoted on the stock exchange and currently trade at $2.00. Growth of profits and dividends has averaged 15 per cent over the last few years. The cost of equity for XYZ plc can be calculated as:

$$\text{Cost of equity capital} = \frac{\text{Current dividend (gross) }\%}{\text{Current market price}} + \text{Growth rate }\%$$

$$= \frac{(\$0.10 \times 100)\%}{\$2} + 15\% = 20\%$$

With this method, dividends are assumed to grow in the future at the constant rate achieved by averaging the last few years' performance.

Capital asset pricing model (CAPM)

Before turning to the next method, we need to clarify some aspects of risk. There are two broad types of risk: specific and systematic.

Specific risk applies to one particular business. It includes, for example, the risk of losing the chief executive; the risk of someone else bringing out a similar or better product; or the risk of labour problems. Shareholders are expected not to want compensation for this type of risk as it can be diversified away by holding a sufficient number of investments in their portfolios.

Systematic risk derives from global or macro-economic events that can damage all investments to some extent and therefore holders require compensation for this risk to their wealth. This compensation takes the form of a higher required rate of return.

A slightly more complicated approach to the cost of equity tries to take the systematic risk element into account. It is known as the 'capital asset pricing model' or CAPM. Put simply, CAPM states that investors' required rate of return on a share is composed of two parts: a risk-free rate similar to that obtainable on a risk-free investment in short-term government securities; and an additional premium to compensate for the systematic risk involved in investing in shares. This systematic risk for a company's shares is measured by the size of its beta factor. A beta of 1.0 for a company means that its shares have the same systematic risk as the average for the whole market. If the beta is 1.4 then systematic risk for the share is 40 per cent higher than the market average. A company's share beta is applied to the market premium that is obtained from the excess of the return on a market portfolio of shares over the risk-free rate of return. The formula to calculate cost of equity capital using CAPM is:

$$Ke = Rf + B(Rm - Rf)$$

where: Ke = cost of equity, Rf = risk-free return, Rm = return on market portfolio of shares and B = beta factor.

For example, if the risk-free rate of return is 5.5 per cent and the return on a market portfolio is 12 per cent, then for a company with a beta of 0.7 for its ordinary shares the cost of equity is:

$$Ke = Rf + B(Rm - Rf)$$
$$= 5.5\% + 0.7(12\% - 5.5\%)$$
$$= 10.05\%$$

Of the two methods described for finding the cost of equity for a company, the CAPM method is the more scientific. Ideally, the risk-free and market rates of return should reflect the future but current rates of return are used as substitutes. Beta factors measure how sensitive each company's share price movements are relative to market movements over a period of a few years.

The weakness of CAPM lies in it assuming all investors are rational and well-informed and that markets are perfect and there is an unlimited supply of risk-free money. There are even more complex models for calculating the cost of equity capital, but none are without their critics.

Weighted average cost of capital

Having identified the cost of equity and the cost of borrowed capital (and that of any other long-term source of finance such as hire purchase or mortgages), we need to combine them into one overall cost of capital. This is primarily for use in project appraisals as justification of those that yield a return in excess of their cost of capital.

An average cost is required because we do not usually identify each individual project with one particular source of finance. Because equity and debt capital have very different costs, we would make illogical decisions and accept a project financed by debt capital only to reject a similar project next time round when it was financed by equity capital. Generally businesses take the view that all projects have been financed from a common pool of money except for the relatively rare case when project-specific finance is raised. The weightings used in the calculations should be based on the market value of the securities and not on their book or balance sheet values.

As an example, assume your company intends to keep the gearing ratio of borrowed capital to equity in the proportion of 20:80. The nominal cost of new capital from these sources has been assessed, say, at 10 per cent and 15 per cent respectively and corporation tax is 30 per cent. The calculation of the overall weighted average cost is as follows:

Type of capital	Proportion (a)	After-tax cost (b)	Weighted cost (a × b)
10% loan capital	0.20	7.0%	1.4%
Equity	0.80	15.0%	12.0%
			13.4%

The resulting weighted average cost of 13.4 per cent is the minimum rate that this company should accept on proposed investments. Any investment that is not expected to achieve this return is not a viable proposition. Risk has been allowed for in the calculation of the beta factor used in the CAPM method of identifying the cost of equity. This relates to the risk of the whole existing business. If a company embarks on a project of significantly different risk, or has a divisional structure of activities of varying risk levels, then a single cost of equity for the whole company is inappropriate. In this situation, the average beta of proxy companies operating in the same field as a division can be used.

Industry norms

Researchers compile data from company accounts to arrive at industry norms. Clearly there are limitations to the value of what is in effect little more than averaging of the numbers of very disparate businesses. Adding Tesco's sales figure (£56 billion) to that of Wholefoods (£94 million), would simply drown out the smaller business's performance.

A better approach is to get the information on your competitors or companies you respect and make your own calculations. Often the basic ratios will have been helpfully provided in the accounts.

Creditguru provides some basic information that will give you a rough idea of the norms in various industry sectors: www.creditguru.com/index.php/financial-analysis/financial-statement-ratio-analysis/107-industry-norms-and-key-business-ratios.

Also, Macrotrends provides basic ratios by business sector: www.macrotrends.net/stocks/research.

Future investment decisions

The cost of capital is an important figure as it is in essence the threshold for future investments. Using the figures shown above, if our weighted average cost of capital is 13.4 per cent, taking on any new activity that makes a lower profit ratio will be lowering the performance, hardly an MBA type of activity.

Investment decisions, where the decisions have cost and revenue implications for years, perhaps even decades, fall into a number of categories:

- *Bolt-on investments:* these are where an investment will be supporting and enhancing an existing operation, for example if part of a production process is being slowed down for want of some new equipment to eliminate a bottleneck.
- *Standalone single project:* this involves a simple accept or reject decision.
- *Competing projects:* this requires a choice of which produces the best results either because only one can be pursued or because of limited finance. In the latter case this is described as *capital rationing*.

What follows is an examination of the financial aspects of investment decisions. There may well be other strategic reasons for taking investment decisions including those that might be more important than finance alone. For example, it could be imperative to deny a competitor a particular opportunity, or if part of achieving a national or global strategy calls for disproportionate expenses in one or more areas. However, there are *no* circumstances when any investment decision should not be subjected to proper financial appraisal and so at least seeing the cost of accepting a lower return than required by the cost of capital being used.

It is also important to note that any methodology for appraising investments requires that cash is used rather than profits, for reasons that will become apparent as the techniques are explained. Profit is not ignored; it is simply allowed to work its way through in the timing of events.

Payback period

The most popular method for evaluating investment decisions is the *payback* method. To arrive at the payback period you have to work out how many years it takes to recover your *cash* investment. Table 4.2 shows two investment projects that require respectively £20,000 and £40,000 cash now to get a series of cash returns spread over the next five years.

Table 4.2   The payback method

	Investment A £	Investment B £
Initial cash cost *now* (Year 0)	20,000	40,000
Net cash flows		
Year 1	1,000	10,000
Year 2	4,000	10,000
Year 3	8,000	16,000
Year 4	7,000	4,000
Year 5	5,000	28,000
Total cash in over period	25,000	68,000
Cash surplus	5,000	28,000

Although both propositions call for different amounts of cash to be invested we can see that both recover all their cash outlays by year four. So we can say these investments have a four-year payback. But as a matter of fact investment B produces a much bigger surplus than the other project and it returns half our initial cash outlay in two years. Investment A has only returned a quarter of our cash over that time period.

Payback may be simple, but it is not much use when it comes to dealing with either the timing or with comparing different investment amounts.

Incremental cash flows

For investment decisions you only consider the cash flows that are incremental. You ignore those that are not affected by the decision (like the money already spent on researching whether or not a new product might work). You then assess the present values of the cash flows that are different, that is, are incremental to current operations.

Discounted cash flow

We know intuitively that getting cash in sooner is better than getting it in later. In other words, a dollar received now is worth more than a dollar that will arrive in one, two or more years in the future because of what we could do with that money ourselves, or because of what we have to pay out to have use of that money (see the cost of capital, above). To make sound investment decisions we need to ascribe a value to a future stream of earnings to arrive at what is known as *the present value*. If we know we could earn 20 per cent on any money we have then the maximum we would be prepared to pay for a dollar coming in one year hence would be around 80 cents. If we were to pay one dollar now to get a dollar back in a year's time we would in effect be losing money.

The technique used to handle this is known as 'discounting' and the process is termed 'discounted cash flow' (DCF) and the residual discounted cash is called the 'net present value'. The first column in Table 4.3 shows the simple cash flow implications of an investment proposition; a surplus of 5,000 comes after five years from putting 20,000 into a project. But if we accept the proposition that future cash is worth less than current cash the only question we need to answer is how much less. If we take our weighted average cost of capital as a sensible starting point we would select 13.4 per cent as an appropriate rate at which to discount future cash flows. To keep the numbers simple and to add a small margin of safety let's assume 15 per cent is the rate we have selected (this doesn't matter too much as you will see in the section on internal rate of return).

Table 4.3   Using discounted cash flow (DCF)

	£ Cash Flow A	Discount Factor at 15% B	Discounted Cash Flow A × B
Initial cash cost *now* (Year 0)	20,000	1.00	20,000
Net cash flows			
Year 1	1,000	0.8695	870
Year 2	4,000	0.7561	3,024
Year 3	8,000	0.6575	5,260
Year 4	7,000	0.5717	4,002
Year 5	5,000	0.4972	2,486
Total	25,000		15,642
Cash surplus	5,000	Net Present Value	(4,358)

The formula for calculating what a £ received at some future date is:

$$\text{Present Value (PV)} = £P \times 1/(1 + r)^n$$

where £P is the initial cash cost, r is the interest rate expressed in decimals and n is the year in which the cash will arrive. So if we decide on a discount rate of 15 per cent, the present value of a £ received in one year's time is:

$$\text{Present Value} = £1 \times 1/(1 + 0.15)^1$$
$$= £0.87 \text{ (rounded to two decimal places)}$$

So we can see that our £1,000 arriving at the end of year one has a present value of £870; the £4,000 in year two has a present value of £3,024 and by year five the present value reduces cash flows to barely half their original figure. In fact far from having a real payback in year four and generating a cash surplus of £5,000, this project will make us £4,358 worse off than we had hoped to be if we wanted to make a return of 15 per cent. The project, in other words, fails to meet our criteria using DCF but may well have been pursued using payback.

Internal rate of return (IRR)

DCF is a useful starting point but does not give us any definitive information. For example, all we know about the above project is that it doesn't make a return of 15 per cent. In order to know the actual rate of return we need to choose a discount rate that produces a net present value of the entire cash flow of zero, known as the 'internal rate of return'. The maths is time-consuming but SpreadsheetML.com has a useful template for working out payback, discounted cash flow, internal rate of return, and a lot more calculations relating to capital budgeting (www.spreadsheetml.com/finance/free-capitalbudgeting.shtml).

Aswath Damodaran, who teaches corporate finance and valuation on the MBA programme at the Stern School of Business at New York University, has a wide range of free spreadsheets for all aspects of finance including DCF and IRR (https://pages.stern.nyu.edu/~adamodar/New_Home_Page/PVPrimer/pvprimer.htm). Using this spreadsheet you will see that the IRR for the project in question is slightly under 7 per cent, not much better than might be obtained through bank interest and certainly insufficient to warrant taking any risks for.

Perpetuities

The example above assumes that the project will come to a natural end after a set number of years, in this case five. This may not be the case if, for example, you launch a new product or open a factory extension. In such cases you might well assume that the investment will last a very long time into the future. Whilst you could simply roll out from year six onwards with ever-diminishing discount factors, there is a convenient short cut.

The present value of a perpetuity – that is, a cash flow where the annual amount does not change – is calculated as follows:

Present value of perpetuity = Annual cash flow / Discount rate

In the example in Table 2.3 this equates to:

$$5,000 / 0.15 = 33,333$$

So a cash flow of £5,000 that lasts forever has a value of £33,333 to the business when it comes to evaluating an investment proposal.

Growing perpetuity

A further twist can be given to the concept of perpetuities. If you believe the cash flow will increase over time by a set amount, the formula can be tweaked to accommodate that fact. The present value of the above perpetuity if it is expected to grow by 10 per cent a year is:

= Cash flow / (Discount rate – Growth rate)

In this example this equates to:

5,000 / (0.15-0.10) = 5,000 / 0.05 = £100,000

The residual discounted cash flow is known as the net present value (NPV).

Shares and markets

The magic of multiples

By the time the business you are working in has successfully grown to the point where profits are above £1 ($1.6/€1.18) million it will be possible to give some serious thought to floating on a stock market. (See Chapter 7 for more on the practical steps to achieve this.) That means selling shares in your business to the public at large and perhaps, in time, getting your company bought out by a bigger fish still. The logic of the maths is as follows. Your business with a profit of £1 ($1.6/€1.18) million would in all probability be valued at £4 ($6.4/€4.720) million, give or take half a million, based on a P/E ratio of 4. However, the same business on a stock market could be valued on a much higher P/E ratio, perhaps as much as double. The logic is that the shares are liquid; that is, investors know their value from day to day and can sell up and move on any time they like. Also, companies on a stock market are subject to a greater degree of scrutiny and so investors can be more confident in their accounts – although the market crash of October 2008 left that argument in some doubt.

You also have a powerful way to accelerate value, once your company has been floated off. If you now buy a private business that is making profits of £250,000 in your business sector it would in all probability be sold on a P/E of around 4, so costing you about £1 million. But now that profit is in a public company and as you are on a P/E of 8 it would add £2 million to your value (8 × £250,000). So, in effect, for £1 million of investment you have instantly added £2 million to your value, and of course the profit stream of

£250,000 should continue and there may well be synergies from cost savings and economies of scale. Thus the alchemy of market multiples.

Share buyback and other market manipulation techniques

Companies can buy back their shares and that reduces the number of shares outstanding, giving each remaining shareholder a larger percentage ownership of the company. This is usually considered a sign that the company's management believes its share price is undervalued. Other reasons for buybacks include putting unused cash to use, raising earnings per share and obtaining stock for employee stock option plans or pension plans.

Buying back shares doesn't actually change anything in the business. Customers, products, employees, operations and strategies are all unchanged: just a piece of financial sleight of hand has been used in an effort to manipulate the share price. But do analysts, the people who tell the market what a share is likely to be worth in the future, really fall for such transparent tricks? Apparently they do. A study, 'A matter of appearances: How corporate leaders manage the impressions of financial analysts', by two academics, James Westphal and Melissa Graebner, published in the *Academy of Management Journal* in February 2010, provides compelling evidence to support that view.

The study of 1,300 analysts and corporate bosses found that the CEO was more likely to resort to managing appearances when his or her company received a negative appraisal from Wall Street, rather than make any substantive changes. Aside from share buybacks, designed to send a signal of confidence in value to the market, other techniques include appointing more independent directors. In theory that should improve corporate governance and hold the working board to account more effectively. In practice, although such external appointments may have no formal ties to the company, they very often have 'friendship' ties to the boss. This is the case in some 45 per cent of the cases in this study. More blatant still are the incidents where CEOs secure jobs and club memberships for analysts in an attempt to prevent stock prices being downgraded.

Apparently these tactics pay off handsomely. Firms that take these measures see the chances of having their stock upgraded, and hence the nominal value of the business increased, by 36 per cent. The chance of a downgrade, the study concluded, falls by 45 per cent. Amazingly, public companies enjoy lasting share price gains from plans that please analysts even when the plans aren't actually implemented. The announcement alone seems sufficient to please the market.

Online video courses and lectures

Break Even Analysis Formulas Chart & Plotting Break Even Point on Chart: At the excelisfun Channel at YouTube: www.youtube.com/watch?v= 7MxlVMzRxa8

How to Calculate the Internal Rate of Return: Alanis Business Academy: www.youtube.com/watch?v=hKyeS-bAf3I

How to Calculate Net Present Value: Alanis Business Academy: www. youtube.com/watch?v=jylJ2r9bklE

How to Calculate the Payback Period: Alanis Business Academy: www. youtube.com/watch?v=ZmvbD0heOAA

How to Calculate the Profitability Index: Alanis Business Academy: www. youtube.com/watch?v=JaEUoMGbmJs

How to Conduct a Breakeven Analysis: Alanis Business Academy: www. youtube.com/watch?v=tXI3Qdu_Qt8

Pricing Objectives and Strategies: Alanis Business Academy: www.youtube. com/watch?v=gPAGip9GOIU

Weighted Average Cost of Capital (WACC): Education Unlocked: www. youtube.com/watch?v=46oLXwClvkw

What is the P/E Ratio? The Wealth Academy presented by Valentine Ventures: www.youtube.com/watch?v=TKk1xdTbOK0

Online video case studies

Coca-Cola's income statement and balance sheet for the last five years, 2021: www.youtube.com/watch?v=vE7Ui7-_Po0

Paul Clarke, Director of Technology at Ocado, talks about how technology is driving their business, outlining why long term value creation for shareholders comes before anything else: www.youtube.com/watch?v= GP4T6tMqWcI

Starbucks financial analysis, 2021: www.youtube.com/watch?v=5Q_ IjcJ62ZM

Tesco accounting scandal, 2014: www.youtube.com/watch?v=_x2lYc0PnTc

Tesla financial analysis, 2021 – Overview by Paul Borosky, MBA: www. youtube.com/watch?v=wDchrU8KBNU

Walmart financial report 2022: www.youtube.com/watch?app=desktop&v= ur-EiSRKk3o

PART TWO
Corporate capital structures

In this part the role of business structures in financing business is examined. Those structures include: sole traders, partnerships, limited partnerships, companies – private and public. In practice sole traders are limited to borrowing as a source of finance, while the others can use equity.

The forms of debt finance examined include those provided by banks such as overdrafts and term loans. Other debt instruments reviewed include bonds and convertibles, syndicated loans, commercial paper, leasing finance, hire purchase, sale and leaseback, factoring, invoice discounting and bills of exchange.

For equity finance the different shares structures – ordinary, preference and convertible – are examined. The alternative sources of equity finance are also discussed in this part, including business angels and seed corn funding, business incubators, venture capital – private and publicly funded, corporate venture funding, stock markets, and hybrid structures such as mezzanine finance and crowdfunding.

05

The role of business structures in financing business

- A brief history of corporate structures
- Working alone
- Forming partnerships
- Limiting liabilities
- Cooperatives

In this chapter we will examine how businesses are legally constituted, how those structures came about and the bearing they have on the financial options open to a firm. In the following chapters we will look at the different financing options in detail.

There are at least two reasons why an MBA student should acquire a basic appreciation of the milestone events that have led up to the current theories of how businesses and organizations are constituted and financed. The first is much the same reason as why most people learn something of the history of their country, its neighbours, its friends and enemies. Such a study lends interest, context and an appreciation of how we got to where we are today. It is much easier to understand, for example, the enmity between the French and the British with a smattering of information on the smouldering commercial and territorial disputes that ranged around the world from the Americas to India as well as across the African continent.

The second reason is perhaps even more important. Harvard Professor Geoffrey Jones, who edited *Business History: Illustrated* (2010, Oxford Handbooks in Business & Management) with University of Wisconsin-Madison Professor Jonathan Zeitlin, claims in his core history text used at Harvard that: 'Over the last few decades, business historians have generated rich empirical data that in some cases confirms and in other cases contradicts many of today's fashionable theories and assumptions by other disciplines.' This loss of history has resulted in the spread of influential theories based on ill-informed understandings of the past. 'For example,' Jones claims, 'current accepted advice is that wealth and growth will come to countries that open their borders to foreign direct investment. The historical evidence shows clearly that this is an article of faith rather than proven by the historical evidence of the past.'

Businesses are themselves legal entities and the complexity of commercial life means that, sooner or later, you will find yourself taking, or defending yourself against, legal action. Ignorance does not form the basis of a satisfactory defence so every MBA needs to know enough law to know when he or she might need legal advice. Some business schools take law very seriously; for example at Northwestern University's Kellogg School and George Washington University MBA students can take a joint MBA and JD (*juris doctor*), the basic professional degree for lawyers. Babson in Wellesley, Massachusetts, has law as one of its core subjects. Penn State, on the other hand, offers only an optional module in the second year on 'Business Law for Innovation and Competition'.

Nevertheless, lawyers dominate big businesses in the United States and both Congress and the Senate. In the UK around 12 per cent of MPs are either barristers or solicitors, the largest professional grouping in the House of Commons. Other than very large businesses it is not usual to have either a qualified lawyer or a legal department in businesses in the UK. Such services are usually bought in either on a contractual or ad hoc basis. Law is an imprecise field (social backgrounds of MPs 1979-2019: https://research-briefings.files.parliament.uk/documents/CBP-7483/CBP-7483.pdf).

Corporate structures

As an MBA it's highly likely that you will be working for a conventional company, private or public. There are, however, a number of distinct forms that a business can take, the choice depending on a number of factors: commercial needs, financial risk and the need for outside capital.

Each of these forms is explained briefly below, primarily as they apply in the UK, together with the procedure to follow on setting them up. You can change your ownership status later as your circumstances change, so while this is an important decision it is not a final one.

Sole trader

Most businesses start up as sole traders and indeed around a fifth of all businesses in the US and UK employing fewer than 50 people still use this legal structure for much of their business life. It has the merit of being relatively formality free and there are relatively few rules about the records you have to keep. There is no requirement for your accounts to be audited, or for financial information on your business to be filed.

As a sole trader there is no legal distinction between you and your business – your business is one of your assets, just as your house or car is. It follows from this that if your business should fail, your creditors have a right not only to the assets of the business but also to your personal assets, subject only to the provisions of the Bankruptcy Acts. The capital to get the business going must come from you – or from loans. There is no access to equity capital.

Partnerships

Partnerships are effectively collections of sole traders and, as such, share the legal problems attached to personal liability. There are very few restrictions to setting up in business with another person (or persons) in partnership, and several definite advantages. By pooling resources you may have more capital; you will be bringing, hopefully, several sets of skills to the business; and if you are ill the business can still carry on.

There are two serious drawbacks that you should certainly consider. First, if one of the partners makes a business mistake, perhaps by signing a disastrous contract, without the knowledge or consent of the others, every member of the partnership must shoulder the consequences. Under these circumstances your personal assets could be taken to pay the creditors even though the mistake was no fault of your own.

Second, if a partner goes bankrupt in his or her personal capacity, for whatever reason, his or her share of the partnership can be seized by creditors. As a private individual you are not liable for your partner's private debts, but having to buy him or her out of the partnership at short notice could put you and the business in financial jeopardy. Even death may not release you from partnership obligations and in some circumstances your estate can remain liable. Unless you take 'public' leave of your partnership by notifying your business contacts and legally bringing your partnership to an end, you could remain liable.

The legal regulations governing this field are set out in the Partnership Act 1890, which in essence assumes that competent businesspeople should know what they are doing. The Act merely provides a framework of agreement that applies 'in the absence of agreement to the contrary'. It follows from this that many partnerships are entered into without legal formalities – and sometimes without the parties themselves being aware that they have entered a partnership!

The main provisions of the Partnership Act state:

- All partners contribute capital equally.
- All partners share profits and losses equally.

- No partner shall have interest paid on his capital.
- No partner shall be paid a salary.
- All partners have an equal say in the management of the business.
- Unless you are a member of certain professions (law, accountancy, etc) you are restricted to a maximum of 20 partners in any partnership.

It is unlikely that all these provisions will suit you, so you would be well advised to get a written 'partnership agreement' drawn up by a solicitor at the outset of your venture.

Limited partnerships

One possibility that can reduce the more painful consequences of entering a partnership is to form a limited partnership, combining the best attributes of a partnership and a company.

A limited partnership works like this. There must be one or more general partners with the same basic rights and responsibilities (including unlimited liability) as in any general partnership, and one or more limited partners who are usually passive investors. The big difference between a general partner and a limited partner is that the limited partner isn't personally liable for the debts of the partnership. The most a limited partner can lose is the amount that he or she paid or agreed to pay into the partnership as a capital contribution or received from the partnership after it became insolvent.

To keep this limited liability, a limited partner may not participate in the management of the business, with very few exceptions. A limited partner who does get actively involved in the management of the business risks losing immunity from personal liability and having the same legal exposure as a general partner.

The advantage of a limited partnership as a business structure is that it provides a way for business owners to raise money (from the limited partners) without having to either take in new partners who will be active in the business, or having to form a limited company. A general partnership that's been operating for years can also create a limited partnership to finance expansion.

Limited companies

How they came about

From the earliest trading times to the present day the most popular legal structure under which to operate has been as a sole trader, which in effect means everyone for themselves. In the beginning merchants always risked their own money, if they had any to invest; if they travelled, as most did, they risked their lives on the journey. The caravan trade of Asia, Asia Minor, and North and Central Africa ploughed its way through the sands that separated distant cities and seaports. The largest caravans comprised thousands of camels and required careful administration. They also stimulated people to band together in partnerships, pooling protection costs and profits to spread the risks. The partnerships would usually last only for the particular journey. Later on, older merchants who had made money from earlier ventures could join such expeditions by putting up money, without the hardship of making the trip themselves. This could be seen as an early form of limited partnership.

As the ventures became more costly and of longer duration, partnership structures of fixed duration of one, three or five years became common, with an ever increasing range of partners with differing shares in the venture. To add to the complications these partners could join and leave, perhaps for no more sinister reason than death, at different times.

The concept of limited liability, where the shareholders are not liable, in the last resort, for the debts of their business, changed the whole nature of business and risk taking. It opened the floodgates, encouraging a new generation of entrepreneurs to undertake much larger scale ventures without taking on all the consequences of failure. As the name suggests, in this form of business liability is limited to the amount you contribute by way of share capital and, in the event of failure, creditors' claims are restricted to the assets of the company. The shareholders of the business are not normally liable as individuals for the business debts beyond the paid-up value of their shares.

The concept itself can be traced back to Roman times, when it was granted, albeit infrequently, as a special favour to friends for large undertakings by those in power. The idea was resurrected in 1811 when New York State brought in a general limited liability law for manufacturing companies. Most US states followed suit and eventually Britain caught up in 1854. Today most countries have a legal structure incorporating the concept of limited liability.

Limited companies today

About a third of all businesses operate under some form of limited liability. As the name suggests, in this form of business your liability is limited to the amount you state that you will contribute by way of share capital, though you may not actually have to put that money in.

A limited company has a legal identity of its own, separate from the people who own or run it. This means that, in the event of failure, creditors' claims are restricted to the assets of the company. The shareholders of the business are not liable as individuals for the business debts beyond the paid-up value of their shares. This applies even if the shareholders are working directors, unless of course the company has been trading fraudulently. Other advantages include the freedom to raise capital by selling shares.

Disadvantages include the cost involved in setting up the company and the legal requirement in some cases for the company's accounts to be audited by a chartered or certified accountant.

Public Limited Company (plc)

A plc is a company that can sell shares to the public at large either through a recognized stock market or by advertising in the press or through intermediaries. It needs to fulfil some minimum conditions which vary from country to country but generally:

- It must state that it is a plc in its articles of association.
- It must have a five-figure authorized share capital.
- Before it can trade a quarter of that must be actually paid up.
- Each allotted share must be paid up to at least a quarter of its nominal value.
- There must be at least two shareholders, two directors and a company secretary who meets certain standards in terms of qualifications or experience.
- It must file accounts with the relevant regulatory body in the country in which it is domiciled.
- Those accounts must follow the format and be prepared under the rules of the relevant national accounting body. If the company offers shares in the major developed economies then it will need to follow the rules outlined in Chapter 2.
- With some minimal exceptions the company's accounts will have to be audited by an approved firm of auditors (see Chapter 9).

Different forms of company

Limited companies come in a number of different shapes and sizes, with different rules governing them dependent on where they operate. In the United States for example, there are S corporations (S corps) and C corporations (C corps), which share many features in common but have a number of important differences. C corporations have no restrictions on ownership, but S corporations are restricted to having no more than 100 shareholders who must be US citizens/residents.

Company limited by guarantee

This type of incorporation is used for non-profit organizations that require corporate status as a means of protecting participants. There are no shareholders but members give an undertaking to contribute a nominal amount towards the winding up of the company in the event of a shortfall when it closes down. It cannot distribute its profits to its members, and is therefore eligible to apply for charitable status if necessary. You may find this type of structure being used by a business as a means of isolating part of its activities such as clubs or sports associations that are not part of its profit-generating business.

Cooperative

A cooperative is an enterprise owned and controlled by the people working in it. Once in danger of becoming extinct, the workers' cooperative is enjoying something of a comeback, and there are over 4,370 operating in the UK, employing 195,000 people. They are growing at the rate of 20 per cent per annum. Worldwide, there are over 3 million cooperatives employing 200 million people and operating in 156 countries. The International Co-operative Alliance (www.ica.coop) represents the movement.

Social enterprise

The term 'social enterprise' describes the purpose of a business, not its legal form. It is defined (by the UK Government, for example) as 'a business with primarily social objectives whose surpluses are principally reinvested for that purpose in the business or in the community, rather than being driven by the need to maximise profit for shareholders and owners'. A social enterprise venture can take a variety of legal forms ranging from sole trader through to limited company. Community Interest Companies (CICs) are an example of how countries are responding to the growing international interest in the sector. Established in the UK in 2004, a CIC is a form of company specifically created for the social enterprise sector. They have to include details of their social purpose in their articles of association and there are restrictions on what they can do with their assets, the objective being to ensure the community retains a continuing benefit from the business's activities.

The CIC form has been growing in popularity, and in 2021 over 100,000 were registered in the UK alone (www.socialenterprise.org.uk/app/uploads/2022/05/State-of-Social-Enterprise-Survey-2021-compressed.pdf).

Online video courses and lectures

Capitalism and Legal Forms of Business: Professor Charles RB Stowe, Lander University: www.youtube.com/watch?v=BTUbnZ2IISc

Forming Strategic Partnerships When Starting Your Business: MSNBC's Your Business OPEN Forum with Peter Wendell, a Stanford Business School lecturer in strategic management and the founder of Sierra Ventures, who has some advice about how to manage your partnerships: www.youtube.com/watch?v=3leadhEk4tA

How Do You Find Soul Mates? Guy Kawasaki of Garage Technology Ventures talks at Stanford's e-corner: http://ecorner.stanford.edu/authorMaterialInfo.html?mid=1184

How to Start a Social Enterprise – Greg Overholt at TEDxYouth@Toronto: www.youtube.com/watch?v=7178mTndI6A

What type of legal entity should my business become? Parrott CPA discusses sole proprietorships, partnerships, C-corporations, S-corporations and LLC's: www.youtube.com/watch?v=g9PBxdpkfR4

Online video case studies

Danger: The three founders of Danger, Andy Rubio, Joe Britt, and Matt Hershenson, came to Silicon Valley in the late 80's or early 90's where they worked for a series of companies, met and formed relationships with each other and started Danger in January of 2000: http://ecorner.stanford.edu/authorMaterialInfo.html?mid=1133

The real reason to form a limited company: www.1stformations.co.uk/blog/the-real-reason-you-should-form-a-limited-company/

PROTSAHAN India: Sonal Kapoor, founder CEO and microbiologist-MBA talks of how she set up her social enterprise: www.youtube.com/watch?v=n6jbr2aiytg

06
Debt finance

- Borrowing options
- Bank finance
- Government-supported lending
- General bonds
- Specialist bonds
- Asset-based lending

Debt finance and its regulation are hardly new: its practice stretches far back before the arrival of firms such as Banca Monte dei Paschi di Siena SpA (MPS) in 1472, though that is now the oldest operating bank. By 1795 BC Hammurabi, a Babylonian lawmaker, had already established a code of behaviour for money lenders and merchants to adhere to. 'If the agent accept money from the merchant, but have a quarrel with the merchant (denying the receipt), then shall the merchant swear before God and witnesses that he has given this money to the agent, and the agent shall pay him three times the sum', is one example of the fine detail of these dozens of interlocking laws. Hammurabi's code was certainly not the earliest. Preceding sets of laws have disappeared, but several traces of them have been found, and Hammurabi's own code clearly implies their existence. He only claimed to be reorganizing a legal system long established. The introduction of coined money in about 600 BC by the Greeks allowed bankers to keep account books, change and lend money, and even arrange for cash transfers for citizens through affiliate banks in cities thousands of miles away.

Despite being remembered mostly for their military prowess during the crusades the Knights Templar became, in part by accident, the first major international banking institution. Their specific forte was in keeping the highways open to allow pilgrims to come to the Holy Land unmolested. This goal inevitably meant the Templars owned some of the mightiest castles, and because of their awesome reputation as fighting men, their castles served as ideal places to deposit money and other valuables. A French knight, for example, could deposit money or mortgage his chateau through the Templars in Paris and pick up gold coins along the route to Jerusalem and on the way back, if he survived! The Templars charged a fee for both the transaction and for converting the money into various currencies along the route. Over the years the business grew and eventually the Templars ran a network of full service banks providing lending and ancillary services across Europe, from England to Jerusalem. At their maximum strength the Templars employed about 7,000 people, owned 870 castles and fortified houses and were the principal bankers to popes and kings.

Bank lending

Towards the lower risk end of the financing spectrum are the various organizations that lend money to businesses. They all try hard to take little or no risk, but expect some reward irrespective of performance. They want interest payments on money lent, usually from day one, though sometimes they are content to roll interest payments up until some future date. While they hope the management is competent, they are more interested in securing a charge against any assets the business or its managers may own. At the end of the day they want all their money back. It would be more prudent to think of these organizations as people who will help you turn a proportion of an illiquid asset such as property, stock in trade or customers who have not yet paid up, into a more liquid asset such as cash, but of course at some discount.

CASE STUDY
Hippychick

When new mother Julie Minchin discovered the Hipseat she knew she had found a helpful product. Anything that makes carrying a baby around all day without ending up with excruciating backache has got to be a benefit. It was only later that she realized that selling the product for the German company that made the Hipseat could be the right way to launch her into business. At first Julie acted as its UK distributor but later she wanted to make some major improvements to the product. That meant finding a manufacturer to make the product especially for her business. China was the logical place to find a company flexible enough to make small quantities as well as being able to help her keep the cost of the end product competitive.

   She funded the business with a small family loan, an overdraft facility and a variety of grants secured with the help of a government-backed initiative. Company accounts for 2021 show over £¼ million profit, for what by any accounts was a challenging year for most of their sector, hit hard by Covid-19 problems. It supplies national chains such as Boots and Mothercare as well as independents. It also sells via its catalogue and website and is in the process of building a network of distributors for its branded products.

Banks are the principal, and frequently the only, source of finance for nine out of every 10 unquoted businesses. Firms around the world rely on banks for their funding.

Bankers, and indeed any other sources of debt capital, are looking for asset security to back their loan and provide a near-certainty of getting their money back. They will also charge an interest rate that reflects current market conditions and their view of the risk level of the proposal; usually anything from 0.25 per cent above the prevailing base rate, to upwards of 3 or 4 per cent for more risky or smaller firms.

Bankers like to speak of the 'five Cs' of credit analysis, factors they look at when they evaluate a loan request. When applying to a bank for a loan, be prepared to address the following points:

1 *Character:* bankers lend money to borrowers who appear honest and have a good credit history. Before you apply for a loan, it makes sense to obtain a copy of your credit report and clean up any problems.

2 *Capacity:* this is a prediction of the borrower's ability to repay the loan. For a new business, bankers look at the business plan. For an existing business, bankers consider financial statements and industry trends.

3 *Collateral:* bankers generally want a borrower to pledge an asset that can be sold to pay off the loan if the borrower lacks funds.

4 *Capital:* bankers scrutinize a borrower's net worth, the amount by which assets exceed debts.

5 *Conditions:* whether bankers give a loan can be influenced by the current economic climate as well as by the amount.

Types of bank funding

Banks usually offer three types of loan:

1 *Overdrafts:* though technically short-term money as they can be called in at a moment's notice, these tend to form a part of the permanent capital of a business, albeit a fluctuating one.

2 *Term loans:* offered for set periods.

3 *Government-backed loans:* these are available to some types of business, usually small or new ventures, where the banker's normal criteria might not be met, but the government would like to encourage the sector.

1. Overdrafts

The principal form of short-term bank funding is an overdraft, secured by a charge over the assets of the business. A little over a quarter of all bank finance for small firms is in the form of an overdraft. If you are starting out in a contract cleaning business, say, with a major contract, you need sufficient funds initially to buy the mop and bucket. Three months into the contract they will have been paid for, so there is no point in getting a five-year bank loan to cover this as within a year you will have cash in the bank and a loan with an early redemption penalty! However, if your bank account does not get out of the red at any stage during the year, you will need to re-examine your financing. All too often companies utilize an overdraft to acquire long-term assets, and that overdraft never seems to disappear, eventually constraining the business.

The attraction of overdrafts is that they are very easy to arrange and take little time to set up. That is also their inherent weakness. The key words in the arrangement document are 'repayable on demand', which leaves the bank free to make and change the rules as it sees fit. (This term is under constant review, and some banks may remove it from the arrangement.) With other forms of borrowing, as long as you stick to the terms and conditions, the loan is yours for the duration. It is not so with overdrafts.

2. Term loans

Term loans, as long-term bank borrowings are generally known, are funds provided by a bank for a number of years. Just over a third of all term loans are for periods greater than 10 years, and a quarter are for three years or less.

The interest can either be variable, changing with general interest rates, or fixed for a number of years ahead. The proportion of fixed-rate loans has increased from a third of all term loans to around one in two. In some cases it may be possible to move between having a fixed interest rate and a variable one at certain intervals. It may even be possible to have a moratorium on interest payments for a short period, to give the business some breathing space. Provided the conditions of the loan are met in such matters as repayment, interest and security cover, the money is available for the period of the loan. Unlike in the case of an overdraft, the bank cannot pull the rug from under you if circumstances (or the local manager) change.

3. Government-backed funds

Governments around the world have an interest in seeing businesses in their country prosper and grow. Their logic is selfish. Successful businesses employ more people and, both directly through tax on profits or sales and indirectly through the taxes their employees pay, pay more into the national coffers. Those employees in turn buy more goods and services, spreading wealth across the wider economy. When the economy is booming businesses can, for the most part, grow unaided. During downturns or periods of unusual turbulence businesses may need stimulation or encouragement to grow and that is where governments believe that, by making finance easier, they can get the economy moving. One method is to make grant finance available to certain types of business, say high tech; or firms in relatively depressed areas. An alternative is to focus on firms at a particular stage; start-up, early growth or when they start exporting.

Government sources of finance comes by way of grants that are, in effect, free money. Soft loans; that is, money that banks would not normally lend and equity participation. The range and types of funding vary from time to time, country to country.

These resources are a useful starting point for an MBA to familiarize themselves with the subject:

- Australia: Grants and assistance: https://business.gov.au/grants-and-programs?
- Canada: Invest in Canada: www.investcanada.ca/programs-incentives
- Developing countries: The International Finance Corporation (IFC), the private-investment arm of the World Bank Group, helps with lending to small businesses in emerging markets, supporting projects that may be considered risky, such as those in conflict areas, women-owned businesses and sustainable energy: www.ifc.org/>Products>Loans
- Europe: Access to finance. To access EU finance, click on your country to locate banks or venture capital funds that provide finance supported by the EU: https://europa.eu/youreurope/business/finance-funding/getting-funding/access-finance/index_en.htm
- India: Department of Financial Services: https://financialservices.gov.in/
- The UK: Finance and support for your business: www.gov.uk/business-finance-support
- The USA: Funding options: www.usa.gov/funding-options

CASE STUDY
BrewDog

In the BrewDog accounts filed in 2021 the company reported revenue of £237,763 million. They also signalled that they were the world's first carbon negative beer brewer. Legend has it that boredom led to James Watt and Martin Dickie setting up BrewDog in Fraserburgh in 2007. The boredom in question was with 'the industrially brewed lagers and stuffy ales' that dominated the UK beer market at that time. Their mission was 'to make other people as passionate about great craft beer as we are'. The solution that the pair, both just 24 at that time, came up with was to brew their own. Operating out of a leased building in Fraserburgh, backed only by bank loans, the pair acquired some stainless steel tanks and started brewing beers to their own recipe. Initially they started with tiny batches, filled bottles by hand and sold their beers at local markets and 'out of the back of our beat up old van'.

Barely twelve months into their venture they launched the UK's strongest ever beer, Tokyo. The resulting media storm signalled, according to the pair, 'the downfall of Western civilization'. Guidance from alcohol industry watchdog the Portman Group pretty much banned all of their beers. Beer consumers, however, had other ideas, quaffing the stuff in industrial quantities. BrewDog started exporting to Sweden, Japan and America, and with a slot on TV with Oz Clark the new company was as hot as its products. In only their second year, BrewDog became Scotland's largest independent brewery.

On the back of this success they persuaded the banks to give them money to buy more tanks and a proper bottling machine. But keeping up with demand meant having to leave the banks behind. Banks' appetite for risk proved rather less than BrewDog's customers' appetite for the company's beer. Crowdfunding was in its infancy in 2009 and Watt and Dickie had to pioneer their own version. They didn't just want money; they wanted to form a community who not only financed the business but also played a part in product development and marketing strategy. These investors became the founding 'legion of brand ambassadors around the globe'. So 'Equity for Punks' was formed, and in 2009 they raised £642,000 from 1,300 investors.

By 2020 subsequent rounds of funding have seen some 133,000 investors pump over £75 million into the business. Investors can put in as little as £25, getting core benefits such as discounts on beer, invites to brew days and entry into their BrewDogs Millionaire Competition. Joining the Dead Pony Club calls for an investment of £200-plus, rising through stages to £4,975-plus, where as a 'Black Eyed King Impvestor' (*sic*) you get discounts of up to 30 per cent.

Bonds, debentures and mortgages

Bonds, debentures and mortgages are all kinds of borrowing with different rights and obligations for the parties concerned. For a business, a mortgage is much the same as for an individual. The loan is for a specific event, buying a particular property asset such as a factory, office or warehouse. Interest is payable and the loan itself is secured against the property, so should the business fail the mortgage can substantially be redeemed.

Companies that want to raise funds for general business purposes, rather than as with a mortgage where a particular property is being bought, issue debentures or bonds. These run for a number of years, typically three years and upwards, with the bond or debenture holder receiving interest over the life of the loan, and the capital is returned at the end of the period.

The key difference between debentures and bonds lies in their security and ranking. Debentures are unsecured and so in the event of the company being unable to pay interest or repay loans holders may well get little or nothing back. Bonds are secured against specific assets and so rank ahead of debentures for any pay-out.

Unlike bank loans that are usually held by the issuing bank, though even that assumption is being challenged by the escalation of securitization of debt being packaged up and sold on, bonds and debentures are sold to the public in much the same way as shares. The interest demanded will be a factor of the prevailing market conditions and the financial strength of the borrower.

Categories of bond

There are several general categories of bond that companies can tap into. *Standard bonds* pay interest, a coupon, half-yearly on the principal amount, known as the face or par value. At the maturity date the principal is repaid. The value of bonds fluctuates depending on market condition, the length of time to maturity and the likelihood of the borrower defaulting. None of these matters are of immediate concern to the recipient of the funds, as long as they can service the interest. The risk is for the bondholder who can see the value of the investment alter over time.

Zero coupon bonds pay no interest over their life but pay a lump sum at maturity equivalent to the value of the interest such an investment would normally bear. The buyer of the bond receives a return by the gradual appreciation of the bonds' price in the marketplace. This could be an attractive financing strategy for a business making an investment that itself will not bear fruit for a number of years.

Junk bonds are bonds usually subordinated to, that is put below in the pecking order of who gets paid in tough times, other regular bonds. Such bonds carry a higher interest burden.

Callable bonds are used when an issuer wants to retain the option to buy back the bonds from the public if general interest rates fall sharply after the issue date. The issuer notifies bondholders that after a certain date no further interest will be paid, leaving the holders with no reason to keep the bond. The company issuing the bond can then go out to the market and launch a new bond at a lower rate of interest and so lower its cost of capital. This process is also known as refinancing.

Commercial paper

Banks and big companies such as General Electric and AT&T regularly raise cash for operations by issuing paper to investors that often matures in six months or less. Private investors, especially money-market funds, buy this debt because as well as being very safe it pays an interest rate slightly higher than comparable US Treasury notes or UK Government Gilts. Although commercial paper is technically repayable in under six months in practice the corporate borrower repays investors by issuing more paper, effectively paying back investors with more borrowed cash. The attraction to the borrower over other forms of lending is that as long as it matures before nine months (270 days) it doesn't have to be registered with any regulatory body, making it in effect 'off-balance sheet', which in turn reduces gearing (see Chapter 8 for more on gearing and financial risk). The exception to this rule is if the proceeds from this type of financing are to be used for anything other than current assets (inventories, debtors, etc), for example fixed assets, such as a new plant. In such cases the relevant regulatory body has to be informed. However, in practice business funds tend to go into a pot and tracing where a particular sum of money came from and what was done with it is virtually impossible.

Syndicated loan

This is a loan offered by a group of lenders (a syndicate) who work together to provide funds usually though by no means always for a single borrower. The borrower could be a business, a large project, or a government. The loans are usually so large as to be potentially fatal to any single lender in the event of a default – hence the syndication. Borrowers who need a sophisticated facility or multiple types of facility find that using a syndicated loan agreement simplifies the borrowing process by using a single agreement covering the whole group of banks and different types of facility rather than entering into a series of separate bilateral loans. A syndicated loan agreement could contain a fixed term or revolving facility that is in effect permanent; or it can contain a combination of both or several of each type (multiple term loans in different currencies and with different maturity dates are fairly typical of the more complex syndicated loan). The syndicated loan can be for one borrower, a group of borrowers or allow for new borrowers to join in under certain circumstances from time to time. Four important pieces of documentation accompany syndicated loans:

1 *Term sheet:* this sets out the terms of the proposed financing, the parties involved, their expected roles and the key features of the loan including the type of facilities, the amounts, the pricing, the term of the loan and the covenant (any conditions and restrictions).

2 *Information memorandum:* this contains a commercial description of the borrower's business, management and accounts as well as details of the proposed loan facilities required. This document contains more information than is usually in the public domain so potential lenders will be expected to sign a confidentiality undertaking.

3 *Syndicated loan agreement:* the loan agreement sets out the detailed terms and conditions on which the facility is made available to the borrower.

4 *Fee letters:* borrower pays fees to those banks in the syndicate that have performed additional work or taken on greater responsibility in the loan process, including the arranger, the agent and the security trustee. Details of these fees are usually put in separate side letters to ensure confidentiality. These fees are in addition to paying interest on the loan and any related bank expenses.

CASE STUDY
Cobra Beer

The latest accounts for the Cobra Beer Partnership, a joint arrangement between Molson Coors Brewing Company (UK) and Bilimoria Holdings, filed in October 2021 show a turnover of £35,700,000 with profits of £3,833,000. These figures were around half that achieved in the years before the Covid-19 pandemic struck.

In 1990 Cambridge-educated and recently qualified accountant Karan Bilimoria started importing and distributing Cobra beer, a name he chose because it appeared to work well in lots of different languages. He initially supplied his beer to complement Indian restaurant food in the UK. Lord Bilimoria, as he now is, started out with debts of £20,000 ($32,000/€23,600), but from a small flat in Fulham and with just a Citroen CV by way of assets he has grown his business to sales of over £100 ($160/€118) million a year.

Three factors have been key to its success. Cobra was originally sold in large 660 ml bottles and so was more likely to be shared by diners. Also, as Cobra is less fizzy than European lagers, drinkers are less likely to feel bloated and can eat and drink more. The third factor was Bilimoria's extensive knowledge through his training as an accountant of sources of finance for a growing business. He was fortunate in having an old-style bank manager who had such belief in Cobra that he agreed a loan of £30,000 ($48,000/€35,400) but since then has tapped into every possible type of funding (see Figure 6.1).

Payment in kind (PIK)

A PIK loan usually doesn't require any cash payment of either capital or interest until it matures. Such loans are typically unsecured with maturity dates usually exceeding five years. These loans usually carry a detachable warrant, which is the right to purchase a certain number of shares at a given price for a certain period of time, or some such mechanism. This allows the lender to share in the future success of the business by way of compensation for its risk.

PIKs are something of a controversial debt structure and can ratchet sub-stantial amounts of interest every year, which can ultimately destroy a com-

Figure 6.1 Cobra Beer's financing strategy

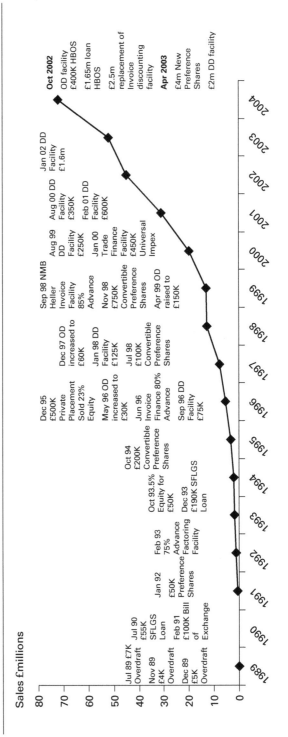

pany. Paramount Restaurants, the owner of Chez Gerard and Cafe Uno, is an example of the distress this form of finance can cause. In March 2010 the company saw its PIK notes stand at over £78 ($125/€92) million, up from £51.5 ($82.4/€60.7) million three years earlier. The debt was provided by Silverfleet, which backed a £107 ($171/€126) million buy-out. The PIK element was rolling up a crippling 15.5 per cent interest annually.

Paramount's bankers, including Royal Bank of Scotland, HSBC and Barclays had to take the company over from Silverfleet, taking a 60 per cent equity stake in the business themselves, in an effort to save the business from failure.

Asset usage financing

The banks are more covert when it comes to looking for security for money lent. Some other major sources of funds are less circumspect; indeed their whole prospectus is predicated on a precise relationship between what a business has or will shortly have by way of assets, and what they are prepared to advance. Such products play an important role in financing businesses.

Leasing companies

Physical assets such as cars, vans, computers, office equipment and the like can usually be financed by leasing them, rather as a house or flat may be rented. Alternatively, they can be bought on hire purchase. This leaves other funds free to cover the less tangible elements in your cash flow.

Leasing is a way of getting the use of vehicles, plant and equipment without paying the full cost all at once. Operating leases are taken out where you will use the equipment (for example a car, photocopier, vending machine or kitchen equipment) for less than its full economic life. The lessor takes the risk of the equipment becoming obsolete, and assumes responsibility for repairs, maintenance and insurance. As you, the lessee, are paying for this service, it is more expensive than a finance lease, where you lease the equipment for most of its economic life and maintain and insure it yourself. Leases can normally be extended, often for fairly nominal sums, in the latter years.

Hire purchase differs from leasing in that you have the option to eventually become the owner of the asset, after a series of payments. You can find a leasing company via International Finance and Leasing Association (www.ifla.com), a network of leading finance companies all over the world. The website also has general information on terms of trade and code of conduct.

Discounting and factoring

Customers often take time to pay up. In the meantime you have to pay those who work for you and your less patient suppliers. So, the more you grow, the more funds you need. It is often possible to 'factor' your creditworthy customers' bills to a financial institution, receiving some of the funds as your goods leave the door, hence speeding up cash flow.

Factoring is generally only available to a business that invoices other business customers, either in its home market or internationally, for its products or services. Factoring can be made available to new businesses, although its services are usually of most value during the early stages of growth. It is an arrangement that allows you to receive up to 80 per cent of the cash due from your customers more quickly than they would normally pay. The factoring company in effect buys your trade debts, and can also provide a debtor accounting and administration service. You will, of course, have to pay for factoring services. Having the cash before your customers pay will cost you a little more than normal overdraft rates. The factoring service will cost between 0.5 and 3.5 per cent of the turnover, depending on volume of work, the number of debtors, average invoice amount and other related factors. You can get up to 80 per cent of the value of your invoice in advance, with the remainder paid when your customer settles up, less the various charges just mentioned.

If you sell direct to the public, sell complex and expensive capital equipment, or expect progress payments on long-term projects, then factoring is not for you. If you are expanding more rapidly than other sources of finance will allow, this may be a useful service that is worth exploring.

Invoice discounting is a variation on the same theme where you are responsible for collecting the money from debtors; this is not a service available to new or very small businesses. The International Factoring Association (www.factoring.org/) has a directory of factoring companies around the world, with the strongest coverage in North America.

Letters of credit and bills of exchange

Until the 19th century the branch banking system was fairly limited and postal services relatively slow. A system of transferring money, in particularly between countries, but also within countries was established. Initially under the general heading of 'bills of exchange' these financial instruments were in effect promissory notes, much like the modern day cheque, drawn up by one party who promises to pay another a certain sum on a certain day. Variations on this theme also became established, letters of credit being one of the most common. These were and to some extent still are used for buyers and sellers of international goods to transfer money to facilitate transactions. These letters can be irrevocable, that is payment must be made if all conditions are met; revocable – these can be cancelled or amended without prior notice; or transferrable where the letter concerned and the money attached can be passed to another party, usually a 'middleman' or agent. An MBA needs only a nodding acquaintance with these types of financial instruments and when you need to know more you can read up on them at LC Consultancy Services, founded by Certified Documentary Credit Specialist (CDCS) Ozgur Eker, which has information on every form of letter of credit, sample contracts, case studies and examples, as well as information on other trade financing instruments (www.letterofcredit.biz/index.html).

Sell and leaseback assets

August 2009 saw broadcaster ITV reporting full-year losses of £2.59 ($4.14/€3.1) billion, a consequence of the collapse in advertising revenue brought about by the prevailing economic crisis. By the time it reported these figures the company had already cut 1,000 jobs, secured £155 ($248/€183) million in cost savings and had its sights set on cutting a further £215 ($344/€254) million out of overheads in 2010. In fact the company's advertising revenue decline of 15 per cent was a little better than that of the market as a whole, which had slipped back 17 per cent. Nevertheless Michael Grade, the outgoing chairman, felt the situation drastic enough to call for further action. He sold the Friends Reunited website to Scottish publisher D C Thompson, of *Beano* fame, for £25 ($40/€29.5) million, some £150 ($240/€177) million less than ITV had paid for it four years earlier. The assets that Grade sold off were considered non-core and so could safely be sacrificed. But what if you want to keep assets but still need cash, perhaps for less pressing needs than survival?

Sale and leaseback can be seen as a less desperate measure than selling off assets. At least using this strategy you live and get to fight another day. The process involves selling some or all of your fixed assets including property and vehicles to another company, becoming a tenant in what were your premises or leasing your former cars and delivery fleet. The benefits are a large slug of cash to help ride out a storm, but also it's a way to reduce operating costs going forward, as amongst other things there is a tax benefit to be realized by offsetting lease costs as an operating expense. IBM, for example, sold and leased back four of its five remaining owned sites in the UK in 2006, leaving only its Hursley software laboratory in company ownership. As well as reducing costs, IBM is increasingly trying to have only sufficient property on the books to meet business demands, and leasing on relatively short terms helps in this respect. Other big users of sale and leaseback include Tesco, which recently made a £366 ($585/€432) million property sale and leaseback of 12 stores and two distribution centres.

Online video courses and lectures

Banking and Money: Khan Academy Course: http://freevideolectures.com/Course/2552/Banking-and-Money#

Banks: Professor Shiller of Yale University traces the origins of banking: http://oyc.yale.edu/economics/econ-252-11/lecture-13#ch2

How to Stay Out of Debt: Warren Buffett talking at the Nebraska Forum: www.youtube.com/watch?v=HM9h9t1vpIE

Introduction to Financial Markets: Alanis Business Academy: www.youtube.com/watch?v=tXURswGIbiE

Small Business Administration Loans – Small Talk with John Guy of Webster Bank – SBA Loans: www.youtube.com/watch?v=pDD0illFW-o

Online video case studies

Bootstrapping with flair: Susan Feldman, One Kings Lane, in conversation with Tina Seelig, Stanford University: https://ecorner.stanford.edu/videos/bootstrapping-with-flair-entire-talk/

Destination London: Rachael Lowe's presentation to Dragons' Den. www.youtube.com/watch?v=PrB2JmyfkrM

Innocent Drinks: Richard Reed, Innocent co-founder, talks about starting and funding, sponsored by Schroders Private Banking: www.youtube.com/watch?v=bUi6lugzFn0

07
Equity

There are many sources of funds available to businesses but not all of them are equally appropriate to all businesses at all times. These different sources of finance carry very different obligations, responsibilities and opportunities for profitable business, and having some appreciation of these differences will enable the MBA to help managers and directors make informed choices.

Most businesses initially and often until they go public, floating their shares on a stock market, confine their financial strategy to bank loans, either long- or short-term, or other financing methods that require the loan to be repaid with interest – this field of finance was the subject of Chapter 6. Often this strategy is adopted as managers view the other financing methods as either too complex or too risky. In many respects the reverse is true. Almost every finance source other than banks will to a greater or lesser extent share some of the risks of doing business with the recipient of the funds. (The appropriate balance of risk to be selected between differing sources of finance is covered in Chapter 10.)

Businesses operating as a limited company or limited partnership have a potentially valuable opportunity to raise relatively risk-free money. It is risk-free to the business but risky, sometimes extremely so, to anyone investing. Essentially this type of capital, known collectively as 'equity', consists of the issued share capital and reserves of various kinds. It represents the amount of money that shareholders have invested directly into the company by buying shares, together with retained profits that belong to shareholders but which the company uses as additional capital. As with debt, equity comes in a number of forms with differing rights and privileges.

Ordinary shares form the bulk of the shares issued by most companies and are the shares, which carry the ordinary risks, associated with being in business. All the profits of the business, including past retained profits, belong to the ordinary shareholders once any preference share dividends have been deducted. Ordinary shares have no fixed rate of dividend; indeed over half the companies listed on US stock markets pay no or virtually no dividend. These include high growth companies such as Google and Microsoft, which argue that by retaining and reinvesting all their profits they can create better value for shareholders than by distributing dividends.

A company does not have to issue all its share capital at once. The total amount it is authorized to issue must be shown somewhere in the accounts, but only the issued share capital is counted in the balance sheet. Although shares can be partly paid, this is a rare occurrence.

Preference shares get their name for two reasons. First, they receive their fixed rate of dividend before ordinary shareholders. Second, in the event of winding up a company, any funds remaining go to repay preference share capital before any ordinary share capital. In a forced liquidation this may be of little comfort as shareholders of any type come last in the queue after all other claims from creditors have been met.

Class A and class B shares are cases where categories of shareholder are singled out for more or less favourable treatment. For example, class A shares are often given up to five votes per share, while class B shares get one. In extreme cases class B shareholders can get no votes at all. Companies will often try to disguise the disadvantages associated with owning shares with less voting rights. Google (a subsidiary of Alphabet Inc.) provides an interesting example. When they launched their initial public offering (IPO) in 2004, they announced that they planned to have three classes of shares, with sufficient structural inequality to rub the wider investing community up the wrong way:

- Class A shares: For the general investing community, offering one vote per share, as is usual for common stock.
- Class B shares: Reserved for Google executives and founding members, offering ten votes per share.
- Class C shares: Offered to general Google employees, these shares came with no voting rights.

'Reserves', a typically misleading term in all accounting, means profits of various kinds that have been retained in the company as extra capital. Also important is what the term 'reserves' does not mean. It does not mean actual money held back in reserve in bank accounts or elsewhere. Reserves come from retained profits over many years but are reinvested in buildings, equipment, stocks or company debts, just like any other source of capital and rarely held in cash. The main categories of reserves are as follows:

- Profit and loss account: the cumulative retained profits from ordinary trading activities.
- Revaluation reserve: the paper-profit that can arise if certain assets are re-valued to current price levels without the assets concerned being sold.

- Share premium account: the excess over the original par value of a share when new shares are offered for sale at an enhanced price. Only the original par value is ever shown as issued share capital.

There are two broad sources of equity: *private equity* usually put in by individuals or small groups of individuals who, for the potential of greater returns, will take on greater risks; or *public capital* through a share issue on a stock market.

Private equity

There are a number of sources of private equity including business angels, venture capital firms, corporate venture funding and a recent addition, crowdfunding. Table 7.1 illustrates what is often referred to as the A, B, C, D and E of funding.

Business angels

One likely first source of equity or risk capital will be a private individual with his or her own funds, and perhaps some knowledge of your type of business. In return for a share in the business, such investors will put in money at their own risk. They have been christened 'business angels', a term first coined to describe private wealthy individuals who back a play on Broadway or in London's West End.

Most angels are determined upon some involvement beyond merely signing a cheque and may hope to play a part in your business in some way. They are hoping for big rewards – one angel who backed Sage with £10,000 ($16,000/€12,000) in its first round of £250,000 ($5000,000/€295,000) financing saw his stake rise to £40 ($64/€47) million.

These angels frequently operate through managed networks, usually on the internet. In the UK and the United States there are hundreds of networks, with tens of thousands of business angels prepared to put up several billion each year into new or small business.

Here are 10 things worth knowing about business angels:

1 40 per cent suffer partial or complete loss of their investment;
2 50 per cent don't conduct research into prospective investments;
3 55 per cent don't take up personal references, compared with only 6 per cent of venture capital providers in general;
4 90 per cent have worked in a small firm or owned their own business;
5 business angels meet owners five times on average before investing, compared with venture capital providers in general who require 10 meetings;

Table 7.1   The A, B, C, D, E and onwards of funding

Round	Investors?	Purpose of the round	Company milestones
Seed	Family/friends Angel investors, early-stage VCs	Validated market – founders selling their vision, building a team, making the prototype. Anything from £20,000 to £1 million – amount varies widely.	• Firm up product/market position. • Make first hires. • Build and launch prototype.
Series A	Crowdfunding – angel investors, early stage VCs	At this stage, business has firmed up on its product offering and prospective customer base. Valuation based on sales level.	• Finalize scale up methods – make or buy in? • Refine prototype. • Firm up business model. • Set KPIs.
Series B	As with series A plus a focus on later-stage growth. Corporate venture firms	Business model confirmed and customer base established. Valuation based on sales and profit plus factors such as intellectual property and high-value industry recruits.	• Scale up sales process. • Increase team, adding star performers. • Build up business department and management structure – sales and marketing teams – finance. • Break even and make a profit. • Expect buy-out offers.
Series C, D, E and onwards	Private equity firms, VC funds, big public companies with corporate venture portfolios	Scaling up. Increasing market share, making acquisitions, growing internationally and preparing for a public listing.	• Rapid growth in market share. • Expand product range. • Expand internationally. • Look for businesses to buy.

6 10 per cent of business angel investment is for less than $10,000 (£6,250/€8,475) and 45 per cent is for over $50,000 (£31,250/€42,370);

7 most business angels invest close to home. Up to 50 miles is usual, with 200 miles as the limit. Angels rarely invest abroad;

8 only 2 per cent have made overseas investments;

9 angels often flock together. Syndicated deals make up more than a quarter of all deals, where two or more angels band together to invest;

10 angels are up to five times more likely to invest in start-ups and early stage investments than venture capital providers in general.

Finding a business angel

The UK Business Angels Association (https://ukbaa.org.uk) has an online directory of UK business angels. The European Business Angels Network (eban) has directories of national business angel associations both inside and outside of Europe at (www.eban.org/membership-directory) from which you can find individual business angels.

Venture capital

Venture capitalists (VCs), sometimes unflatteringly referred to as 'vulture capitalists', are investing other people's money, often from pension funds. They have a different agenda from that of business angels, and are more likely to be interested in investing more money for a larger stake. In general, VCs expect their investment to have paid off within seven years, but they are hardened realists. Two in every 10 investments they make are total write-offs, and six perform averagely well at best. So, the one star in every 10 investments they make has to cover a lot of duds. VCs have a target rate of return of 30 per cent plus, to cover this poor hit rate.

Raising venture capital is not a cheap option and deals are not quick to arrange either. Six months is not unusual, and over a year has been known. Every VC has a deal done in six weeks in its portfolio, but that truly is the exception. Fees will run to hundreds of thousands of pounds, the sweetener being that these can be taken from the money raised.

Although the 100 billion or so invested by VCs sounds impressive, they only back around 35,000 businesses in any one year. (You can see a chart showing more history and detail provided by KPMG at: https://assets.kpmg/is/content/kpmg/global-venture-financing-5?scl=1.)

Finding venture capital

The British Private Equity and Venture Capital Association (www.bvca.co.uk) and Invest Europe (www.investeurope.eu) both have online directories giving details of hundreds of venture capital providers. The National Venture Capital Association in the US has directories of international venture capital associations both inside and outside the United States (www.nvca.org>Resources).

You can see how those negotiating with or receiving venture capital rate the firm in question at The Funded website (www.thefunded.com) in terms

Figure 7.1 Global venture financing, 2019–22

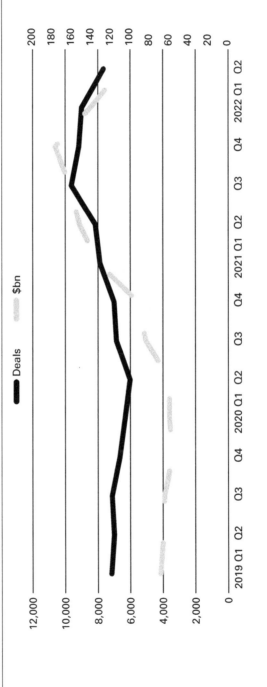

of the deal offered, the firm's apparent competence and how good it is at managing the relationship. There is also a link to the VC's website. The Funded has 21,226 members.

The Internet Bookshop case below tells something of the way that raising investment funds can propel a business. Alternatively, putting too little funding in place can lead to missed opportunities to grow.

CASE STUDY
The Internet Bookshop and why it was eclipsed by Amazon

UK entrepreneur Darryl Mattocks, a software engineer and computer enthusiast, entered the market in 1994 a year ahead of Amazon, but his approach was profoundly different. Mattock went into a bookshop in Oxford and picked up a book he had ordered a few days before. He paid for it, walked a few doors down to the Post Office and despatched it to the customer who had e-mailed his order the previous week. He was constrained initially to financing the business using credit cards, though later a friend introduced him to James Blackwell, a member of the family behind the Oxford booksellers, who put up £50,000 ($80,000/€59,000) for a 50 per cent stake in the venture.

Jeff Bezos, a former investment banker, raised $11 (£6.9/€9.3) million from Silicon Valley venture capitalists before starting up, and invested $8 (£5/€6.8) million of that in marketing. Mattocks' Internet Bookshop had a database of 16,000 books, while Amazon was selling nearly $16 (£10/€13.5) million worth of books. In 1998, around the time it was buying Waterstones, WH Smith bought out bookshop.co.uk, parent company of the Internet Bookshop, for £9.4 ($15/€11) million. Amazon was then valued at $10.1 (£6.3/€8.6) billion.

Corporate venturing

Venture capital firms often take a hand in the management of the businesses they invest in. Another type of venturer is also in the risk capital business, without it necessarily being their main line of business. These firms, known as corporate venturers, usually want an inside track to new developments in and around the edges of their own fields of interest.

Sinclair Beecham and Julian Metcalfe, who started with a £17,000 ($27,000/€20,000) loan and a name borrowed from a boarded-up shop, founded Prêt a Manger. They were not entrepreneurs content with doing their own thing. They had global ambitions and it was only by cutting in McDonald's the burger giant that they could see any realistic way to dominate the world. They sold a 33 per cent stake for £25 ($40/€29.5) million in 2001 to McDonald's Ventures LLC, a wholly-owned subsidiary of McDonald's Corporation, the arm of McDonald's that looks after its corporate venturing activities.

They could also have considered Cisco, Apple Computers, IBM and Microsoft, which also all have corporate venturing arms. Other corporate venturers include Deutsche Bank, which set up DB eVentures to get a window on the 'digital revolution'. Reuters Greenhouse has stakes in 85 companies and even the late and unlamented Enron had venture investments (totalling $110/£176/€130 million). For an entrepreneur this approach can provide a 'friendly customer' and help open doors. For the 'parent' it provides a privileged ringside seat as a business grows and the opportunity to decide if the area is worth plunging into more deeply, or at least provides valuable insights into new technologies or business processes.

Bain & Company, an American management consulting company, reckons corporate venture capital (CVC) deal value has increased more than tenfold over the decade to 2022. The annual volume of deals has grown at about 7 per cent: www.bain.com/insights/corporate-venture-capital-m-and-a-report-2022.

CASE STUDY
Innocent

In the summer of 1998 when Richard Reed, Adam Balon and Jon Wright had developed their first smoothie recipes but were still nervous about giving up their jobs, they bought £500 ($800/€590) worth of fruit, turned it into smoothies and sold them from a stall at a London music festival. They put up a sign saying, 'Do you think we should give up our jobs to make these smoothies?' next to bins labelled 'YES' and 'NO', inviting people to put the empty bottle in the appropriate bin. At the end of the weekend the 'YES' bin was full, so they went in the next day and resigned. The rest, as they say, is history. Virtually a household name, the business has experienced a decade of rapid growth. But the business stalled in 2008, with sales slipping back and their European expansion soaking up cash at a rapid rate.

The founders, average age 28, decided that they needed some heavyweight advice and talked to Charles Dunstone, Carphone Warehouse founder, and Mervyn Davies, chairman of Standard Chartered. The strong advice was to get an investor with deep pockets and ideally something else to bring to the party to augment the youthful enthusiasm of the founders. They launched their search for an investor the day that Lehman Brothers filed for bankruptcy. In April 2009 the Innocent team accepted Coca-Cola as a minority investor in their business, paying £30 ($48/€35) million for a stake of between 10 and 20 per cent. They chose Coca-Cola because as well as providing the funds, it can help get their products out to more people in more places. Also, with Coca-Cola having been in business for over 120 years, there will be things they can learn from it.

Family, friends and business associates of the board

Those close to your company, family and friends of the board of directors, key suppliers or customers can often be persuaded to either lend or invest in your business. This helps you avoid the problem of pleading your case to outsiders and enduring extra paperwork and bureaucratic delays. Help from friends, relatives and business associates can be especially valuable if your business has credit problems that would make raising money from a commercial funding source difficult or impossible.

Such sources of finance bring a range of extra potential benefits, costs and risks that are not a feature of most other types of finance. You need to decide if these are acceptable and incorporate this into your assessment of whether or not to recommend going down this route.

Some advantages of raising money from people you know well are that you may get easier terms, may be able to delay paying back money until you are in better financial shape and may be given more flexibility if your firm gets into difficulties. But once the loan or investment terms are agreed, the same legal obligations apply as with any other source of finance.

In addition, raising money from such sources can have a major disadvantage. If your business does poorly and those close to you end up losing money, you may well damage a good personal relationship. So, in dealing with friends, relatives and business associates, be extra careful not only to establish clearly the terms of the deal and put them in writing but also to make an extra effort to explain the risks. In short, it's your job to make sure your helpful friend, relative, supplier or customer won't suffer a true hardship if you're unable to meet your financial commitments. Don't accept money from those who can't afford to risk it.

Here are 10 things to remember about raising money from family, friends and business associates:

1 Do agree proper terms for the loan or investment.

2 Do put the agreement in writing and if it involves a share transaction or guarantee, have a legal agreement drawn up.

3 Do make an extra effort to explain the risks of the business and the possible downside implications to their money.

4 Do make sure when raising money from parents to advise those concerned that other siblings are compensated in some way, perhaps via a will.

5 Do make sure you or your fellow directors want to run a family business before raising money in this way as family investors always want to get involved.

6 Don't borrow from people on fixed incomes.

7 Don't borrow from people who can't afford to lose money.

8 Don't make the possible rewards sound more attractive than you would to any other investor.

9 Don't offer jobs in your business to anyone providing money unless they are the best person for the job.

10 Don't change the normal pattern of social contact with family, friends or business associates after they have put up the money.

Crowdfunding

Over the past few years, the business world has seen the birth and rapid growth of what appears to be a new way of raising funds, known as crowdfunding. *Crowdfunding* is an organized means for a large group of people to make mostly small individual donations to fund a business or an idea. It uses the power of the internet to bring the two sides together. Crowdfunding replicates some of the more traditional funding activities in an online format, such as pitching for a desired amount of finance. As finance for business goes, this new vehicle puts the entrepreneur in the driving seat, and empowers members of the public and the investor community – the *crowd* – to get a piece of the action as paying passengers in a number of companies.

Crowdfunding can raise funds in one of four ways or in any combination of all of them:

- *Equity.* Offers some share in the business for money invested, much as you would with a venture capital provider or business angel. By some accounts crowdfunding raises more money than VCs and business angels combined. Palo Alto-based smartwatch maker Pebble is one of the highest-funded campaigns in crowdfunding history, having raised over €20 million. It's also the fastest funded, raising $1 million in less than an hour.

- *Loans.* You can also pay interest treating the funds as a loan in the same way as with bank finance. The interest is likely to be higher than with comparable bank finance and the time horizon for paying the loan back will be shorter. Chilango, a London chain of fast-service Mexican restaurants founded by two ex-Skype executives, raised money through what they entertainingly called a Burrito Bond to help roll out more restaurants across London. They offered an interest rate of 8 per cent repayable over four years.

- *Reward-based.* This involves exchanging gifts or rewards based on the amount of giving. Smith & Sinclair completed a successful reward-based crowdfunding campaign to finance their Immersive Edible Alcohol Shop, creating inventive sweet treats for adults. The founders met their goal of £23,000 in only 49 days from 96 backers offering as rewards speciality alcohol-based jewellery. Chilango sweetened their deal by offering all investors two free burrito vouchers and those that put in more than £10,000 get free food for the entire duration of the bond.

- *Invoice financing platforms.* This works in much the same way as cash flow financing (see earlier in this chapter). Once approved, the business can sell an invoice (as small as £1,000 and as large as £1 million+) on the invoice trading platform. Once verified, the invoice is sold on the platform, where multiple investors buy slices of the invoice. The business receives funds in their account as an advance of up to 90 per cent of the invoice face value within 24–48 hours. When the invoice is settled in full the invoice trading platform makes the remaining balance available to the business, minus their fees. The advantages to the users of this service are speed – you can be up and funded in 24 hours; you only fund the invoices you want to, unlike conventional discounters who require to take on your whole debtors ledger; and there is no lengthy lock period – you just operate invoice by invoice.

Crowdfund providers

There are now literally hundreds of crowdfunding platforms around the world. And the last word in that sentence is the key to the competitive advantage of this type of funding. Unlike banks and private equity providers which tend to operate on a country or at best continent basis, crowdfunders can be anywhere.

You can find a complete list of crowdfunding sites in a directory that's produced by Nesta or the UK Crowdfunding Association website.

Here are a handful of operators just to get a flavour of the players.

CROWDCUBE

Crowdcube was the first UK-based crowdfunding website, and the first crowdfunding website in the world to enable the public to invest in and receive shares in UK companies. They have 359,856 registered investors and have raised over £220 million of new capital for thousands of businesses.

The range of businesses that have used the site include:

- Darlington Football Club, which raised £291,450 from 722 investors over 14 days to help fend off closure after going into liquidation.
- Universal Fuels raised £100,000, making founder Oliver Morgan, at 20 the youngest entrepreneur to successfully raise investment through the process.

KICKSTARTER

Kickstarter is predominantly for creative projects, be they films, games, art, design or music. It has its roots in the United States. In 2012, a UK version was launched to encourage local giving for local projects, and nearly 10 million people have pledged nearly £2 billion. The site is a resounding success, demonstrating the power of people and the life-changing achievements that happen when people get behind each other.

In much the same way that other financially incentivized sites demand that projects reach full pledge subscription, Kickstarter is an *all-or-nothing site*, meaning that you get nothing unless your project is fully funded. You set the pledge amount and you set the deadline, but you must then go shake the trees and make the golden fruit drop into your funding crate. To some people this seems harsh, but it does mean that you need to mobilize the power of your crowd and get people doing something versus talking about doing something for your idea, so it's a great financial firecracker.

To date, an impressive 36 per cent of projects have reached their funding goals. Creators keep 100 per cent ownership of their work, but a 5 per cent success fee goes to Kickstarter.

INDIEGOGO

Founded in San Francisco in 2008, Indiegogo, one of the first crowdfunding sites, has a global audience. It covers the spectrum from creative ideas to start-up business ideas to charity projects.

The success rate is lower than Kickstarter's, at 34 per cent. Its success fee starts at 5 per cent on a fully funded pledge, and 5 per cent on a partially funded pledge (Kickstarter doesn't offer partial funding). Indiegogo also charges up to 9 per cent on credit card and PayPal pledges, so the fees can add up. On the plus side, it refunds 5 per cent if the campaign reaches its target.

In 2014, it launched Indiegogo Life (now called Generosity), enabling people to raise funds for life events, such as celebrations, and also for emergencies, medical expenses and so forth. Generosity is different from Indiegogo with regard to the fees it charges for the funds raised, allowing fundraisers to keep more of the money they raise.

Both loan- and equity-based crowdfunding platforms are regulated by the FCA (Financial Conduct Authority), which helps protect investors. Peer-to-peer (P2P) lenders have to adhere to strict guidelines around capital, money and disclosure requirements. Investment-based platforms, both debt and equity, also fall under this umbrella.

Incubators and accelerators

Tempting though it might be to believe that business accelerators are an internet phenomenon, incubators, science parks, innovation centres, technology parks and a whole variety of other names have been coined over the years to describe the task that accelerators and incubators perform.

The first serious attempt at incubation is credited to a near-derelict building near New York. The name came into common usage more by way of a joke than as a serious description of the task in hand. One of the incubators' first tenants was involved in incubating real chickens. Several waves of accelerators followed this inauspicious start and by the 1980s several hundred such facilities were scattered around the US, Canada, Europe and Australia. Later incubator progressions took in the developing economies and the internet variation, which came into being in the mid-1990s, swept across the US, Europe, India, China, Malaysia, Singapore, the Philippines and elsewhere, bringing the total to some 4,000 facilities worldwide

The terms *incubator* and *accelerator* are often used interchangeably, and although you can get funding from both, incubators are most useful in the idea or pre-start stage. An accelerator is helpful to speed up your growth using funding, education, learning, mentoring and showcasing.

An *accelerator* provides services to support your business, often in return for equity, as your business begins to scale and grow. *Incubators* focus on very early-stage, small companies that have an idea that needs developing into more of a business.

INCUBATORS

While there is no single model for business incubators, in most cases the concepts go beyond the simple provision of a shared office or workspace facility for small business clients. The hallmark of any effective business incubator programme should be its focus on the added value that it brings to small business 'tenants' in terms of strengthened business skills; access to business services; improved operating environment; and opportunities for business networking, etc, to nurture early-stage small businesses, increasing the prospects for business survival and growth compared with the situation outside the incubator.

ACCELERATORS

The McKinsey Accelerators were a response to the challenges of the first wave of internet businesses. Their service set out to turbocharge the launch and growth of new e-businesses worldwide. They aimed to offer access to their extensive network of 'best in class' third-party service providers and their Fortune 500 client and alumni database. McKinsey's Accelerators offered four main types of assistance, which is very much the model adopted as standard:

- *intensive business building* (six to 12 months). For ventures that need to move at maximum speed McKinsey offers a large team to provide day-to-day execution of the marketing plan, including product launch itself;
- *targeted projects* (one to six months). Accelerator teams provide in-depth analytical services to enable start-ups to pinpoint their market opportunities, position and vulnerabilities. They can also screen merger and acquisition projects;
- *burst services* (two days to two months). Based on the hypothesis that

few start-ups have the resources for lengthy analysis and drawn-out marketing studies, McKinsey consultants can provide rapid-fire market data and other short-term targeted analysis needed for short-term decision making;

- *senior counselling* (as needed). Access to McKinsey partners for open, unbiased dialogues on any key business issues.

The National Business Incubation Association (NBIA) is the world's leading organization advancing business incubation and entrepreneurship. It has 1,900 members in 60 countries.

CASE STUDY
Chilango – how the Burrito Bond was born

When former Skype employees Eric Partaker and Dan Houghton started Chilango they had in mind supplying mouth-watering Mexican food, something of a rarity when they launched seven years ago. Eric developed an appetite for tacos, burritos and the like in his native Chicago, but when he came to work in London was faced with a veritable Mexican cuisine desert. When Eric met Dan, by coincidence also a Mexican food fanatic, the pair made it their mission to plug what they saw as a gap in the market.

Eric Partaker, an American and Norwegian national, graduated from the University of Illinois at Urbana-Champaign with a Bachelor of Science degree in Finance, and is also an alumnus of Katholieke Universiteit Leuven, Belgium, where he studied History, Philosophy, and Literature. Dan is a Cambridge mathematics graduate, leaving with a 1st. They met up in 2005 when they were both on the new business ventures team reporting to the CEO of Skype Technologies.

By 2014 with seven London Mexican food outlets open, one opposite the Goldman Sachs headquarters, they had proved there was an appetite for their business model. But with each new restaurant costing around £500,000 to launch they discovered another gap – an urgent need for cash to achieve their goal to launch six new Chilango restaurants around London quickly.

In 2014 they hit the headlines for financial rather than culinary innovation. Using the Crowdfunding website they set out to raise £1 million in two months offering 8 per cent interest with the capital to be repaid in four years. With the minimum investment set at £500, those putting up £10,000 get free lunch once a week at one of their restaurants. Hence the name 'Burrito Bond' was born.

One day after books on the bond opened, investments had already been received from executives in the food and drinks business, including the chief executive officer and chief financial officer of café-chain Carluccio's, the former CEO of Domino's Pizza UK and the former CEO of Krispy Kreme UK, according to the prospectus website. By 3 July 2014, according to information on the Crowdfunding website the company had received £1,140,500 from 344 investors.

The Covid-19 pandemic saw the business hit the buffers, as did much of the restaurant business world. Investment group RD Capital Partners took the business over in August 2020. June 2021 saw the business start expanding again, spurred by the use of dark kitchens.

Private capital preliminaries

Two important stages will be gone through before a private investor will put cash into a business. The emphasis put on these stages will vary according to the complexity of the deal, the amount of money and the legal ownership of the funds concerned. For example, business angels investing on their own account can accept greater uncertainty than, say, a venture capital fund using a pension fund's money.

1. Due diligence

Usually, after a private equity firm signs a letter of intent to provide capital and you accept, it will conduct a due diligence investigation of both the management and the company. During this period the private equity firm will have access to all financial and other records, facilities, employees, etc, to investigate before finalizing the deal. The material to be examined will include copies of all leases, contracts and loan agreements in addition to copious financial records and statements. The equity firm will want to see any management reports such as sales reports, inventory records, detailed lists of assets, facility maintenance records, aged receivables and payables reports, employee organization charts, payroll and benefits records, customer records and marketing materials. It will want to know about any pending litigation, tax audits or insurance disputes. Depending on the nature of the business, it might also consider getting an environmental audit and an insurance check-up. The sting in the due diligence tail is that the current owners of the business will be required to personally warrant that everything they have said or revealed is both true and complete. In the event that proves not to be so, they will be personally liable to the extent of any loss incurred by those buying the shares.

2. Term sheet

A term sheet is a funding offer from a capital provider. It lays out the amount of an investment and the conditions under which the new investors expect the business owners to work using their money.

The first page of the term sheet states the amount offered and the form of the funds (a bond, common stock, preferred stock, a promissory note or a combination of these). A price, either per 1,000 units of debt or per share of stock, is quoted to set the cost basis for investors 'getting in' on your company. Later that starting price will be very important in deciding capital gains and any taxes due at acquisition, IPO (initial public offering) or shares/units transferred.

Another key component of the term sheet is the 'post-closing capitalization'. This is the proposed cash value of the venture on the day the terms are accepted. For example, investors may offer £500,000 in series A preferred stock at 50 pence per share (1 million shares) with a post-closing cap of £2 million. This translates into a 25 per cent ownership stake in the firm (£500,000 divided by £2 million).

The next section of the term sheet is typically a table that summarizes the capital structure of your company. Investors generally start with preferred stock to gain a priority of distribution, should the enterprise fail and the liquidation of assets occur. The typical way to handle this is to have the preferred stock convertible into common stock on a 1:1 ratio at the investors' option, such that the preferred position is essentially a common stock position, but with priority of repayment over the founders' own common stock position.

Other terms included on the sheet could cover rents, equipment, levels of debt vs equity, minimum and maximum time periods associated with the transfer of shares, vesting in additional shares, option periods for making subsequent investments and having 'right of first refusal' when other rounds of funding are sought in the future.

Public capital

Stock markets are the place where serious businesses raise serious money. It's possible to raise anything from a few million to tens of billions; expect the costs and efforts in getting listed to match those stellar figures. The basic idea is that owners sell shares in their businesses, which in effect brings in a whole raft of new 'owners' who in turn have a stake in a business's future profits. When they want out they sell their shares to other investors. The share price moves up and down to ensure that there are as many buyers as sellers at any one time.

Going public also puts a stamp of respectability on you and your company. It will enhance the status and credibility of your business, and it will enable you to borrow more against the 'security' provided by your new shareholders, should you so wish. Your shares will also provide an attractive way to retain and motivate key staff. If they are given, or rather are allowed to earn, share options at discounted prices, they too can participate in the capital gains you are making. With a public share listing you can join in the takeover and asset-stripping game. When your share price is high and things are going well you can look out for weaker firms to gobble up – all you have to do is to offer them more of your shares in return for theirs; you do not even have to find real money. But of course this is a two-sided game and you also may now become the target of a hostile bid.

You may find that being in the public eye not only cramps your style but also fills up your engagement diary. Most CEOs of public companies find that they have to spend up to a quarter of their time 'in the City' explaining their strategies, in the months preceding and the first years after going public. It is not unusual for so much management time to have been devoted to answering accountants' and stockbrokers' questions that there is not enough time to run the day-to-day business, and profits drop as a direct consequence.

The City also creates its own 'pressure' both to seduce companies onto the market and then by expecting them to perform beyond any reasonable expectation. There have been a number of high profile examples of companies that have floated their shares on a stock market then changed their minds and withdrawn, buying out all outside shareholders. The rationale for taking a company back into private hands is that owners feel that they can run the company better without the need to justify their decisions to other shareholders, or the complex and burdensome regulations that public companies must comply with.

CASE STUDY
The Card Factory

The Card Factory is the UK's leading manufacturer and retailer of greetings cards. It was founded in 1997 by husband and wife Dean and Janet Hoyle, with a single shop in Wakefield, Yorkshire. By 2022 it operated through 1,016 stores across the UK and Ireland, employing over 8,000 staff, and generating some £205 million revenue. The company is the leading specialist retailer in the large and competitive UK greetings card market; adults on average send 31 cards a year and spend some £1.37 billion on single cards. There are approximately 800 card publishers in the UK, most of which are small businesses with fewer than five employees. Approximately one third of the company's sales are from gift dressings, small gifts and party products, a market estimated to be worth £1–2 billion.

With 16 years of unbroken revenue growth sales turnover reached £327 million in the year to 31 January 2014. The Card Factory took that performance as an opportunity to launch on the London Stock Exchange. They listed on 20 May 2014 selling £90 million worth of shares, representing about 13 per cent of the value of the business as a whole. The Card Factory was the 23rd new company listed in the first half of 2014, which saw £1.6 billion of new money raised for these businesses. Investors have had something of a roller-coaster ride. The shares entered the market at 200p, doubled in value over the next two years and steadily slipped back. On 30 September 2022 the shares stood at 44p, barely a quarter of their price when the company launched onto the stock market eight years earlier.

Initial public offer – criteria for getting a stock market listing

The rules vary from market to market but these are the conditions that are likely to apply to get a company listed on an exchange.

Getting listed on a major stock exchange calls for a track record of making substantial profits with decent seven-figure sums being made in the year you plan to 'float', as this process is known. A listing also calls for a large proportion, usually at least 25 per cent, of the company's shares being put up for sale at the outset. In addition, you would be expected to have 100 shareholders now and be able to demonstrate that 100 more will come on board as a result of the listing.

As you draw up your flotation plan and timetable you should have the following matters in mind:

- *Advisers:* you will need to be supported by a team that will include a sponsor, stockbroker, reporting accountant and solicitor. These should be respected firms, active in flotation work and familiar with the company's type of business. You and your company may be judged by the company you keep, so choose advisers of good repute and make sure that the people work effectively together. It is very unlikely that a small local firm of accountants, however satisfactory, will be up to this task.

- *Sponsor:* you will need to appoint a financial institution, usually a merchant banker, to fill this important role. If you do not already have a merchant bank in mind, your accountant will offer guidance. The job of the sponsor is to coordinate and drive the project forward.

- *Timetable:* it is essential to have a timetable for the final months in the run-up to a float – and to adhere to it. The company's directors and senior staff will be fully occupied in providing information and attending meetings. They will have to delegate and there must be sufficient back-up support to ensure that the business does not suffer (see below for an example of a timetable).

- *Management team:* a potential investor will want to be satisfied that your company is well managed, at board level and below. It is important to ensure succession, perhaps by offering key directors and managers service agreements and share options. It is wise to draw on the experience of well-qualified non-executive directors.

- *Accounts:* the objective is to have a profit record that is rising but, in achieving this, you will need to take into account directors' remuneration, pension contributions and the elimination of any expenditure that might be acceptable in a privately owned company but would not be acceptable in a public one, namely excessive perks such as yachts, luxury cars, lavish expense accounts and holiday homes.

Accounts must be consolidated and audited to appropriate accounting standards and the audit reports must not contain any major qualifications. The auditors will need to be satisfied that there are proper stock records and a consistent basis of valuing stock during the years prior to flotation. Accounts for the last three years will need to be disclosed and the date of the last accounts must be within six months of the issue.

Junior stock markets

Many countries have experimented with introducing stock markets with less onerous entry conditions than those required by main markets. These usually require shorter trading histories and less rigorous regulations. Arguably the most successful of these is AIM (Alternative Investment Market) where since its launch in 1995, over 3,000 companies from across the globe have raised billions.

Table 7.2 shows the funds raised by the seven main European junior stock markets. AIM accounts for more investment than all the other markets.

Table 7.2   Europe's main junior stock markets, 2021 – capital raised and market share

Market	Capital raised (£m)	Percentage (nearest whole %)
Borsa Italiana	740	4
First North Denmark	184	1
First North Finland	870	5
First North Stockholm	5,370	30
Frankfurt stock exchange – Scale	315	2
Paris Alternet	827	5
AIM (Alternative Investment Market) UK	9,525	53
Total	18,018	100

SOURCE: Hacker Young, www.uhy-uk.com/insights/uk-aim-dominated-european-junior-markets-making-over-half-all-fundraising-2021

CASE STUDY

Meraki: Corporate venture multi-million dollar pay day

Meraki (may-rah-kee), a Greek word that means doing something with passion and soul, could soon stand for how to make a billion in under a decade. Meraki was formed in 2006 by three PhD candidates from MIT, Sanjit Biswas, John Bicket and Hans Robertson, all currently on leave from their degree programme.

Meraki, according to its website, 'brings the benefits of the cloud to edge and branch networks, delivering easy-to-manage wireless, switching, and security solutions that enable customers to seize new business opportunities and reduce operational cost. Whether securing iPads in an enterprise or blanketing a campus with WiFi, Meraki networks simply work'. With over 10,000 customers worldwide ranging from the English public school Wellington College to fast-food chain Burger King, Meraki was initially backed by Californian venture capital firm Sequoia Capital and Google, two early venture investors. Rajeev Motwani, the Stanford University professor who taught Google co-founders Larry Page and Sergey Brin, made the necessary introductions.

Payday came on 19 November 2012 when Cisco, who had been in exclusive talks since September with Meraki bought the company for US $1.2 billion (£754 million). The founders had been considering a flotation and at first rejected Cisco's overtures. Analysts think Cisco has overpaid, but with their greater market presence and cash resources the company is confident it will be able to expand Meraki's technology using their global networks. Cisco has included a retention package to keep Meraki's co-founders at Cisco to consummate the deal. Sujai Hujela, an executive at Cisco, also stated: 'We are making sure we want to preserve and pollinate the culture (at Meraki) into Cisco.'

Stock markets – a brief history

One thing that truly separates MBAs from the rest is having some appreciation of the history of major business milestones. Having such a grasp, used judiciously, never fails to impress. Stock markets have an interesting and longer pedigree than most people in business would guess. Many would put them down as a fairly modern phenomenon, perhaps even giving the start of the last century as their starting point. They would, however, be seriously wrong, if that were their view.

The need for stock exchanges developed out of early trading activities in agricultural and other commodities. During the Middle Ages, traders found it easier to use credit that required supporting documentation of drafts, notes and bills of exchange. The history of the earliest stock exchange, the French stock exchange, goes back to the 12th century when transactions occurred in commercial bills of exchange. To control this budding market,

Phillip the Fair of France (1268–1314) created the profession of *couratier de change*, which was the predecessor of the French stockbroker. At about the same time, in Bruges, merchants began gathering in front of the house of the Van Der Buerse family to engage in trading. Soon the name of the family became identified with trading and in time a 'bourse' came to signify a stock exchange. At the same time, stock exchanges began to materialize in other trading centres like the Netherlands (Amsterdam Bourse) and Frankfurt (the Deutsche Stock Exchange, formerly the Börse).

In 1698, when one John Castaing in 'Jonathan's Coffee-house' in Exchange Alley in the City of London began publishing a list of stock and commodity prices called 'The Course of the Exchange and other things', the business of stock exchanges really got under way. By 1761 a group of 150 stockbrokers and jobbers had formed a club at Jonathan's to buy and sell shares. In 1773 the brokers erected their own building in Sweeting's Alley, with a dealing room on the ground floor and a coffee room above. Briefly known as 'New Jonathan's', members soon altered the name to 'The Stock Exchange'.

It was not until 1791 that the United States had its first bourse when the Philadelphia traders organized a stock exchange. The following year, 21 New York traders agreed to deal with each other under a buttonwood tree on Wall Street. By 1794 the market had moved indoors. India's premier stock exchange, the Bombay Stock Exchange (BSE), can trace its origins as far back as 125 years when it started as a voluntary non-profit-making association. In the 1870s, a securities system was introduced in Japan and public bond negotiation began. This resulted in the request for a public trading institution, and the 'Stock Exchange Ordinance' was enacted in May 1878. Based on this ordinance, the Tokyo Stock Exchange Co. Ltd was established on 15 May 1878 and trading began on 1 June.

These early stock exchanges were gentlemen's clubs governed only by a few house rules. Trading rarely started before 10.30 am and was over by 15.30 pm. No records were filed, no rules governed the case of a trader who could not deliver what he had sold and nothing prevented prices being manipulated.

The world's stock markets

How many stock exchanges are there? You may have heard of the LSE (London Stock Exchange) and NYSE (New York Stock Exchange), with the more informed adding Frankfurt, Tokyo and perhaps Paris. Those guessing five, or even 10 or 20, are way off. The answer is around 200. The big markets compete with alternative platforms, brokerage networks for market share and about a third of equities trading occurs off-exchange. The World Federation of Exchanges (www.world-exchanges.org/) is a useful source for facts and figures on these markets. There is a directory of world stock markets at: www.world-exchanges.org/membership-events#member-list.

Timetable to a float

While you may never have done an IPO, as the first launch of shares to the public is known, an MBA Business Finance will have to be able to appear as though he or she knows the ropes thoroughly. Copenhagen Business School's Professor Luiss Guido Carli lectures on the dangers of underpricing IPOs and Harvard Business School has a whole library of articles on IPO strategies.

The process used to take about six months to execute; now it is routinely being done in half that time. Though it may vary from exchange to exchange the timetable looks broadly like the following.

Week 1. Pick underwriters to take your company to market. This involves listening to a dozen or more bankers telling you why they are number one in doing your type of IPO. At the rate of three a day this can be a wearying experience, listening to depressingly similar presentations. The bankers will all have done successful IPOs before, probably by the dozen, so you will be looking more for empathy than technical competence. At the end of the week you need to have chosen a lead and probably a couple of co-managers to help spread the good word about your great business to the share-buying community.

Week 2. The lead manager begins drafting the company's prospectus. This involves sucking dry the board, management team and your accountants of background information. Your CFO will be involved full-time in this process, so better get some financial back-up in place to deal with routine matters.

Week 3. The company team and bankers collaborate on the prospectus. By now fairly junior staff will be handling the process. The stars your company met on week one's presentations have moved on to sell the next deal. This process can involve several eight-hour days with people from your law, banking and accounting firms going through the documentation line by line.

This involves a delicate balance between outlining the risks while simultaneously describing the business and the investment prospects in a way that will appeal. You can see how other companies have gone about this process by looking at their filings on the London Stock Exchange and Securities and Exchange Commission (SEC) websites. In the end this due diligence process should have flushed out any worries and concerns about you or your business.

Week 4. The lead manager files the registration document with the LSE/SEC, or its equivalent in the country you plan to list.

Weeks 5–8. The lead bankers and you and your team prepare the roadshow presentation and wait for the LSE/SEC to digest your documents.

Week 9. The LSE/SEC responds with 20 pages of nitpicking questions: 'What do you mean by "online response times"?' and, 'Can you provide evidence that your client x is one of the largest drinks manufacturers in

Spain?' There may well be a second round of questions a few weeks later, but by now you will have got the measure of how to reply.

Probity is important in this whole process. What is required is transparency, the Nirvana of the share-dealing community. The World Online float on the Amsterdam Exchange (AEX) in the spring of 2000 is a salutary warning on disclosure. The company was at the time Europe's largest internet service provider. It generated an enormous amount of interest among Dutch private investors, the company's home base, with 150,000 subscribing in the March IPO at a price of €43 (£36.4/$58.2). Within six weeks the price was down to €14.80 (£12.5/$20). The reason given for the slump in price was that World Online's chairman, Nina Brink, had disposed of some of her shares to US private equity fund Baystar Capital, three months before the float. The price she sold at was €6.04 (£5.11/$8.19) and Baystar sold in the first few days of trading at over €30 (£25.4/$40.7). Brink was accused of making allegedly misleading statements during the offer period, and was forced to resign. Unhappy shareholders immediately reached for their lawyers.

Week 10. The lead manager plans the roadshow. Your team go to the bank and sell the company to its institutional sales force. They then get to work with their clients to persuade them to subscribe for your stock. Everyone is bound by what are known as 'the rules' that govern the 'quiet period', which extends from due diligence until a set time after the IPO. Over this period the company must be careful not to hype the stock or do anything that would lead to speculation about your firm's performance in the press.

There are also rules explaining exactly what you can and cannot say to the press. It's generally best to say nothing. If one of your competitors is doing an IPO their quiet period is a good time to hit at them in the press, or to go out and buy a business you know they might want. They are in effect in limbo and can't retaliate.

This is where the institutional sales team come into their own. Via an ancient ritual of winks, nudges, passive verbs, rhetorical questions and comparisons, they get their story across. The lead bank's sales team can be a mighty force indeed. Goldman Sachs, for example has several hundred frontline sales people in its IPO team, and that can result in a very big message reaching a lot of potential investors.

Weeks 11–12. A glorified travel agent in the bank fixes up a punishing schedule, known as the 'roadshow'. This is the reverse of week one, when people were selling to you. Now your team are selling the stock to institutional investors. This could involve as many as 80 meetings across three continents in 13 days. A lot can be said at roadshow meetings, but the only document that can be handed out is the approved prospectus. Anything else could be a violation of the rules.

Commitments start to come in from the institutions. 'I'll take 250,000, but only if it's priced below £20. At £25 I'll only take 100,000.' The bank's syndicate manager has to make sense of this anticipated demand to come up with an IPO price.

Week 13. The day of the IPO. Assuming stock markets have not gone into one of their all too frequent nose dives, the bank's market maker figures out the highest price someone will sell and someone will buy at and sets a price, usually above the opening price and the price at which the institutions have bought. If the markets have plunged and you have to pull the IPO, it's like slipping down a long snake back to the bottom of the snakes and ladders board. You may get another crack at it in six months, or perhaps never. One entrepreneur likened doing his IPO to childbirth: painful, glorious, but not to be done again.

Your company is now public, the bank collects 7 per cent of the proceeds, your board and shareholders are rich, as are you if you negotiated stock options into your employment terms. Your company now has the funds and credibility to get back to growing the business.

If the market maker has got the price too high and the shares plunge quickly it will leave a sour taste in everyone's mouth. The pre-float share-holders can't realize their gain for months after the float, and having a paper profit slashed in half, as for example with lastminute.com's float, will not endear you to the staff. The institutions will be sitting on a loss, and while they are grown up enough to take it on the chin, they will be very wary when you come back for more money. It is usually best to set the price at a rate that will see the shares rising in the weeks and months following a float. That makes for better press coverage too, which inevitably impacts on cus-tomers, suppliers and potential employees.

Though IPOs are an important aspect of corporate finance, they are something of a minority activity. Stock Analysis, a website that aims to be the internet's best source of free stock data and information, reckons that in the USA, the largest market for this funding category, there have been '5,916 IPOs between 2000 and 2022. The least was in 2009 with only 62. The full year 2021 was an all-time record with 1035 IPOs, beating the previous record of 480 in the year 2020' (https://stockanalysis.com/ipos/statistics/).

What investors want

The legal structures – partnerships and limited companies in their various forms (see Chapter 5) – have made it easier and safer for entrepreneurs to raise money. But what exactly do investors want in return? Well, unsurpris-ingly they too are using something like the factors outlined in Chapter 3, which I recommend you use to evaluate a business opportunity for yourself. Investors would like the problem your product or service addresses to be a big one; they would like to see that your solution is scalable and that there is some discernable barrier preventing others entering your market too quickly. They want a few other things as well.

Evidence of customer acceptance

Backers like to know that your new product or service will sell and is being used, even if only on a trial or demonstration basis. The founder of Solicitec, a company selling software to solicitors to enable them to process relatively standard documents such as wills, had little trouble getting support for his house conveyancing package once his product had been tried and approved by a leading building society for its panel of solicitors. If you are only at the prototype stage, then as well as having to assess your chances of succeeding with the technology, financiers have no immediate indication that, once made, your product will appeal to the market. Under these circumstances you have to show not only that the 'problem' your innovation seeks to solve is substantial but that your product is one that a large number of people will have a compelling need for, and be willing to pay for, in a foreseeable time-scale.

Fake meat, plant- or cell-based meat substitutes are a case in point. Until early 2022 the prevailing view was that this was a hot business sector. However, by the autumn of that year vegan venture capitalist Beyond Meat, heavily supported by venture capital, had crashed from a share price of $234 to under $15. McDonalds had ditched Beyond's "McPlant" burger in the US. It seems unlikely that this sector will get much support from investors any time soon.

There really is a market

One inventor from the Royal College of Art came up with a revolutionary toilet system design that, as well as being extremely thin, used 30 per cent less water per flush and had half the number of moving parts of a conventional product, all for no increase in price. Although he had only drawings to show, it was clear that with domestic metered water for all households a distinct possibility and a UK market for half a million new units per annum, a sizeable acceptance was reasonably certain. As well as evidence of customer acceptance, entrepreneurs need to demonstrate that they know how and to whom their new product or service must be sold, and that they have a financially viable means of doing so.

Figure 7.2 shows the funding appetite of various sources of funds. VCs, business angels and indeed any source of share capital will only be attracted to propositions that combine high growth potential with a high risk/reward potential. Banks and other lenders will be attracted to almost the opposite profile, looking instead for a stable less risky proposition that at least offers some security for the capital sum they are putting up.

Figure 7.2   Funding appetite

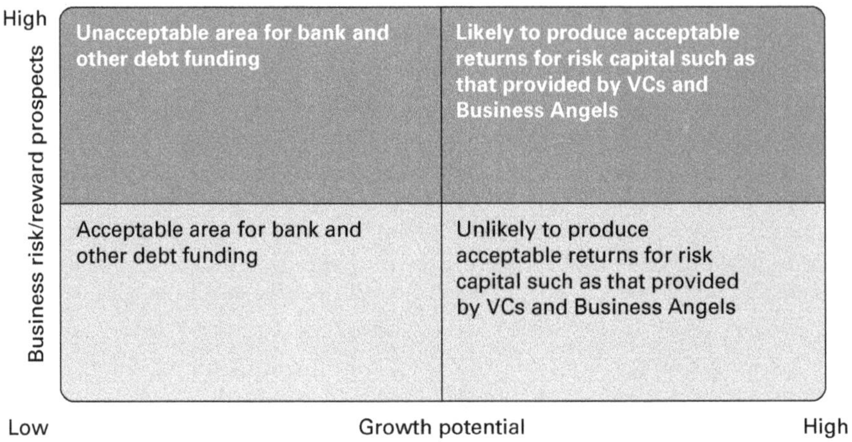

High	Unacceptable area for bank and other debt funding	Likely to produce acceptable returns for risk capital such as that provided by VCs and Business Angels
	Acceptable area for bank and other debt funding	Unlikely to produce acceptable returns for risk capital such as that provided by VCs and Business Angels
Low	Growth potential	High

(y-axis: Business risk/reward prospects)

Personal qualities

At the end of the day every investment boils down to people. So you, your career progression, your knowledge, skills and experience will all be upper-most in an investor's mind when reviewing your proposition. Tim Waterstone, for example, the founder of the Waterstones bookstore chain, had first-hand experience of running a chain of bookshops.

Team worker

Investors are rarely interested in supporting one-man bands. They want the security that having a team brings, even if it's only a team of two. They also know that few people have all the skills needed to get a substantial venture off the ground. Bebo and Money Supermarket (see the case studies below) are examples of the different skill sets that teams can bring beyond that of a single entrepreneur. Investors also know that teamwork is essential if the business is to become valuable and the sooner they see that attribute being exhibited the better.

Hybrids

A number of financing methods straddle the debt and equity boundary. These try to mitigate taking a bit more risk for the potential of a bit more return that would be usual with debt financing. But they also limit the upside that might be expected from pure equity, which would retain all of any increase in value from the outset.

Convertible preference shares operate as with preference shares, in that their holders rank before ordinary shareholders for dividend payments, or return of funds in the case of failure. They also have the option at some specified date in the future to convert to ordinary shares and so enjoy all of any increase in value.

Mezzanine finance has one or all of these characteristics: it ranks after other forms of debt but before equity for any payout in the event of a business failing; it pays higher, often significantly higher, interest than other debt; it can be held for up to 10 years; and it can be converted into ordinary shares. It is popular with VCs for management buy-outs.

Money for free – grants

There is little an MBA can do that is viewed with greater favour than bringing cost-free money into a business. It's never easy to do, takes longer than you think and much more effort than the word 'free' might encourage you to think. But it can be done and the payback for both the business and the MBA who secures the funds can be disproportionately large.

Government agencies at both national and local government level as well as some extra-governmental bodies such as the EU offer grants, effectively free or nearly free money in return for certain behaviour. It may be to encourage research into a particular field, stimulate innovation or employment, or to persuade a company to locate in a particular area. Grants are constantly being introduced (and withdrawn), but there is no system that lets you know automatically. You have to keep yourself informed.

GRANTfinder is a UK database that includes details in excess of 8,000 funding opportunities (www.grantfinder.co.uk). They also offer a range of fee based support, including advice on bid writing and training on grant searching.

For the European Commission, see 'Funding – loans and grants from the European Union': www.eubusiness.com/funding.

CASE STUDY
TomTom

In Q1 2022 TomTom announced revenues of €128 million, as well as confirming it had sealed a deal to integrate their technology in the Nissan Ariya, the brand's latest EV. The company has come a long way since 1991, when TomTom was founded and began a journey that would change the way people drive forever.

Harold Goddijn and Corinne Vigreux, married for more than two decades, are the co-founders of the satellite navigation device that has come to define the sector. Vigreux studied at a Paris business school starting out at a French games firm before moving to the UK to Psion, then a FTSE 100 technology company famed for its handheld PDA (Personal Digital Assistant). Goddijn read economics at Amsterdam University and whilst working for a venture capital firm came across some of Psion's handheld computers and organizers and was impressed. He approached Psion suggesting a joint distribution venture selling the company's products in the Netherlands. Vigreux was sent to the Netherlands to negotiate with Goddijn, the first time the pair had met. They married in 1991 and Vigreux resigned from Psion and moved to Amsterdam.

A brief spell working for a Dutch dairy co-operative saw Vigreux suffering from technology withdrawal symptoms. With software wizards Peter-Frans Pauwels and Pieter Geelen, she started Palmtop Software, later to become TomTom, designing software such as dictionaries, accounting packages and diet books that could be loaded on to Palm Pilots and Pocket PCs. In late 1998 Goddijn and Vigreux saw a navigation system built for a computer and gradually the idea took shape. Three years and €4 million later the quartet had created the TomTom, launching it at €799. Even at this price it was far cheaper than existing products and superior in that it featured a touch screen, a first for the sector.

The year after launch the company floated, selling 50 per cent of the business to fund the growth and acquisition. But 2008 saw them hit turbulence. The credit crunch, market saturation, a high level of debt, and Google starting to offer maps for free represented more serious problems in a single year than many face in a lifetime. The company restructured, reduced debt and now generate half their revenue from selling licences to their maps, constructing in-built systems for the car industry, and telematics. TomTom Telematics is now recognized as a leading provider of telematics solutions with over 350,000 subscriptions worldwide. In 2013 TomTom launched its own branded GPS sport watches to help runners, cyclists and swimmers keep moving towards their fitness goals, by providing essential performance information at a glance. The company now employs 3,600 people and is a globally recognized brand.

Online video courses and lectures

Bocconi, private equity and venture capital: www.coursera.org/learn/private-equity

Corporate Finance Essentials: Prof Javier Estrada of IESE Business School offers this course each year. It consists of six sessions requiring no previous knowledge or preparation. Each session will consist of a video lecture of around 45–60 minutes and one or two recommended readings: www.coursera.org/learn/corporate-finance-essentials

Crowdfunding, Wharton: www.coursera.org/learn/wharton-crowdfunding

Mastering the VC Game: How to Raise Your First Round of Capital with Jeff Bussgang, Senior Lecturer in Entrepreneurship at HBS and a General Partner at Flybridge Capital Partners: www.youtube.com/watch?v=aNfB4sBBwEc

Understanding financial markets, University of Geneva: www.coursera.org/learn/understanding-financial-markets

Online video case studies

Crowd-funding Case Studies with Fundit.ie: www.youtube.com/watch?v=phX1q9CHmkY

Endeca. Co-Founders Steve Papa and Pete Bell simulate the founding and early growth of their company, walking through key terms and legal due diligence. Harvard i-lab. Strategy: www.youtube.com/watch?v=0QTProGpc1o

Funding Strategies at Apperian. Mark Lorion, CMO of Apperian, talks about his company's funding strategy at the Harvard i-lab: www.youtube.com/watch?v=5CtUNS5kERw

Meraki: Co-founder and CEO Sanjit Biswas presents the history of the company, from its roots at MIT in Cambridge, MA to February 2012, immediately prior to the deal with Cisco: www.youtube.com/watch?v=-btII98nZVE8

Sowing seeds – 4 Case Studies. The Sowing SEEDS Action Group successfully secured £1.6m of funding for the area: www.youtube.com/watch?v=FVoqDJ7XJPI

Tesla raising up to $5 billion: www.bloomberg.com/news/articles/2020-12-08/tesla-raising-up-to-5-billion-in-third-capital-raise-this-year#xj4y7vzkg

PART THREE
Financial strategies and special topics

MBAs are expected to have a grasp of financial management that goes substantially beyond the basics of accounting reports and sources of finance. Sitting near or in the boardroom will give an MBA a ringside seat on mergers, acquisitions, joint ventures and the like. In fact they should be in on every aspect of business planning and strategy formulation as this is where the next rungs up the career ladder will start to appear.

Though the MBA will rarely have much to do directly with tax or foreign exchange, for example – these are more likely to be under the wing of the treasury function – he or she must have a basic appreciation of the impact of these areas on business risk and performance. Tax affairs, if poorly managed, can consume a fifth of a business's hard-won profits and the vagaries of exchange rate fluctuations can erode that further still.

In addition to knowing where a business can raise funds, the MBA needs a sound appreciation of the risks associated with each source and in particular how funding sources can be best balanced to reduce those risks.

These areas are the subject of the third part of the book.

08
Risk management

- Setting an acceptable gearing level
- Dealing with defaulting customers
- Resorting to law
- Managing foreign exchange risks
- Protecting investors
- Finding financial facts

Neither in 'Small business survival and COVID-19' (Giunipero et al, 2022, www.sciencedirect.com/science/article/pii/S0739885921000597) nor '35 years of studies on business failure' (Balcaen and Ooghe 2006, www.researchgate.net/publication/222400744) is any definitive reason why business fail clearly explained. However, a useful fact for the MBA to know is that the rumour of calamities awaiting most ventures is just that – an unfounded and incorrect piece of oft-repeated misinformation. An exhaustive study of the eight-year destinations of all 814,000 US firms founded in a particular year, by Bruce A Kirchoff, Professor of Management at New Jersey Institute of Technology, revealed that just 18 per cent actually failed, meaning that the entrepreneurs were put out of business by their financial backers, lack of demand or competitive pressures. True, some 28 per cent of businesses closed their doors voluntarily, their founders having decided for a variety of reasons that either working for themselves or this particular type of business was just not for them.

But the majority of the businesses studied in Kirchoff's mammoth and representative study survived and in many cases prospered. The European Observatory study carried out a few years later than Kirchoff's and using a smaller sample came to a similar conclusion on survival rates. However, this study added one important extra fact. The failure rate in the early years is much higher than in later years, and by year five of a firm's life the failure curve is flattening off (see Figure 8.1, produced from data in the quoted research studies). Interestingly the general pattern of performance of the

Figure 8.1   The truth about the risk of failure

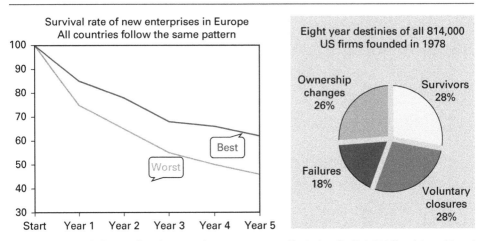

Various sources: Including Small Business Development Center, Bradley University (Feb 2015) and *Annual Report on European SMEs 2013/2014*, European Commission

SOURCE: *Entrepreneurship and Dynamic Capitalism*, Kirchhoff, 1993.

countries designated as weakest in the period covered by the European study (Croatia, Cyprus, Czech Republic, Hungary, Greece, Ireland, Portugal, Romania, Slovenia and Spain) were broadly the same as for the stronger countries though the absolute performance was not. Nevertheless, businesses face real and constant dangers from areas of risk that managers can and should understand, and they should take action to limit the potential damage.

Gearing – leverage

Despite the esoteric names – debentures, convertible loan stock, preference shares – businesses have access to only two fundamentally different sorts of money. *Equity*, or owner's capital, including retained earnings, is money that is not a risk to the business. If no profits are made, then the owner and other shareholders simply do not get dividends. They may not be pleased, but they cannot usually sue, and even where they can the advisers who recommended the share purchase will be first in line.

Debt capital is money borrowed by the business from outside sources; it puts the business at financial risk and is also risky for the lenders. In return for taking that risk they expect an interest payment every year, irrespective of the performance of the business. 'High gearing' is the term used when a business has a high proportion of outside money to inside money. High gearing has considerable attractions to a business that wants to make high returns on shareholders' capital. But as with economies and consumers, the most common financial risk a business faces is borrowing more money than it can safely service given the vagaries of economic cycles.

Table 8.1   The effect of gearing on shareholders' returns

	No gearing N/A	Average gearing 1:1	High gearing 2:1	Very high gearing 3:1
Capital structure				
Share capital	60,000	30,000	20,000	15,000
Loan capital (at 12%)	–	30,000	40,000	45,000
Total capital	60,000	60,000	60,000	60,000
Profits				
Operating profit	10,000	10,000	10,000	10,000
Less interest on loan	None	3,600	4,800	5,400
Net profit	10,000	6,400	5,200	4,600
Return on share capital	10,000	6,400	5,200	4,400
	60,000	30,000	15,000	15,000
As percentage	16.6%	21.3%	26%	30.7%
Times interest earned	N/A	10,000	10,000	10,000
		3,600	4,800	5,400
	N/A	2.8 times	2.1 times	1.8 times

How gearing works

Table 8.1 shows an example of a business that is assumed to need 60,000 of capital to generate 10,000 operating profits. Four different capital structures are considered. They range from all share capital (no gearing) at one end to nearly all loan capital at the other. The loan capital has to be 'serviced', that is, interest of 12 per cent has to be paid. The loan itself can be relatively indefinite, simply being replaced by another one at market interest rates when the first loan expires.

Following the table through you can see that return on the shareholders' money (arrived at by dividing the profit by the shareholders' investment and multiplying by 100 to get a percentage) grows from 16.6 to 30.7 per cent by virtue of the changed gearing. If the interest on the loan were lower, the ROSC, or return on shareholders' capital, would be even more improved by high gearing, and the higher the interest, the lower the relative improvement in ROSC. So in times of low interest rates, businesses tend to go for increased borrowings rather than raising more equity, that is money from shareholders.

At first sight this looks like a perpetual profit-growth machine. Naturally shareholders and those managing a business whose bonus depends on shareholders' returns would rather have someone else 'lend' them the money for the business than ask shareholders for more money, especially if by doing so they increase the return investment. The problem comes if the business does not produce the £10,000 operating profits shown in the table. Very often a drop in sales of 20 per cent means profits are halved. If profits were halved in this example, the business could not meet the interest payments on its loan. That would make the business insolvent, and so not in a 'sound financial position'; in other words, failing to meet one of the two primary business objectives.

What is an acceptable level of gearing?

Bankers tend to favour 1:1 gearing as the maximum for a business, although they have been known to go much higher. As well as looking at the gearing, lenders will study the business's capacity to pay interest. They do this by using another ratio called 'times interest earned'. This is calculated by dividing the operating profit by the loan interest. It shows how many times the loan interest is covered, and gives the lender some idea of the safety margin. The ratio for this example is given at the end of Table 8.1. Once again rules are hard to make, but much less than 3 × interest earned is unlikely to give lenders confidence. (See Chapter 3 for a comprehensive explanation of the use of ratios.)

Any decisions about gearing levels have to be taken with the level of business risk involved. Certain categories of venture are intrinsically more risky than others. Businesses selling staple food products where little innovation is required are generally less prone to facing financial difficulties than, say, internet start-ups, where the technology may be unproven with a short shelf-life and the markets themselves uncertain; see Figure 8.2.

Off balance sheet activity

High gearing levels upset investors, who think their dividend stream will be threatened, and lenders, worried that their loans won't get serviced or repaid. So it's hardly surprising that financial whiz-kids are always looking for smoke and mirrors techniques to get liabilities either off the balance sheet or at least massaged favourably. The crucial date for any activity is the year end, and if that were, say, 31 March, whisking anything damaging out of the way on 30 March only to have it reappear on 1 April would render that item effectively invisible to anyone outside the enterprise. As long as the auditors will sign off the accounts, assuming they spot it, then all will be well.

Figure 8.2   Risk and gearing

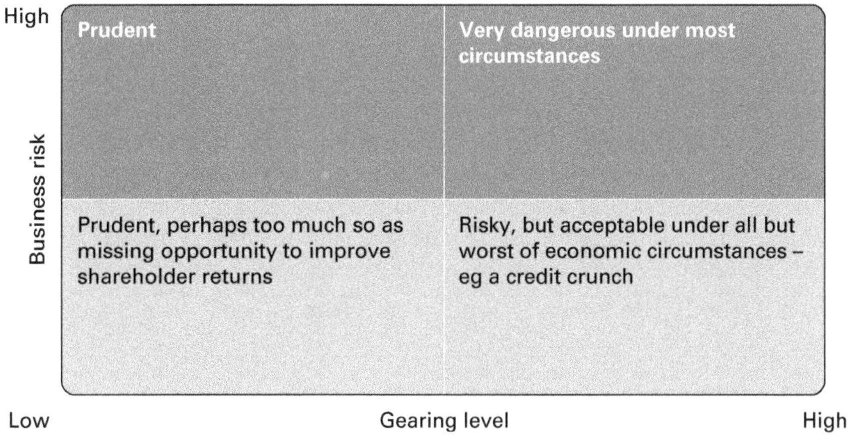

So how does this work? Suppose a company has offices bought for £100 million, with £80 million of that provided by way of a commercial mortgage. That £80 million will form part of the company's borrowings and so serve to push up its gearing level. If, using the year end above, the offices could be 'sold' to a third party on 30 March for at least £100 million, both the asset (the office) and the liability (the £80 million mortgage loan) would not show up in the year-end balance sheet. The net effect would be to artificially reduce the company's gearing, which in turn would reassure investors and make lenders more susceptible to approaches for more borrowings. On 1 April, an appropriate date as it happens, both asset and liability re-appear only to be banished again the following year. In reality the company carries the liability (and asset) throughout. No one, save perhaps the board of directors, the CFO and the auditors, will be any the wiser.

This was the technique, known in the trade as Repo 105, used by Lehman Brothers and approved by their auditors, Ernst and Young (E&Y). The sums made invisible in this way while Lehman was in its death throes exceeded $50 billion, sufficient to flatter even the most over-geared balance sheet. Although Repo 105 and similar techniques are in line with internationally acceptable accounting standards, their effect is to mislead. E&Y's annual fees earned from Lehman Brothers were $31 million and they and other financial magicians are often worth paying if the other option is failure.

Customer default

The sale process is not complete until, as one particularly cautious sales director put it: 'the customer has paid, used your product and not died as a consequence'. Although there are theoretically regulations to ensure that big firms pay small businesses promptly there is little evidence they do. Figure 8.3 shows some facts about credit collection. What is noticeable is that a significant proportion of customers exceed the payment terms and that the smaller you are the more likely it is that you will be paid late. Behaviour varies enormously in different countries – for example, late payment is four times as likely to be a problem in the UK as it is in the Netherlands.

One of the top three reasons that businesses run into cash flow problems or in the worst cases fail is that a customer doesn't pay up in full or on time. You can take some steps to make sure this doesn't happen to your firm by setting prudent terms of trade and making sure the customers are creditworthy before you sell to them.

Set your terms of trade

You need to decide on your terms and conditions of sale and ensure they are printed on your order acceptance stationery. Terms should include when and how you require to be paid and under what conditions you will accept cancellations or offer refunds.

Check creditworthiness

There is a wealth of information on credit status for both individuals and businesses of varying complexity, so there is no need to trade unknowingly with individuals or businesses that pose a credit risk. The major agencies that compile and sell business credit histories include Experian (www.experian.co.uk/business-express/credit-report/company-credit-check/) and Dun & Bradstreet (www.dnb.co.uk/solutions/risk-management-solutions). Both these companies offer worldwide business coverage as well as a range of risk and financial insights on more than 250 million organizations worldwide. Between them they offer a comprehensive range of credit reports instantly online, including advice on credit limits and CCJs (County Court Judgments). Figure 8.4 shows part of a 16-page credit report that culminates in a specific score, giving the user some idea of the likelihood of getting paid, and an indication of how much credit should be extended to the company.

Get credit insurance

If your company can get a factoring company or invoice discounter to take on your clients, most of the risk of default will be covered by them. In return for a fee they will even take on responsibility for collecting money owed and pursue late payers. An independent research study of 2,000 businesses in 10 European economies by the Credit Management Research Centre at Leeds University Business School indicates that bad debts represent an average of

Figure 8.3 The extent to which late payments from customers impact your business – 2020

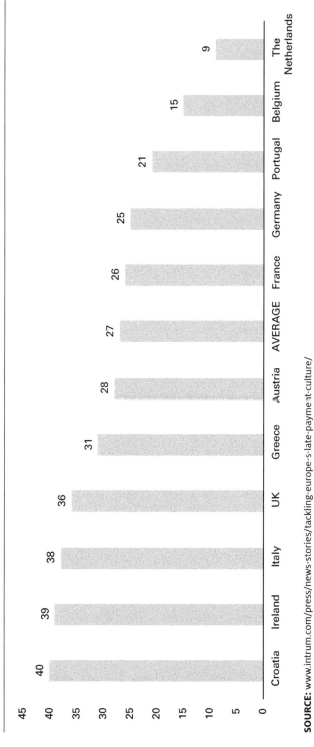

SOURCE: www.intrum.com/press/news-stories/tackling-europe-s-late-payment-culture/

Figure 8.4 Part of a credit report

Risk Score

Today's:	59
Previous:	27 until (28/06/2008)

Historical Trend

56 until (28/06/2008)
54 until (30/06/2007)
42 until (24/06/2006)
43 until (25/06/2005)

Score Key

0–35	Caution, High risk potential.
36–50	Caution, Moderate risk. Measured exposure.
51–60	Normal, Limited risk potential, Normal terms.
61–100	Confidence, Low risk potential.

There was a very significant Increase in Sales from £49,359,000 to £68,142,000 for the period ending 28/06/08.

The latest Accounts show an increase in Pre-tax Profits from £3,175,000 to £3,874,000.

Credit Limit (GBP)

Today's:	430,000
Previous:	100,000 until (28/06/2008)
Contract Limit (GBP):	6,000,000

Shareholders-Funds increased from £1,247,000 to £5,584,000, while Total Assets Increased from £23,342,000 to £30,246,000.

The percentage of Profit in each unit of sales of 5.69 is above the industry average of 3.30.

The business activity in which this company is involved contains a higher amount of insolvencies compared to total population averages.

The company has been established for more than 13 years.

County Court Judgments Summary:	Number of exact unsatisfied CCJs: None
	Number of probable unsatisfied CCJs: None
	Number of possible unsatisfied CCJs: None

0.74 per cent for non-insured companies against 0.38 per cent for companies using credit insurance. While that may not sound too dramatic, when you consider that most companies make less than 10 per cent profit, losing 0.36 per cent through lack of insurance (0.74 – 0.38) is a hefty slice – around 3.6 per cent of potential extra gains.

Credit insurers' business proposition rests simply on the fact that they have better information – the big ones track the performance of over 40 million companies worldwide. Also, they don't have to base their credit decisions on short-term risks solely on the basis of an 18-month old P&L and balance sheet and a rough credit score. Regional risk offices established in the major cities are in charge of making direct contact with buyers (the clients of their clients) and of obtaining the most up-to-date information on their financial position. You can read more on this subject in Chapter 6 in the section on discounting and factoring.

Do your own due diligence

There may be occasions when even the most creditworthy customers can't get credit insurance. The pressures caused by the Covid-19 pandemic and the Russo/Ukraine war are good recent examples, but the credit crunch of 2008–10 and that of 1973–74 were both severe also. So a company may have to make its own judgement on whether to risk supplying a customer. First off you will have to read the accounts. The important measures will be those that affect liquidity (a company's ability to meet short-term obligations) and solvency (the current level of borrowed money compared to the owners' investment).

Use the knowledge acquired in Chapter 3 to decide whether or not to supply to EAT Ltd on credit, based on the information in the company's accounts (see Figures 8.5 and 8.6).

The first slightly worrying observation is that while turnover is up – £75,544,025 compared to £68,141,924, profits are down – £2,110,808 compared to £4,336,980. Still, this is hardly surprising given the seriously difficult trading conditions during the worst recession the UK has experienced since the Second World War.

There are, however, three pieces of positive information. First, the company has a lot more cash in 2009 (£6,227,385) compared to 2008 (£5,425,881). Also it is paying its creditors (which will include us if we decide to supply) faster, in 54.52 days (£11,284,968/£75,544,025 × 355) compared to 65.07 days in 2008 (£12,147,727/£68,141,924 × 365). Finally, although it is heavily geared – 1.62:1 (£12,476,344/£7,695,390) that is a lot lower gearing than in the previous year, which was 2.24:1 (£12,514,104/£5,584,582). The EAT case study gives the company's own analysis of the situation.

Figure 8.5   EAT Ltd profit and loss account for the years to June 2008 and June 2009

Profit and loss account

	Period from 29 Jun 08 to 27 Jun 09 £	Period from 1 Jul 07 to 28 Jun 08 £
Turnover	75,544,025	68,141,924
Cost of sales	29,418,496	26,698,725
Gross profit	46,125,529	41,443,199
Distribution and administrative costs	43,425,803	37,682,701
Operating profit	2,699,726	3,760,498
Interest receivable	36,968	113,209
Profit on ordinary activities before taxation	2,736,694	3,873,707
Tax on profit on ordinary activities	(625,886)	463,273
Profit for the financial period	2,110,808	4,336,980

CASE STUDY
EAT – an in-house credit risk assessment study

EAT was founded by Niall MacArthur (49), son of a Scottish Tory MP and his Canadian wife Faith (47). He took an MBA at City University Business School, then for the next 13 years worked in investment banking at Bankers Trust. The first EAT opened beside London's Charing Cross station in 1996.

EAT's strategy is based on MacArthur's first-hand experience of the shortening of City workers' 'lunch hour' to less than half that time and recognizing that the break from the office was very important: 'It had to be open-ended, fun, sexy and rewarding.' His competitive edge on Prêt a Manger (making sandwiches fresh onsite every day) is where they pride themselves: EAT makes all its own food – sandwiches, sushi, salad and soup – in its 15,000 sq ft (1,394 sq m) kitchen in Wembley. That in turn means they can serve faster food.

The board comprises managing director, founder and main shareholder Niall MacArthur, owning more than 35 per cent of the company, who is mainly concerned with property acquisitions and funding of the chain. His wife Faith is the company's brand director and the power behind EAT's shop design and

Figure 8.6   EAT Ltd balance sheets for June 2008 and June 2009

	27 Jun 09 £	28 Jun 08 £
Fixed assets		
Tangible assets	19,430,664	19,243,215
Current assets		
Stocks	649,140	644,978
Debtors	5,149,512	4,932,339
Cash at bank and in hand	6,227,386	5,425,881
	12,026,038	11,003,198
Creditors: amounts falling due within one year	11,284,968	12,147,727
Net current assets/(liabilities)	741,070	(1,144,529)
Total assets less current liabilities	20,171,734	18,098,686
Creditors: amounts falling due after more than one year	12,476,344	12,514,104
	7,695,390	5,584,582
Capital and reserves		
Called-up share capital	4,400,368	4,400,368
Share premium account	1,438,315	1,438,315
Profit and loss account	1,856,707	(254,101)
	7,695,390	5,584,582

menu. Also on the board are retail director Colin Hughes, formerly of Prêt a Manger and Marks & Spencer; finance director Fraser Hall, who cut his teeth at pharmaceutical chain McCarthy and restaurant chain Pizzaland; and Stephen Lynn, the non-executive director who came in when 3i bankrolled the company six years ago. In August 2005, 3i sold its stake to private equity firm Penta Capital in a refinancing of the business.

In June 2008 it was announced that MacArthur planned to sell EAT inspired by the successful £345 ($552/€407) million sale of rival fast-food group Prêt a Manger to Bridgepoint. The company and its shareholders appointed advisers at PwC to carry out a strategic review of the business to facilitate the sale.

The last five audited years' accounts are all listed as 'clean' and show sales growing at a compound rate of 21.5 per cent per annum to the current level of circa £70 ($112/€82.6) million. The last year's post-tax profit as filed was £4.3 ($6.9/€5.1) million, up from £3.3 ($5.3/€3.9) million in the preceding year.

The gross margin is 60 per cent, there is no debt, either long or short term, the net worth is about £6 ($9.6/€7) million with some £5.4 ($8.6/€6.4) million of cash in the bank. Although not able to match its current assets to its current liabilities, the litmus test of sound liquidity, its position is fast improving. Over the past five years the current ratio has improved each year, moving from 0.29 to 0.82 (greater than 1 is the optimal ratio). Normally a business selling food to retail customers for cash while taking around 40 days to settle its bills would be highly liquid, but EAT has used all the cash it can get to fuel its growth.

As far as credit rating is concerned the position improved. Until 2007 it was ranked as being moderately risky; since then it has moved well into the normal risk bracket as its current score of 59 puts it just two points away from the score of 61 that is required to move into the lowest risk bracket. The company's total assets exceed £30 ($48/€35) million, up from £23 ($37/€27) million last year, and it is significantly more profitable than the average for the sector (EAT makes 5.69 per cent net profit compared to the industry average of 3.3 per cent).

So why wouldn't credit insurers cover them? The main problems seem to be that the sector contains a much higher than average rate of insolvencies, so insurers will err on the side of caution; and the company has used supplier credit to fuel its fast growth, in effect using that money instead of providing more share capital or taking on any borrowings. This means suppliers have become bankers and investors, without any of the security that bankers would normally expect, or any of the upside that would accrue to shareholders from the business's success. That in turn makes credit insurers wary as they too are carrying more risk than they would like.

Should we supply EAT without credit insurance cover?

The question hinges on EAT's capacity to survive and prosper in the present economic climate. In its favour is its relatively low price point, meaning it is still affordable, despite the fact that there are fewer people in jobs and more of them are bringing in their own lunches. Also, the company is very profitable, has a strong board of directors with both the expertise and track record to raise outside funds, and it has the capacity to take on borrowings if necessary. If EAT is one of the very few customers being supplied without insurance it would seem a risk worth taking on a measured basis.

Postscript

EAT was bought out by rival chain Prêt a Manger in May 2019 and closed in March 2020.

Keep track of aged debtors

An important responsibility of management is to track how those who owe money for services and products comply with their obligations. Figure 8.7

shows that 14 per cent of debtors have exceeded the due date. As well as having the overall picture, a print out of the individual picture, account by account, will enable management to pursue debtors with the appropriate vigour. Not all late payers will become delinquent. In some cases the inflexibility of their payment systems is to blame. For example, some companies have cheque runs once a month only, so if an invoice comes in just after that date it could be close to eight weeks before it would have any chance of being paid. Creditor policies calling for payment in 30 days would register such cases as being in default, so clearly some oversight of the system is required.

Figure 8.7 Age analysis of debtors' invoices

Duration from invoice date	% of total debtors	Cumulative total %	Number of accounts
0–14 days	28	28	264
15–28 days	25	53	205
29–42 days	19	72	147
43–56 days Due date	14	86	82 Due date
57–70 days	7	93	38
71–84 days	4	97	16
85–98 days	2	99	20
99+ days	1	100	7

Warning signals that creditors are getting into financial difficulties include:

- cheques bouncing;
- partial payments being offered;
- post-dated payments being offered;
- claims that payments have been lost in the post;
- claims that the necessary signatories or payment approvers are away.

Dealing with delinquents

It usually falls to the finance department to deal with any problems relating to late or non-payment of accounts. However prudent your terms of trade and rigorous your credit checks, you will end up with late payers and at worst non-payers. There are ways to deal with them, but experience shows that once something starts to go wrong it usually gets worse. There is an old investment saying: 'the first loss is the best loss' that applies here.

Chasing debtors

The most cost-effective and successful method of keeping late payers in line is to let them know you know. Nine out of 10 small businesses do not routinely send out reminder letters advising customers that they have missed the payment date. Send out a polite reminder to arrive the day after payment is due, addressed to the person responsible for payments, almost invariably someone in the accounts department if you are dealing with a big organization. Follow this up within five days with a phone call, keeping the pressure on steadily until you are paid.

If you are polite and professional, consistently reminding them of your terms of trade, there is no reason your relationship will be impaired. In any event, the person you sell to may not be the person you chase for payment.

Resorting to law

There are a number of ways in which you can use the courts in a cost-effective manner to recover money owed, short of appointing your own lawyers:

- *The Small Claims Court* is for people whose claim is for relatively small sums that would not be worth pursuing if you had to hire lawyers. Be warned, however, even if you win in the Small Claims Court you can still have problems enforcing the judgement and getting bad debtors to pay up. Most countries have a small claims legal process. There is a useful directory of small claims courts by country at: https://en.wikipedia.org/wiki/Small_claims_court.

- *Arbitration*, which involves an independent person listening to the arguments of both sides and making a commonsense decision, is a less expensive, faster and less threatening way of getting disputes resolved. You have to agree to be bound by the decision and as with any other 'judgment', you still have to get the loser to pay up. But at least there is no dispute that the money is owed you. The Chartered Institute of Arbitrators supports more than 17,000 alternative dispute resolution practitioners in 149 countries around the world (www.ciarb.org/our-network/).

Before you resort to law

You should take one last precautionary measure before you chase debtors too hard. Make sure you are legally entitled to payment. Nothing will get as much egg on an MBA's face as discovering after a lengthy and expensive exercise in trying to force payment that the customer has a 'get out of gaol card' tucked away.

Customers buying products are entitled to expect that the goods are 'fit for purpose' in that they can do what they claim and, if the customer has informed you of a particular need, that they are suitable for that purpose. The goods also have to be of 'satisfactory quality', ie durable and without defects that would affect performance or prevent their enjoyment. For services you must carry the work out with reasonable skill and care and provide it within a reasonable amount of time. The word 'reasonable' is not defined and is applied in relation to each type of service. So, for example, repairing a shoe might reasonably be expected to take a week, while three months would be unreasonable.

If goods or services don't meet these conditions customers can claim a refund. If they have waited an excessive amount of time before complaining or have indicated in any other way that they have 'accepted' they may not be entitled to a refund, but may still be able to claim some money back for a period of up to six years.

Online and distance trading

The fastest growing and potentially the most complex area of business is selling by mail order via the internet, television, radio, telephone, fax or catalogue. Such activities require that you comply with some additional rules over and above those concerning the sale of goods and services described above. In summary, you have to provide written information, an order confirmation, and the chance to cancel the contract. During the 'cooling off period' customers have the unconditional right to cancel within seven working days, provided they have informed you in writing by letter, fax or e-mail.

There are, however, a wide range of exemptions to the right to cancel including accommodation, transport, food, newspapers, audio or video recordings and goods made to a customer's specification. The Complete Guide to Global E-commerce Regulations is a useful resource that provides an overview of the subject and links to country-specific resources (https://jumpseller.co.uk/learn/the-complete-guide-to-global-ecommerce-regulations/).

Foreign exchange

It is almost inconceivable that an MBA will be working in a company that has no dealings with either overseas customers or foreign suppliers. This in turn means handling money in at least two currencies, your own and the country you will trade in or with. Many countries have their own currency, but not all currencies are equally stable. The less stable the currency the more cost and risk is involved in any transaction.

Key factors to consider about foreign currencies

There are four types of foreign currencies and each have very different risk profiles and need to be managed accordingly:

1 *Not fully convertible*, which means that the government of the country concerned exercises political and economic control over the exchange rate and the amount of its currency that can be moved in or out. China and India are amongst many countries that fall into this category. These currencies can be very volatile and you will need permission to repatriate money.

2 *Pegged* is the most favourable way to obtain currency stability; it means the local currency is 'pegged' to a major convertible currency, such as the euro or dollar. While the local currency may move up and down against all other world currencies, it will remain or at least attempt to remain stable against the one it is pegged against.

3 *Dollarized* is a slight misnomer as the term is used to describe a country that abandons its own currency and adopts the exclusive use of the US dollar or another major international currency, such as the euro.

4 *Fully convertible* is a currency that stands on its own two feet and fluctuates as the country in question and its economy succeeds or fails. Russia, for example, lifted currency controls in July 2006 as a sign of economic confidence, making the rouble fully convertible.

Types of foreign exchange risk to be managed

A business has two distinct types of foreign exchange risk to consider when it comes to considering which, if any, risk management strategy to pursue.

1. Transaction exposure

Transaction exposure occurs when a business incurs costs or generates revenues in any currency other than the one shown in its filed accounts. Two types of event can lead to an exchange rate risk: a mismatch between cost of sales (manufacturing, etc) incurred in one currency and the actual sales income generated in another; and any time lag between setting the selling price in one currency and the date the customer actually pays up. As it is unlikely that there will have been no movement in exchange rates, transaction risk is real and potentially could have serious consequences.

2. Translation exposure

Translation exposure refers to the effects of movements in the exchange rate on the balance sheet and profit and loss account that occur between reporting dates on assets and liabilities denominated in foreign currencies.

In practice any company that has assets or liabilities denominated in a currency other than the currency shown on its reported accounts will have to 'translate' them back into the company's reporting currency when the consolidated accounts are produced. This could be up to four times a year for major trading businesses. Any changes in the foreign exchange rate between the countries involved will cause movements in the accounts that have nothing to do with the underlying economic performance of the company.

Take the case of a UK-based company buying a US company when the exchange rate was £1 to $1.20. The abbreviated balance sheet of the US company (see Figure 8.8) shows that translating at the time of purchase back into £ results in a £ balance sheet total of £200. The following year, however, the dollar has weakened, resulting in an exchange of $1.50 to £1. This is reflected in the second GBP column, with £ totals of 160. This has the wholly unwelcome effect of showing shareholders' funds reduced by £6 million – but actually the effect is entirely due to translation and might be reversed if the exchange rates move in the dollar's favour at a later date. Nevertheless, a company may feel obliged to manage its way out of the exchange rate effect if, for example, the result was an acceptable debt to equity ratio.

Figure 8.8   Foreign exchange translation exposure in millions

Assets	USD	GBP 1.20	GBP 1.50	Liabilities	USD	GBP 1.20	GBP 1.50
Cash	30	24	20	Creditors	190	158	126
Investments	40	34	26	Bank loans	14	12	10
Debtors	130	108	88				
Fixed Assets	40	34	26	Shareholder Funds	36	30	24
	240	200	160		240	200	160

Help with managing foreign exchange risk

These organizations can help an MBA keep on top of foreign exchange matters.

The Reuters Forex Poll ranks HiFX plc within the top three most accurate foreign exchange forecasters globally, beating many of the world's leading banks. As well as carrying out all the functions of dealing in foreign exchange and having the near-ubiquitous currency converter on its website, there is some further information useful to the property investor.

OANDA (www.oanda.com) was first to market in making comprehensive currency exchange information available over the internet, and now licenses out to hotels and airlines providing exchange rate information on their website. On their site you will find an extensive range of valuable tools including Select FXConverter (Foreign Exchange Currency Converter) to access the multilingual Currency Converter with up-to-date exchange rates covering any of the 190 currencies used around the world. The date function is a neat addition as you can see what rate you would have got in the past. For example, £1 sterling would have bought only $1.41 in 1985, while it bought $1.89 in September 2006, a sizeable 34 per cent appreciation. By March 2015 the rate was down to $1.49, more or less its starting point.

The Financial Markets Association website (https://acifma.com/) has links to the websites of some 9,000 members in over 60 countries, listed by continent. The country associations contain directories of members.

Cyber security

A major new risk facing businesses is the myriad of combined risks caused by any online activity, from the relatively universal email communication arena, through to ecommerce. Tesco disclosed in its 2022 annual report that it had carried out a cyberattack stress test and that a data breach could cost it up to £2.4 billion in fines.

These statistics provide a flavour of the damage that can be caused:

- Ransomware attacks are estimated to have reached epidemic proportions. Industry analysts estimate the frequency of these attacks to be one every two seconds, with a cost to industry expected to reach $265 billion by 2031.

- A quarter of the companies hit with a ransomware attack were shut out of their systems for up three days. A quarter were down for a week, while a sixth had outage of two weeks.

- Fewer than a third of ransomware victims recovered their data without paying up.

- Two billion passwords or user names were compromised in 2021, up a third on 2020.

- Breaches caused by security issues in supply chains were up by a third in 2021 compared with 2020.

- The average data breach in the USA cost $9.5 million.

- Social media, whist only responsible for 1 per cent of the breaches in 2021, paid out a third of the total $744 billion in breach costs.

- Fewer than one in four companies are reckoned to provide cyber awareness training on a regular, ongoing basis.

These resources provide a useful backdrop to the subject: 2022 ForgeRock, 'Consumer identity breach report': www.forgerock.com/thank-you/2022-consumer-identity-breach-report; mimecast, 'The state of email security 2022': www.mimecast.com/state-of-email-security/download-hub/; Veritas ransomware solutions: www.veritas.com/en/uk/solution/ransomware.

Ethics – a risk to brand value

Russia's invasion of Ukraine on 24 February 2022 proved a challenge to the ethical values of the corporate world. Russia was the fifth largest European retail market globally in 2021, valued at circa £350 billion. BP, with large stake in Russian energy giant Rosneft, announced within days of the war starting the operation would be hived off. Some brands were hesitant to burn their bridges, in case of a chance of returning when the dust settled. H&M, which had about 170 stores in Russia, paused sales in March. Ikea suspended imports and exports, but continued operating Mega, its major chain of shopping centres, to 'ensure that customers have access to essentials'. Nestlé suspended sales of 'the vast majority' of products sold in Russia, including pet food, coffee and candy sold under KitKat and Nesquik brands. It halted 'non-essential' imports and exports, and halted advertising and capital investment.

Within weeks, when the scale of the disaster became evident, much of the business world moved decisively to distance their brands from an ethical disaster zone. Levi's, a symbol of post-Soviet business in Russia, with around 4 per cent of sales from Russia and Eastern Europe, closed its shops, with concern for human suffering clearly trumping business considerations. Marks & Spencer, with 48 shops in Russia operated by Turkish franchise company FiBA, could only react by suspending shipments of its goods to FiBA, but the Russian shops stayed open.

Online video courses and lectures

Credit risk management: frameworks and strategies. New York Institute of Finance: www.coursera.org/learn/credit-risk-management

Cybersecurity for everyone. University of Maryland: www.coursera.org/learn/cybersecurity-for-everyone

Introduction to cyber security specialization. NYU: www.coursera.org/specializations/intro-cyber-security

Introduction to cybersecurity tools and cyber attacks. IBM Security Learning Services: www.coursera.org/learn/introduction-cybersecurity-cyber-attacks

Introduction to risk management. New York Institute of Finance: www. coursera.org/learn/introduction-to-risk-management

Managing risk and cash flow in international trade. Delivered by Export Development Canada: www.youtube.com/watch?v=XRNxSZ7Ry7Y

Term-structure and credit derivatives. Columbia University: www.coursera. org/learn/financial-engineering-termstructure

The universal principle of risk management: pooling and the hedging of risks. Professor Robert J Shiller – Yale University: www.youtube.com/ watch?v=WMkD8HKJQCM

Online video case studies

BP: Risk management failure at BP. QBE Insurance Europe Ltd: www. youtube.com/watch?v=mGq2kVPVuig

Challenger – A Case Study in Risk Management: History Channel: www. youtube.com/watch?v=shP2JGIfnGg

Facebook: risk management in action: https://corporatesolutions.swissre. com/insights/knowledge/risk-management-action-dialogue-with-facebooks-janaize-markland.html

Profit Pollution and Deception BP and the Oil Spill BBC Documentary: Best Documentaries: www.youtube.com/watch?v=8zGFvzMMO9w

Royal Dutch Shell – How management accountants manage risk – Simon Henry, CFO: www.youtube.com/watch?v=rKNv2hVCfNU

Why Hydro chose to be transparent during cyber-attack: www.youtube. com/watch?v=C6MDz-AgQuE

09
Business tax and profit reporting procedures

- Tax principles
- The role of auditors
- Filing company reports
- Protecting investors
- Responsibilities of directors
- Ethics and enterprise

One reason a business produces accounts and reports is to enable internal staff to keep track of performance, but while that is an important reason it is not the only one or the most important. It is the parties external to the business, shareholders and government authorities in particular, that have specific expectations and requirements that must be adhered to. Furthermore it's the responsibility of the directors, and by extension their advisers – accountants, MBAs and legal staff – to keep the business on the straight and narrow. Tax is very much a hot topic globally, with over 140 countries signing up for ensuring the world's biggest companies pay at least 15 per cent tax by 2023.

Some business schools take tax and reporting very seriously indeed. California State University, Northridge (CSUN) offers a Master's of Science in Taxation, consisting of eight courses aiming to provide students with in-depth knowledge of all the key areas of taxation. The University of Southern Maine's MBA Program offers a number of specializations in taxation including Advanced Business Taxation, as well as providing the opportunity for an internship in taxation.

Principles of taxation

Tax in its various forms can account for up to half of a business's turnover. Taxes constitute the largest single creditor, the most likely event to cause a business to fold and ranks first in the pecking order when it comes to the disposal of assets in such an event. These two judgments against the Inland Revenue Commissioner gave the spur to the 'inventive' approach taken to the subject of tax by many businesses and their accountants:

> Every man is entitled if he can to order his affairs so as that the tax attaching under the appropriate Acts is less than it otherwise would be. If he succeeds in ordering them so as to secure the result, then, however unappreciative the Commissioners of Inland Revenue or his fellow taxpayer may be of his ingenuity, he cannot be compelled to pay an increased tax. (Lord Tomkin – IRC v Duke of Westminster, 1936)
>
> No man in this country is under the smallest obligation, moral or other, so to arrange his legal relations to his business or his property as to enable the Inland Revenue to put the largest possible shovel into his stores. (Lord Clyde – Ayrshire Pullman Motor Services and Ritchie v IRC, 1929)

For business people the justification for tax minimization is overwhelming. No other activity can enhance net profits so dramatically. Every pound, dollar or euro in tax saved drops straight to the bottom line.

Tax evasion, avoidance and mitigation

The opportunities are endless, from the seemingly prudent – Marks & Spencer seeking to obtain group tax relief in respect of losses incurred by certain European subsidiary companies in Belgium, France and Germany – to the plain criminal – stuffing the business with false invoices. China has the dubious distinction of being the world capital of false invoicing. In 2007/8 police there investigated 3,511 cases involving issuing false or tax-offsetting invoices, arrested 2,979 suspects, confiscated 10,510,000 fake invoices, smashed 101 illegal invoice-printing operations and retrieved 9.2 billion yuan in under-declared taxes.

The challenge for directors and managers is to recognize the distinction between different types of behaviour when it comes to tax law:

- *Tax fraud*, often called tax evasion to soften the underlying meaning, involves the intentional behaviour or actual knowledge of the wrongdoing, for example reducing the tax burden by underreporting income, overstating deductions, or using illegal tax shelters; this is a criminal matter.

- *Tax mitigation* involves the taxpayer taking advantage of a fiscally attractive option afforded by the tax legislation and 'genuinely suffers the economic consequences that Parliament intended to be suffered by those taking advantage of the option', as one Law Lord summed up the subject. For example, if a business is allowed to offset the cost of an asset against tax, then so long as it actually buys the asset it is mitigating its tax position.

- *Tax avoidance* lies in the blurred line between tax mitigation and tax fraud and is usually defined by the test of whether your dominant purpose – or your sole purpose – was to reduce or eliminate tax liability.

Transfer pricing

International firms have a degree of flexibility as to where they incur charges and make profits if they have operations in more than one country. For example, if a company buys components in one country, manufactures in another and has a marketing or administrative function in a third country, which is itself incurring cost and adding value, that business has a range of options on where it takes its final profits. By paying a subsidiary a high price for elements of their activities it is possible to lower taxable profits in the company's domestic market. This is not a strategy that appeals much to tax authorities, who work hard to limit the scope of such activities.

Tax types

As a business you are responsible for paying a number of taxes and other dues to the government of the day, both on your own behalf and for any employees you may have as well as being an unpaid tax collector required to account for end-consumers' expenditure.

There are penalties for misdemeanours and you are required to keep your accounts for six years, so at any point should tax authorities become suspicious they can dig into the past even after they have agreed your figures. In the case of suspected fraud there is no limit to how far back the digging can go.

The amount of tax paid on profits varies from country to country and year to year. Data from the OECD (see Figure 9.1) show that corporation tax rates vary from zero in the case in Jersey and half a dozen other so-called tax havens, up to 35 per cent in Malta.

Corporation tax

Corporation tax covers the profit made in an accounting period, usually of one-year duration; it can be shorter under special circumstances, but never longer. Companies are responsible for working out their own tax liability,

Figure 9.1 Global corporation tax rates, 2021

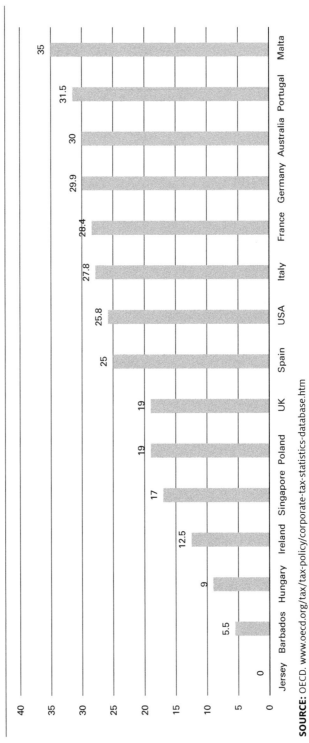

SOURCE: OECD. www.oecd.org/tax/tax-policy/corporate-tax-statistics-database.htm

paying the tax due and filing their tax return no later than 12 months after the end of the accounting period.

Capital allowances

The purchase of capital items such as plant, machinery and equipment, buildings and any such long-term assets are treated for tax purposes in a particular manner. In the profit and loss account these costs are usually shown as an item of depreciation spread over the working life of the asset(s) concerned. For tax purposes, however, depreciation is not an allowable expense; it is replaced with a 'writing down allowance' the amount of which varies according to the policies favoured by the government of the day.

Capital gains tax

Any asset a business disposes of other than the goods it normally trades in is liable, in the event of there being a profit, to pay capital gains tax (CGT). Once that tax was complicated and subject to tapers and indexing depending on the type of asset and how long it was owned. Now in the UK as in many other countries a single rate of tax, in the case of the UK 19 per cent, is applied.

Capital losses

Many sales of assets, old vehicles, computers and so forth, involve a loss rather than a gain. Subject to offsetting any tax relief already claimed from writing down allowances during the asset's life, such losses are usually offset against gains made on the sale of other assets within a set time period, usually several years.

Pay roll tax

Employers are responsible for deducting income tax from employee's pay and making the relevant payment to your tax authority. You will need to work out the tax due. This is a complex area as no two employees are likely to have the same tax circumstances due to the myriad tax credits on offer for various circumstances.

Subcontractors

Companies often seek to circumvent the complexities of pay roll and employment law by using subcontractors. This is particularly so in industries such as construction, but there are strict and precise rules. Subcontractors must hold the appropriate Tax Certificate.

Value Added Tax (VAT) or Sales Tax

VAT, a tax common throughout Europe though charged at different rates, is a tax on consumer spending, collected by businesses. Basically it is a game of pass the parcel, with businesses that are registered charging each other VAT and deducting VAT charged. At the end of each accounting period the amount of VAT you have paid out is deducted from the amount you have charged out and the balance is paid over to the tax authorities.

In the US a sales tax is applied on a state-by-state basis ranging from zero in Alaska up to 7 per cent in Indiana and Tennessee. To make life more complicated some states apply variable rates on many items. The Sales Tax Institute has a useful calculator for having a stab at working out your position (www.salestaxinstitute.com/resources/rates).

Perhaps the most useful resource in this area is the free services provided by Avalara. Their strap line, 'Powering global commerce in a world of tax complexities', is facilitated through an extensive menu of free resources. These are EU, global and US rates for VAT and Sales Taxes.

Help and advice with international tax

These two information sources, between them, contain most of what an MBA needs to know to keep abreast of international tax matters.

The European Commission provides links to the tax authority throughout Europe and most of the developed world: https://taxation-customs.ec.europa.eu/national-tax-websites_en. Their 'Essential links to taxes' provides an eclectic range of services from books and guides, tax software and tax law: www.el.com/elinks/taxes/.

The OECD maintains a database covering comparative information on a range of tax rates including personal income tax rates, social security contributions, corporate tax rates and statistics, effective tax rates, tax rates on consumption, and environmental taxes: www.oecd.org/tax/tax-policy/tax-database/.

Auditors – the gatekeepers

All companies of any size – in the UK that is with a turnover in excess of £5 million and in the United States above $5 million – are required to have their accounts audited, as do most companies with money invested by external shareholders. The audit is carried out annually by a qualified accountant appointed by the directors and approved by the shareholders, to examine evidence and give an opinion about the financial statements. To do so they carry out these main tasks:

- Evaluate the design and operating dependability of the business's accounting system and procedures.

- Evaluate and test the business's internal accounting controls that are established to deter and detect errors and fraud.

- Identify and critically examine the business's accounting methods to ensure they conform to the generally accepted accounting principles of the country in which the company is registered.

- Inspect documentary and physical evidence for the business's revenues, expenses, assets and liabilities, and owners' equities. This can involve carrying out a physical stock check, albeit on a sample basis, checking the condition of that stock, and confirming bank account balances.

The goal of all the audit work is to provide a convincing basis for expressing an opinion on the business's financial statements, and being able to confirm whether or not the company's financial statements and any directly supporting tables and schedules can be relied on. The auditor puts that opinion in the auditor's report.

Most audit reports give the business a clean bill of health, stating that the accounts give a true and fair view. In the case of relatively minor problems matters are usually cleared up before the accounts are filed. Just the threat of an adverse opinion almost always motivates a business to give way to the auditor and change its accounting methods for the figures to be reported. An adverse audit opinion, if it were actually given, indicates that the financial statements of the business are misleading, and by implication possibly fraudulent. The LSE and the SEC do not tolerate adverse opinions and would stop trading in the company's shares on an adverse opinion from its auditor.

The MBAs, unless they are also accountants, don't get involved in doing audits, but they are expected to know who's who in the auditing world; *Accountancy Age* (www.accountancyage.com/rankings/) will keep you informed.

PricewaterhouseCoopers, Tesco's auditors made it clear that, in their view, the accounts:

- 'give a true and fair view of the state of the Parent Company's affairs as at 22 February 2014';

- 'have been properly prepared in accordance with United Kingdom Generally Accepted Accounting Practice'; and

- 'have been prepared in accordance with the requirements of the Companies Act 2006.'

That statement should provide investors and anyone else interested in their figures that they can rely on their having been properly prepared.

What auditors may uncover

Having an audit of a business's financial statements does not guarantee that all fraud, embezzlement, theft and dishonesty will be detected. Audits have to be cost-effective; auditors can't examine every transaction that occurred during the year. Instead, auditors carefully evaluate businesses' internal controls relying on sampling. That in turn means that some problems may remain undetected.

The auditors may uncover some or all of the following in their examination of a business's accounting records:

- *Errors in recording transactions*: these honest mistakes happen from time to time either through lack of experience or failure to pay attention to details. In such cases there is no indication of theft or fraud and all that management wants is the errors corrected and to be confident it won't happen again.

- *Theft, embezzlement and fraud*: this involves staff either alone or in collusion with others taking advantage of weak internal controls to remove cash, product or other assets.

- *Accounting fraud* (also called *financial fraud* or *financial reporting fraud*): this refers to top-level managers who know about and approve the use of misleading and invalid accounting methods with the objective of concealing the business's financial problems or artificially inflating profit. This is usually done for the benefit that accrues, say, by propping up the market price of the company's shares to make the stock options more valuable.

- *Management fraud*: in such cases managers may accept kickbacks or bribes from customers or suppliers.

Going concern – or perhaps not!

A *going concern* is a business that has sufficient financial wherewithal and momentum to continue its normal operations into the foreseeable future and would be able to absorb a bad turn of events without having to default on its liabilities. A business could be under some financial distress, but overall still be judged a going concern. Unless there is evidence to the contrary, the auditor assumes that the business is a going concern.

In some cases the auditor may see unmistakable signs that a business may not be able to convince its creditors and lenders to give it time to work itself out of its present financial difficulties. The creditors and lenders may force the business into involuntary bankruptcy, or the business may make a preemptive move and take itself into voluntary bankruptcy. (See Chapter 8 for more on handling the risk associated with business failure.)

Filing accounts

A company's financial affairs are in the public domain. Companies have to file their accounts with their relevant country tax authority. Accounts should be filed within 10 months of the company's financial year-end. Small businesses can file abbreviated accounts that include only very limited balance sheet and profit and loss account information and these do not need to be audited. Businesses can be fined for filing accounts late.

UK companies file their accounts with Companies House (www.gov.uk/file-your-company-accounts-and-tax-return). US company accounts can be obtained from The Securities Exchange Commission (www.sec.gov).

IRSCalculators.com have a mission 'to help as many taxpayers as we can get fast, easy to understand, accurate, and bug free tax information'. Their directory of world tax authorities is at: www.irscalculators.com/world-tax-authority-list.

They also have a personal tax calculator, which is helpful if you are considering relocating: www.irscalculators.com/international-tax-calculator.

Typical content of the annual report and accounts

The contents of the annual report and accounts for a listed company quoted on a stock exchange (see Chapter 7 for more on stock markets) is more comprehensive than the requirements of private companies, which reduce in line with their size. Disclosure requirements for any substantial business come from three sources:

1 statutory law embodied in Companies Acts;

2 accounting standards as laid down in FRSs and SSAPs (Statements of Standard Accounting Practice);

3 if the business is listed on a stock market, the regulations specified by that market will apply.

The following main items are disclosed in the annual report and accounts:

Chairman's statement – a broad review of progress, changes in strategy and management and a guide to future prospects. For large organizations this may be supplemented by a CEO's (chief executive officer's) review of each individual business's performance.

Strategic report – a review of the business during the financial year and of the future risks faced by the company.

Operating and financial review – a detailed commentary on the financial results and influential factors.

List of directors – details of service, responsibilities and other directorships.

Directors' report – a formal report on specific required items, eg dividend declaration, principal activities, share capital and substantial shareholdings, political and charitable contributions, directors' shareholdings, employment policy, creditor payment policy, close company status (a company with no more than five controlling parties) and appointment of auditors.

Report of the remuneration committee – policy statement on how the total remuneration package of executive and non-executive directors is set.

Corporate governance – a statement of compliance, or otherwise, with the Code of Best Practice on board structure and directors' remuneration.

Auditors' report – a statement of auditors' responsibility and their report on whether or not the financial statements give a true and fair view of the state of affairs.

Financial statements – comprising consolidated profit and loss account, balance sheet, cash flow statement, statement of total recognized gains and losses and parent company balance sheet only.

Notes to the financial statements – additional breakdown and analysis of figures appearing in the main financial statements.

Historic record of financial performance – a 10-year summary of the main financial figures and ratios reflecting profitability, dividends and shareholders' funds.

Notice of meeting – notice of the time and venue of the annual general meeting and the business to be conducted.

You can find more information on the content of accounts at: www.gov.uk/government/publications/life-of-a-company-annual-requirements/life-of-a-company-part-1-accounts.

Notes to the accounts

Look back to the audited accounts for Tesco plc in Table 3.7. To save confusion an important element has been left out of the figures that was included in the auditor's report. Against many of the categories in the table was a number to advise the reader that an explanation of how the figure was arrived at appears at the end of the accounts. The notes to Tesco's accounts run from 1 to 35, covering the best part of 80 of the 147 pages of accounts. Note 35, the smallest, reads:

Note 35 Events after the reporting period

On 21 March 2014, the Group entered into an agreement with Trent Limited, part of the Tata Group, to form a 50:50 Joint Venture in Trent Hypermarket Limited ('THL') which operates the Star Bazaar retail business in India. The Group's investment is £85 million.

On 2 April 2014 the Group, through its subsidiary dunnhumby Limited, acquired Sociomantic Labs ('Sociomantic'), a Berlin-based global leader in digital advertising solutions, for £124m. Sociomantic operates in 14 countries worldwide, with clients in retail, financial services and travel services.

Directors' responsibilities and duties

Any MBA worth his or her salt is either a director of the company he or she works for, or aspires to become one. Be warned, however: a director also has to cope with some technical, more detailed requirements, for example sending in the accounts to Companies House, appointing an auditor if required, holding regular board meetings and keeping shareholders informed. More onerous than just signing them, a director is expected and required in law to understand the significance of the balance sheet, profit and loss account and cash flow statement.

A director's duties, responsibilities and potential liabilities include:

- To act in good faith in the interests of the company; this includes carrying out duties diligently and honestly.

- Not to carry on the business of the company with intent to defraud creditors or for any fraudulent purpose.

- Not knowingly to allow the company to trade while insolvent ('wrongful trading'); directors who do so may have to pay for the debts incurred by the company while insolvent.

- Not to deceive shareholders.

- To have a regard for the interests of employees in general.

- To comply with the requirements of the relevant government regulations, such as providing what is needed in accounting records, appointing auditors and filing accounts.

- Appoint a company secretary, who for a public company must be appropriately qualified.

A good brief working summary of these responsibilities is summarized in 'The Principal Fiduciary Duties of Boards of Directors' by Professor Bernard S Black of Stanford Law School (www.oecd.org/corporate/ca/corporategovernanceprinciples/1872746.pdf).

The Deloitte LLP Centre for Corporate Governance supports boards of directors by providing them with resources relating to current boardroom issues and governance trends. They have a very useful Global Centre for Corporate Governance with 40 centres of Corporate Governance in the Americas, Asia, Europe, and Africa (www2.deloitte.com/us/en/pages/risk/articles/global-site-selector.html). One slight drawback is that not all the centres have their information in English on their website.

Holding board meetings

Board meetings have to be held sufficiently regularly to allow the directors to 'discharge their duties effectively'. On average the boards of public companies meet eight to nine times a year and smaller companies once a quarter. The purposes of board meetings are to take major decisions and to keep everyone informed of events affecting business performance. Having regular board meetings ensures that important matters are properly considered and the various views and outcomes are recorded. Guidelines for successful board meetings are:

- Have as small a number of directors as possible, bearing in mind the size of the business. The amount of useful work a board can do is in inverse proportion to its size.
- Hold meetings regularly and set a timetable a year ahead, updated at the half year. This is vital if there are non-executive directors.
- Have an agenda, and stick to it. Start with the minutes of the previous meeting, get them accepted, move through the agenda and finish with AOB (any other business), and confirm the date and venue for the next meeting.
- Take and circulate minutes of the meeting.
- Have a board chairman whose role is to keep the board meeting on track.

Non-executive directors

Despite the comforting sound of the prefix in this title, 'non-executive' directors carry all the responsibilities of full-time directors, but are rarely close enough to the business to know exactly what the true financial position is. Big companies like to have them, usually to chair the remuneration committee that determines board salaries and bonuses and to provide further safeguards for shareholders. For small companies having a heavyweight outsider can sometimes lend extra credibility to a business proposition.

Directors' misdemeanours

There are three types of activities that directors need to steer clear of if they don't want to join the several thousand or so directors on both sides of the Atlantic who are disqualified and fined each year, or the rather smaller number who end up in prison. Disqualification means that not only can't you run a company but if you issue your orders through others, having them act as a director in your place, you will leave them personally liable. You will be in breach of a disqualification order that can in turn lead to imprisonment and fines. In addition, you can be made personally liable for the debts and liabilities of any company in which you are involved.

Trading while insolvent occurs when your liabilities exceed your assets. At this point the shareholders' equity in the business has effectively ceased to exist and when shareholder equity is negative, directors are personally at risk and owe a duty of care to creditors – not shareholders. If you find yourself even approaching this area you need the prompt advice of an insolvency practitioner. Directors who act properly will not be penalized, and will live to fight another day.

The two areas most likely to lead disqualification are, 1) wrongful trading, which can apply if, after a company goes into insolvent liquidation, the liquidator believes that the directors (or those acting as such) ought to have concluded earlier that the company had no realistic chance of survival. In these circumstances the courts can remove the shelter of limited liabilities and make directors personally liable for the company's debts; 2) fraudulent trading, which is rather more serious than wrongful trading. Here the proposition is that the director(s) were knowingly party to fraud on their creditors. The full shelter of Limited Liability can be removed in these circumstances.

Values and the accounting reports

Values are the ethical concepts of right and wrong behaviour that govern the way in which we discharge our responsibilities. While many responsibilities lie within the scope of the law – shareholder protection, discrimination at work, misleading advertising and so forth – in those areas and the grey area that surrounds them lies the province of ethics and social responsibility. Right and wrong in themselves are often not too difficult to separate out. The problem usually stems from competing 'rights' – giving shareholders a better return versus saving the planet for example.

The owner, operating alone in a small business, or the board of directors are the custodians of the moral tone and in setting standards of behaviour towards everyone the business has dealings with. They are in some ways encouraged by legal constraints placed on them to take a narrow view of those responsibilities. They are required 'to act in good faith in the interests of the company', 'not to deceive shareholders and to appoint auditors to oversee the accounting records', 'not to carry on the business of the company with intent to defraud creditors or for any fraudulent purpose' and 'to have regard for the interests of employees in general'.

Directors and managers also have responsibilities to protect their customers when using their products or services or when visiting company premises, and to follow rules inhibiting pollution in the operating processes. But it is only relatively recently that companies have been required to take a wider view of their responsibilities to other 'stakeholder' groups. Enlightened managers, or those who are particularly astute depending on your level of cynicism, have often taken on broader responsibilities, sponsoring charities, funding social amenities such as play areas or providing low-cost housing. These initiatives are often spurred on by enlightened self-interest, say to help with recruiting and retaining employees, with getting favourable PR or in the case of low-cost housing, providing amenities that are a usual requirement in getting planning consent for a property development or a site for, say, a supermarket. All such activities are reported in the company annual report and accounts.

CASE STUDY
Bayer AG

Founded in Wuppertal, Germany, in 1863, Bayer has more than 30,000 employees, making it one of the biggest employers in the country. The company, best known in consumer markets for aspirin, is one of the world's largest and oldest chemical and health-care products companies. The Bayer Group is truly international, in 2022 comprising 374 companies in 83 countries. Their central purpose is captured in these statements: 'Science for a better life' and 'Helping more people thrive within planetary boundaries' (www.bayer.com/en/investors/sustainability-socially-responsible-investing). These statements conceal a much more complex organization with a range of goals beyond the short-term financial results.

Bayer puts social responsibility at the heart of every aspect of their business. In 2000 they became a founding member of the UN Global Compact and in so doing made a clear commitment to 10 principles relating to human rights, employment standards, environmental protection and the fight against corruption. In 2004 they became the first company to partner with the United Nations Environment Programme in the area of youth and the environment. The development of the Bayer Climate Program, launched in 2006, was a milestone in their commitment to sustainable development. As well as substantially reducing their greenhouse gas emissions, they have set themselves further ambitious targets. Bayer was the only European company in the chemical and pharmaceutical industry to be listed for the fifth time in succession in the world's first global climate index, and in 2009 was rated as the world's best company in the Carbon Disclosure Leadership Index. The Bayer Science & Education Foundation supports innovative school projects in Germany that make science lessons more attractive. Each year they provide a total of about €45 million in funding for the 300 projects they support as part of their social commitment.

In August 2022 Bayer topped pharma rankings for their diversity, equity and inclusion (DE&I) efforts. Ranked on a scale of −100 to +100, Bayer rated +67, comfortably ahead of Astellas (+11), Eli Lilly (+21) and Teva Pharma (+28).

'Social Responsibility' took something of a knock in September 2015 when Volkswagen fell from grace. Recently ranked as the 11th best in the world for its CSR (Corporate Social Responsibility) work by The Reputation Institute, in 2014 it collected the Gold Medal Award for Sustainable Development from the non-profit World Environment Center, and its own sustainability report runs to 156 pages. There is a view gaining ground that CSR departments are simply providing an insurance policy, allowing companies to take risks with their own internal standards.

Online video courses and lectures

Corporate Governance: Presentation to students at the Tepper School of Business by William Pounds, a former senior adviser to The Rockefeller Family: www.youtube.com/watch?v=PC_acEzfL9Q

Introduction to Corporation Tax and the Corporation Tax computation – ACCA Taxation TX – UK lectures: www.youtube.com/watch?v= QrS85qXhquk

The Role of the Audit Committee: John Palmer, managing partner of ICS Consulting Partners, reviews the basic skills and requirements that every audit committee needs to be successful today: www.youtube.com/ watch?v=zJJfFOLcCXU

Taxation of business entities I: corporations. The University of Illinois at Urbana-Champaign: www.coursera.org/learn/taxation-business-entities-part-1

Online video case studies

Bernie Madoff: Scamming of America – The $50 Billion Ponzi Scheme: www.dailymotion.com/video/x27ulpg

The collapse of Lehman Brothers – a simple overview: www.youtube.com/ watch?v=BnDbdQa_r38

The rise and fall of JC Penney: www.youtube.com/watch?v=3i4GrDXNd_w

10
Mergers and acquisitions

- Why most mergers miscarry – and why some don't
- Planning an acquisition strategy
- Valuing businesses
- Limiting the risks

Acquisitions and mergers are areas that an MBA is almost certain to encounter early in his or her career. On some MBA programmes there may well be some unique content in specialized electives. For example, at the London Business School there is an elective on 'Financial analysis of mergers, acquisitions and other complex corporate restructurings', or the partially related subject, 'Dealing with financial crime', on offer at Bayes (formerly Cass) Business School.

Figure 10.1 gives the history of the world's mergers and acquisitions by volume and value over the period 1993-2021. The world recessions in 1991 and 2009 and the Covid-19 pandemic in 2020 put a partial brake on the ever-upward trend. At the time of writing in 2022, the effects of the Russo/Ukraine war on mergers and acquisitions are largely unknown. Nevertheless, nearly 3,000 deals worth over $2 trillion had been banked by September 2022. Oracle's acquisition of Cerner put $28 billion into the stats, and Orange's purchase of Grupo MásMóvil created a new force in Spain's mobile phone market.

Figure 10.1 Global mergers and acquisitions – deals and values, 1993–2021

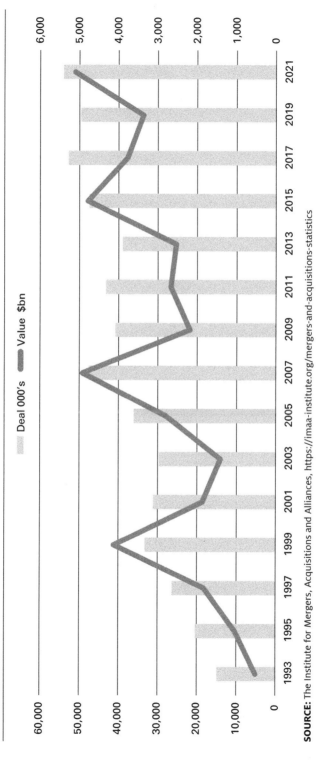

SOURCE: The Institute for Mergers, Acquisitions and Alliances, https://imaa-institute.org/mergers-and-acquisitions-statistics

CASE STUDY
Shell bids for BG

On 9 April 2015, Shell announced that it was paying £47 billion for BG (British Gas), the British multinational oil and gas company headquartered in Reading, United Kingdom. The offer represented a 50 per cent premium to BG's closing share price on the previous day's closing share price. Shell shares closed down more than 4 per cent whilst BG's raced ahead by 38 per cent. Shell claimed that owning BG would allow it to focus on fewer, safer bets and make the most of their mutual assets by integrated gas and deep-water activities whilst pulling back from more risky early stage projects such as the Arctic.

For Helge Lund, BG Group's boss of barely two months, the deal stood to make him up to £32 million of bonuses. For Shell, according to the Economist, 'the acquisition will increase its energy reserves by 25 per cent and make it the world's third-biggest producer of liquefied natural gas'.

Lund built his reputation at the helm of Norway's Statoil, transforming the company from a small domestic operator into a global business. With an MBA from the INSEAD Lund had a range of opportunities when he decided to quit Statoil, but decided instead to join the much troubled BG. In 2014 BG's first-half operating profits of $4 billion was sunk by its cash capital expenditure of $4.8 billion. The view on the street was that BG didn't have the operational capacity or financial scale required to realize the potential of its impressive portfolio. In short it was an ideal takeover target.

Roll the clock forward to September 2022 and this deal proved astute, given Russia's attack on Ukraine that sparked a global scramble for gas.

Here in a nutshell you have all the ingredients of a mega merger. A business with more opportunity than cash; a giant with cash and a need to lower risk and milk assets – realize synergy in the jargon of the merger world. Stoke these up with a leavening of ego and personal wealth creation and the stage is set. Not all mergers are anywhere near this scale, but the mix is the same.

Although M&As are popular with CEOs the research literature produces, at best, inconclusive evidence to support the hypothesis that M&As generally create increased shareholder value for the owners of the acquiring firm. Since Kitching's seminal work 'Why do mergers miscarry?' (*Harvard Business Review*, November–December, 84–101) there has been a big question mark over the subject of acquisitions and shareholder value. Porter ('From competitive advantage to corporate strategy', *Harvard Business Review*, 65 (3), 43–59, 1987) concluded that 'acquisitions have been largely unsuccessful when one considers that over half were subsequently divested'. A clear majority of the academic studies published over the past 50 years come down on the side of the doubters.

So why, you might wonder, do acquisitions capture so much of top management's attention? That arrogance plays a major part in this process is supported by the way that most corporate acquisitions are carried by relatively inexperienced individuals operating almost alone. This quotation from *The Wall Street Journal*, 'a struggle between a few ambitious men using public companies in which they owned a fractional share, for their own gain', captures the dominance of ego and arrogance in the merger process. A light-hearted but statistically sound study was conducted by two academics from Columbia University. They found a way of confirming what we all knew already: there is a link between the premiums paid by bosses and their own inflated self-esteem. They measured such factors as the boss's salary relative to his peers and the acres of flattering press coverage and proved that the higher the self-esteem the higher the premium they paid to acquire the business and consequently the less likely it was that they would create additional value for their shareholders.

The other factor that draws top management to M&A is the immediacy of the apparent reward. Most business strategies present few opportunities to produce clear winners and losers in a very short time frame. But with an acquisition strategy the successful bidder is declared the 'winner' by employees, middle management, competitors, their industry and the financial community at large, all within a matter of weeks. And even if the bid fails, the business community sees the management as a virile aggressor. The consequences of failure take years, even decades to emerge. Time Warner's acquisition of AOL and eBay's of Skype are two such examples where nothing of much value to the acquirers has arisen save copious positive press coverage in the early weeks after the event.

Of course the protagonists are invariably cheered on by their professional advisers who stand to make a healthy profit whatever the outcome. There are, however a number of conditions that research shows are more likely to lead to success.

1. Size matters

Deals between equals in terms of size are more likely to work well than not. The converse is also true. Where the acquired business is much smaller the chances of success are low.

2. Experience counts

For example, M&A is viewed as a cornerstone of the strategy of Cisco, whose top management have made such a study of the subject that management consultants from around the globe take their advice. In the United States, which has the greatest experience base of every type of M&A, buyers are more sophisticated and are less likely to overpay for their acquisitions than are Europeans, for example. In the United States, the medium control premium paid for a public company has been dropping steadily over the past decade from 58 per cent to just 26 per cent. In Europe by contrast, the average premium increased from 31 to 37 per cent.

3. Cash is king

One much vaunted reason for medium-sized firms to go public is the opportunity to use paper to fund acquisitions. But much academic research suggests that both bidders and targets lose in stock-financed deals, as opposed to those financed by cash. The reasons for this are:

- Cash deals are quicker and less costly to implement than share deals.
- A stock offer opens up the bidding to a wider group (ie any firm with or without cash). This in turn increases the competitiveness, which tends to be a disadvantage to the bidder.
- Issuing new stock can be viewed negatively by the capital markets, leading to a drop in the share price of the bidder. This in turn can make the deal more expensive for the acquiring firm.

Avoid firms where the management owns a large slice of the business. It seems reasonable to assume that increased managerial share ownership, through options and the like, encourages managers to maximize shareholder value rather than simply to pursue aggrandizement strategies for their own sake. Giving managers a share of ownership requires them to bear a higher part of the cost of poor decisions. At the same time, greater ownership gives company managers greater control of the company, a power that can be used to resist acquisitions. Managers often resist bids, even when the bid looks likely to create greater shareholder value. Research bears these views out conclusively.

4. Cross-border deals work well

It seems that when firms expand into a new geographic market the shareholders of the acquiring firm are highly likely to experience significant increases in shareholder wealth, but not if they try to repeat the process in the same market. One interesting study (Doukas, J and Travlos, N G, 1988, 'The effects of corporate multinationalism on shareholder's wealth: Evidence from international acquisitions', *Journal of Finance*, 43, 1161–75) found that US bidders going abroad for the first time made significant positive abnormal gains. Those making further acquisitions in the overseas countries in which they were operating did not fare so well. They made either zero or insignificant gains from second and subsequent acquisitions.

Going on the acquisition trail

M&A strategies are often messy, and in hostile bids there can be blood on the carpet. But just because they may end up messy – that is almost inevitable in corporate warfare – they don't have to start off that way. Getting information on public companies is relatively easy. They are required by the rules of the stock exchange they are listed on to provide comprehensive and current – usually quarterly – information on performance. If any major event occurs, for example a serious profit warning, a legal dispute or anything that could materially affect the current profit forecast, that will have to be disclosed immediately. Searching out private companies will call for a bit more digging.

These are some steps you can advise to be taken to improve the chances of making a successful acquisition, merger or joint venture.

Know why you want to buy

Ideally the reasons to buy a business need to be practical and down-to-earth and embedded in the firm's core strategy. Sound reasons for acquisitions include the following:

- to increase market share and eliminate a troublesome competitor;
- to broaden your product range or give you access to new markets;
- to diversify into new markets, acquiring the necessary management, marketing or technical skills to enable you to capture a reasonable slice of the market relatively quickly;
- to get into another country or region;
- to protect an important source of supply that could be under threat from a competitor;
- to acquire additional staff, factory space, warehousing or distribution channels, or to get access to additional major customers more quickly than by starting up yourself.

Your company should produce a written statement explaining the rationale behind your reason to buy – before you start looking for companies to buy – otherwise you could end up pursuing a bargain just because it seems cheap, that has absolutely nothing to do with your previously defined commercial goals. It is also worth remembering that companies available at knockdown prices are likely to need drastic surgery. So unless you fancy your chances as a company doctor, stay well away.

Decide what you want to buy

It can take over one person-year of work, on average, to find and buy a business. The more accurately you describe your ideal purchase the simpler, quicker and cheaper your search will be. Just imagine trying to buy a house without any idea where you wanted to live, how much you wanted to spend, how many bedrooms you needed, whether you wanted a new house or a listed building, or if you wanted a garden. The search would be near impossible to organize, it could take forever, and the resultant purchase would almost certainly please no one. The same problems arise when buying a company. The definition of what you want to buy should explain:

- the business area/products/service the company is in;
- the location;
- the price range and the cash you have available;
- the management depth and the management style you are looking for;
- the minimum profitability and return on capital employed you could accept. It is worth remembering that if the company you plan to buy only makes 1 per cent profit while you make 5 per cent, and you are of equal size, the resultant profit will be 3 per cent: $(5 + 1)/2$;
- the image compatibility between your company and any target;
- scope for integration and cost savings;
- the tax status – for example a business nursing a substantial loss could be worth looking at if that can be offset against your company's profits, so reducing tax due.

Outside of the factors listed above, you may have vital reasons that, if not met, would make the acquisition a poor bet. For example, if you want to iron out major cash flow or plant capacity cycles, there is little point in going for a business similar to your own. That will only make the peaks and troughs more pronounced.

Investigate and approach

Once you have your shopping list of prospective purchases you need to arm yourself with everything you can find out about them. Get their literature, get samples, copies of their advertising, press comment and, of course, their accounts. Then get out and see their premises and as much of their operation as possible. If you cannot get in, get one of your salespeople in to look over the business for you. This investigation will help you both to shorten your shopping list and to put it into order of priority. Now you are ready for the approach. Although you are technically buying, psychologically you would be well advised to think of acquiring a company as a selling job. As such you cannot afford to have any approach rejected either too early or without a determined effort.

You have three options as to how to make the initial approach and each has its merits. You can telephone, giving only the broadest reason for your approach – saying, perhaps, that you wish to discuss areas of common interest. You could write and be a little more specific about your purpose, following that up with a phone call to arrange a meeting, perhaps over lunch. Finally, you could use a third party such as an accountant or consultant (reasons of secrecy could make this method desirable) or a corporate finance house: if executive time is at a premium, there may be no other practicable way.

The first meeting is crucial and you need to achieve two objectives. First, you must establish mutual respect, trust and rapport. Nothing worthwhile will follow without these. Then you need to establish in principle that both parties are seriously interested. Time scale, price, methods of integration, etc can all be side-stepped until later, except in the most general sense.

Valuing a target

There are two special situations that make an initial valuation relatively easy, at least in theory.

1. Share price

First, if your target is already floated on a stock market its value is measured by buyers and sellers every day, or perhaps more often in turbulent times. For example, during the banking meltdown in the autumn of 2008 HBOS's shares oscillated by as much as 40 per cent on an almost daily basis. It was not alone in seeing violent swings and indeed some stock markets, most prominently the Russian main market, actually had to shut down as the volume of selling orders and the spread of prices were too great to comprehend yet alone manage. Nevertheless, the market sets the value of every business on a stock exchange for every transaction. This market price is not necessarily the price that the owners will get for their shares, but in more normal times it is a reasonably close approximation.

2. Asset value

Ongoing businesses are all valued by some measure of future expected profits. In fact the accounts don't even attempt to put a value on the assets. Fixed assets, except for freehold property, are recorded as the cost at date of purchase, reduced by a notional depreciation amount that's sole purpose is to allocate costs over an asset's working life. The asset itself could be of virtually no value at all, such as, say, second-hand office furniture. But that would not be revealed in the balance sheet, whose purpose in this respect is only to show where money has come from and what has been done with that money. The exception to this rule is if a business is not going to continue trading, for example if no buyer can be found. In those circumstances the assets now all have to be valued and sold off piecemeal.

Price/earnings rules

The simplest and most usual way for businesses to be valued is using a formula known as the price/earnings ratio. The P/E ratio is calculated by dividing the share price into the amount of profit earned for each share. For example, if a business makes £100,000 profit and has 1,000 shares, the profit per share is £100. If the share price of that company is £10, then its P/E ratio is 10 (£100/10). So much for the science, now for the art. P/E ratios vary with the business sector and the current market sentiment for that sector. For example, the high tech sector may have a P/E ratio of 30 or more at times – Google had a P/E of 100 at one point. That means that shareholders were prepared to pay $100 for every $1 of profit the company was making. For Barclays Bank, however, they were only paying £10 for every £1 of profits and in the market mayhem of 2008 the banking sector slipped well below that. The market as a whole trades with P/Es between 10 and 20.

Discounting future earnings

A valuation technique popular with the venture capital community is to discount future earnings. We know intuitively that getting cash in sooner is better than getting it in later. In other words, a dollar received now is worth more than a dollar that will arrive in one, two or more years because of what we could do with that money ourselves, or because of what we ourselves have to pay out to have use of that money. So anyone buying your business will need to ascribe a value to a future stream of earnings to arrive at what is known as *the present value*. If we know we could earn 20 per cent on any money, we know the maximum we would be prepared to pay now for a £ coming to us in one year's time would be around 80p. If we were to pay £1 now to get £1 back in a year's time we would in effect be losing money.

The process used to handle this process is known as discounting and the technique is termed 'discounted cash flow' (DCF). The residual discounted cash is called the 'net present value'. The first column in Table 10.1 shows the simple cash flow implications of an investment proposition: a surplus of 5,000 comes after five years from putting 20,000 into a project. But if we accept the proposition that future cash is worth less than current cash, we need to know how much less. If we assume an investor wants to make at least a 15 per cent return on his or her investment then that is the discount rate selected (this doesn't matter too much as you will see in the section on internal rate of return).

The formula for calculating what a dollar received at some future date is worth is:

$$\text{Present Value (PV)} = \$P \times 1/(1 + r)^n$$

Table 10.1 Discounting a stream of future earnings

£	Cash Flow A	Discount Factor at 15% B	Discounted Cash Flow A × B
Initial cash cost NOW (Year 0)	20,000	1.00	20,000
Net cash flows			
Year 1	1,000	0.8695	870
Year 2	4,000	0.7561	3,024
Year 3	8,000	0.6575	5,260
Year 4	7,000	0.5717	4,002
Year 5	5,000	0.4972	2,486
Total	25,000		15,642
Cash surplus	5,000	Net Present Value	(4,358)

where $P is the initial cash cost, r is the interest rate expressed in decimals and n is the year in which the cash will arrive. So if we decide on a discount rate of 15 per cent the present value of a dollar received in one year's time is:

$$\text{Present Value} = \$1 \times 1/(1 + 0.15)^1$$
$$= 0.87 \text{ (rounded to two decimal places)}$$

So we can see that our 1,000 arriving at the end of year one has a present value of 870; the 4,000 in year two has a present value of 3,024 and by year five present value reduces cash flows to barely half their original figure. In fact far from having a real payback in year four and generating a cash surplus of 5,000, this project will make us 4,358 worse off than we had hoped to be if we needed to make a return of 15 per cent. The investment in buying this business fails to meet the criteria using DCF.

SpreadsheetML.com has a useful template (www.spreadsheetml.com/finance/freecapitalbudgeting.shtml).

Aswath Damodaran, who teaches corporate finance and valuation on the MBA programme at the Stern School of Business at New York University, has a wide range of free spreadsheets for all aspects of finance including DCF and IRR (https://pages.stern.nyu.edu/~adamodar/New_Home_Page/spreadsh.htm).

Rules of thumb

Some business sectors have their own yardsticks for estimating the value of a business. For example, sales turnover is often used for computer maintenance and mail order businesses; the number of customers for mobile phone airtime providers; the number of outlets for an estate agency, restaurant or pub chain; and grocery shops are valued partly on their turnover and partly on the value of the stock they hold. The City Flyer Express case study below reveals that landing slots are one of the key metrics used in airline acquisitions. BizStats (www.bizstats.com/reports/valuation-rule-thumb.php) has a nifty table giving a list of these rules.

CASE STUDY
City Flyer Express

Robert Wright, a Cranfield MBA who started up his venture, Connectair, immediately after completing his MBA, sold out to Harry Goodman, late of International Leisure fame, for around £7 ($11/€8.3) million. Not bad for just under five years' work. However, negotiations with Goodman took nearly a year, and the opening offer was barely a seventh of that sum. In the end the deal was valued on a multiple of landing slots, as Goodman planned to use these for his fleet of much larger planes and so create value. Things didn't quite work out as planned and International Leisure went bust. Robert bought the business back from receivership for a nominal £1 and with venture capital from 3i built up the business again, this time under the name City Flyer Express. A decade later he sold the business to British Airways for a healthy £75 ($120/€88.5) million.

Update

Robert was a founder shareholder and former non-exec director (May 2004 – April 2011) at Wizzair, the Hungarian low-cost airline with its head office in Budapest.

Multiple models

Some valuation techniques, particularly those used by business brokers that help sell private companies, involve using a number of adjustments to the basic P/E method. One such approach is based on the following formula:

$$\text{add-back profitability} \times \text{industry sector P/E} + \text{adjustment for assets and liabilities}$$

The add-back profitability involves trying to arrive at what the profit might be in the hands of the acquiring company. In the case where the reported profit of a business for sale is say £500,000 it might be argued that the £50,000 of interest charges should be added back to the profits on the basis that new owners would finance the company in a different way and would have access to these funds as disposable profits. The same argument could be made for the two directors who are paying themselves a hefty £300,000 a year, when in fact the business could be run with a divisional manager by the acquirer paying around £100,000 including a performance-related bonus. That would add a further £200,000 to the profits available in the business. There could be deductions to profits too, if the acquiring firm doesn't expect to be able to retain the income stream post-purchase: specialist consultancy income from work done by one of the owners or the rental income arising from letting out part of the business premises, if that won't continue, for example. To carry our example on let's assume that amounts to a deduction of £100,000. So the business's continuing profits would be assessed as: £500,000 + £50,000 + £200,000 – £100,000 = £650,000. That figure would then be the basis on which to apply the P/E multiple. In the case where the sector P/E is 5, the value would be £3.25 million rather than the £2.5 million that would otherwise have been assumed.

There is one further adjustment made in this valuation approach: an adjustment for assets and liabilities by calculating the net assets, that is the surplus of assets over liabilities. The argument for this is that this represents the current value of the owner's stake in the business. The P/E approach gives the value of future earnings, so adding one to the other gives the 'real' value. In practice any valuation approach is just the starting point for negotiations.

Valuing minority shareholdings

If you are not buying an entire business but taking a minority stake, perhaps putting down a marker for a later bid or as part of a strategic alliance strategy, the rules on value are specialized. The value of your stake will not just be smaller because you have fewer shares, but a minority stake usually can neither force nor prevent the sale of a business. Discounts are applied to most share calculations for a lack of marketability.

EBITDA adjustments

Look back to Chapter 3, where we examined the components of EBITDA. Even having stripped out the elements of cost (interest, tax, depreciation and amortization), there are some other costs that can reasonably be expected to terminate when a business changes hands. Those costs, once added back, will have the effect of increasing profits and hence the potential value of the enterprise. Some such costs might be the rent of any property that won't be required to run the business going forward. That might well be the case if some functions are to be consolidated into the parent company.

It may also be that directors of the company being bought are being paid above the market rate; this is fairly common where the business founder is still in the business. There may also be some directors with very nominal roles but far from nominal pay cheques.

Limit the risks

Buying a business will always be risky. If you have done your homework and got the price right, with any luck the risks will be less. Here are some other things you can do to lessen the risks:

- *Set conditional terms*: for example, you could make part of the price conditional on a certain level of profits being achieved.
- *Handcuff key employees*: if most of the assets you are buying are on two legs, get service contracts or consultancy arrangements in place before the deal is signed.
- *Non-competitive clauses*: make sure that neither the seller nor the key employees can set up in competition, taking all the goodwill you have just bought.
- *Tax clearances*: obviously you want to make sure any tax losses you are buying, or any tax implications in the purchase price, are approved before committing yourself.
- *Warranties and indemnities*: if, after you have bought, you find there is a compulsory purchase order on the vendor's premises and the patent on its exciting new product is invalid, you would quite rightly be rather miffed. Warranties and indemnities set out the circumstances in which the seller will make good the buyer's financial loss, so you could try to include anything crucial that looks worrying under this heading. Not unnaturally, the seller will resist, but you need to be firm on key points.

Manage the acquisition

However well negotiated the deal, most acquisitions that go wrong do so because of the human factor, particularly in the first few weeks after the deal is made public. Some important rules to follow are listed below. Have an outline plan for how to handle the merger and be prepared to be flexible. (Interestingly enough, only one buyer in five has a detailed operational plan of how to manage their acquisition, but as 67 per cent of those being bought believe the buyer has such a plan, it is psychologically important.)

- Let business go on as usual for a few weeks as you learn more about the internal workings of the company. Then you can make informed judgements on who or what should go or remain in post. This rule is followed by 90 per cent of successful acquisitions.

- Hold management and staff meetings on day one to clear up as much misunderstanding as you can. This should be done by the CEO.

- Never announce takeovers on a Friday. Staff will have all weekend to spread rumours. Wednesdays are best: just enough time to clear up misunderstandings, followed by a useful weekend breathing space.

- Make cuts/redundancies a once-only affair. It is always best to cut deep, and then get on with running the business. Continuous sacking saps morale, and all the best people will leave, before it is their turn.

- Set limits of authority and reporting relationships and put all banking relationships in the hands of your own accounts department, as quickly as possible.

CASE STUDY
Till death us do part

When Emad Tawfilis became an investor in Dahl Vineyards, owned by Robert Dahl, he would perhaps have expected something other than being chased through the vines and shot with a .22-caliber semi-automatic handgun by his business partner. Dahl Vineyards opened in mid-summer 2014 on the site of the old Chateau Napa Winery, founded in the late 1980s but vacant for much of the past decade. Physically in poor shape but under new ownership with a new owner and new money the business looked like it may have a future. Dahl was not a wine expert – he was involved in ownership of a Chemical Manufacturing business in Minnesota. The Napa Wine Project, researched and maintained by David Thompson who commented on these events on 15 March 2015: 'Robert has enjoyed wine for many years – one of his father's clients used to trade out wine, and it was this client's wine enjoyed at dinner with his family that, in part, helped nurture his appreciation for wine. He found himself being the only one at parties in college bringing wine, while all his friends were bringing beer.'

In search of a more pleasant way to spend his winters he bought the vineyard, along with a dilapidated range of buildings. Dahl moved quickly to get into contract bottling for négociants and the private labels of several celebrity branded wines. Napa Point Brewing Company, in the hand crafted premium beer business, was added to his portfolio.

On 15 March 2015 Dahl decided the time had come to close down his partnership with Tawfilis. They had filed lawsuits against each other over a $1.2 million investment, with Dahl claiming that the interest Tawfilis was charging on the loan was illegally high. Tawfilis took a rather different position. He asserted that Dahl had tricked him into investing in defunct companies and misused the money invested. Dahl's attorney, Kousha Berokim, said on the day in question the two men were in a meeting that 'was peaceful and held to develop a framework to resolve their dispute,' he said. 'There was certainly no indication of violence.' At 11.30am, Dahl's attorney suggested a short break in what seemed like potentially successful negotiations. Less than 30 minutes later, Tawfilis called 911 saying he was being chased and shot at. He was dead by the time the police reached the scene. When deputies pursuing Dahl by car and helicopter caught up with him on a mountain road, he had shot himself.

Clear the regulators

You may have one further hurdle to face before signing off on an acquisition. If the combination looks like creating a monopoly (this is covered in Chapter 2) you may need to get regulatory clearance. It is not always obvious what is likely to create a monopolistic situation. Europe's long running battle with Microsoft over its domination of the operating system market and Google's stranglehold of search engines seem reasonable areas for the regulator to question. But quite why the Competition and Markets Authority, the UK's monopoly regulator, announced on 9 April 2015 that 'the anticipated acquisition by Poundland plc of 99p Stores Limited will be referred for an in-depth investigation by the CMA' is less clear. The regulator case revolves around their claim that these two stores operate in a unique market with a distinctive price sensitive group of customers selling at a 'single price point'.

The Poundland deal is for a fairly modest £55 million ($80/€75 million), hardly likely to cause a ripple in a retail market worth billions. The company's chief executive, Jim McCarthy told the *Daily Telegraph* that he was 'particularly frustrated that the CMA considered the deal on the basis that the retailer's rivals only main rival was 99p Stores Limited and its other competitors were B&M, Home Bargains, Wilko and Poundstretcher'. He, on the other hand, believes it competes against a wide collection of retailers, including the major supermarket chains.

The main bodies that oversee 'fair competition' are: in the United States, The Federal Trade Commission (www.ftc.gov); in the UK, the CMA (Competition and Markets Authority) (https://commission.europa.eu/business-economy-euro/doing-business-eu/competition-rules_en) and in Europe the European Commission (https://ec.europa.eu/info/business-economy-euro/doing-business-eu/competition-rules_en). Their websites contain information on what they view as potentially problematic to acquisitive companies.

Online video courses and lectures

Advanced valuation and strategy: M&A, private equity and venture capital. Erasmus University Rotterdam: www.coursera.org/learn/advanced-valuation-and-strategy

Alanis Business Academy has a short video taking you through the IRR process: www.youtube.com/watch?v=hKyeS-bAf3I

Developing a Successful Acquisition Strategy: Positioning Your Business for Growth. Georgetown University Alumni Career Services, John Dearing (MBA '96), Managing Director at Capstone Strategic: www.youtube.com/watch?v=NtbwR48FmjM

Enterprise value: Khan Academy: www.khanacademy.org/economics-finance-domain/core-finance/stock-and-bonds/valuation-and-investing/v/enterprise-value

Finance of mergers and acquisitions: valuation and pricing. The University of Illinois at Urbana-Champaign: www.coursera.org/learn/mergers-acquisitions-valuation-pricing

International business venturing abroad. University of Colorado Boulder: www.coursera.org/learn/international-business-venturing-abroad

Price to Earnings Ratio (or P/E ratio): Khan Academy: www.khanacademy.org/economics-finance-domain/core-finance/stock-and-bonds/valuation-and-investing/v/introduction-to-the-price-to-earnings-ratio

Online video case studies

Apple's acquisition strategy: CNBC's Josh Lipton and USA Today San Francisco Bureau Chief Jon Swartz discuss what Apple's acquisition plans say about its hardware business: www.cnbc.com/video/2014/07/28/apples-acquisition-strategy.html

Cisco: an example of best practice in mergers and acquisitions: https://hstalks.com/t/4221/cisco-an-example-of-best-practice-in-mergers-and-a/

Is Facebook's acquisition strategy successful? Scott Redler, Chief Strategic Officer at T3live.com, describes how the tech giant is using acquisitions to penetrate the market: www.cnbc.com/video/2014/03/25/is-facebooks-acquisition-strategy-successful.html

Microsoft closes on $16 billion acquisition of nuance: www.cnbc.com/2021/04/12/microsoft-hunts-for-big-acquisitions-as-antitrust-spotlight-on-rivals.html

Walmart case study – strategic marketing. Rod McNealy, Johnson & Johnson marketing executive: www.youtube.com/watch?v=cFhfOj36s4I

What's Behind Alibaba's Acquisition Strategy? GGV Capital Managing Partner Glenn Solomon discusses Alibaba's acquisition strategy and possible Apple partnership on 'Bloomberg West'. www.bloomberg.com/news/videos/2014-11-04/whats-behind-alibabas-acquisition-strategy

11
Business plans and budgets

- Forecasting sales
- Monitoring economic cycles
- Preparing business plans
- Setting budgets
- Checking on performance

All management decisions have to be set out in a form that will ensure that they can be successfully implemented. For the business or enterprise as a whole that form is a business plan setting out in detail the role each part of the organization has to play for the next three to five years. That period is needed as recognizing an opportunity, developing a product or service to exploit that opportunity and bringing it to market all take time and the plan has to encompass all these stages to be of any value. The dichotomy here is that while strategy takes time for the results to show, the world in which the business is implementing its plans is changing. As one military strategist succinctly put it, all plans disintegrate on contact with the enemy. So three- to five-year business plans need to be reviewed fundamentally each year and progress monitored at least quarterly. It goes without saying that revenue and expenses will be the subject of routine consideration by operating managers on a monthly, weekly and (where fresh produce or similar products are involved) daily basis.

All aspects of preparing the business plan, the supporting forecasts, budgets and economic overview, are tasks that MBAs are invariably expected to be able to carry out, or support line managers in doing so. It calls for a broad level of understanding of key aspects of the business – cash flow, profit margins, funding issues, marketing and selling and human resource issues – that few others in the organization are likely to have. It is an opportunity for an MBA to broaden and deepen his or her relationships with all key executives as well as the board of directors. Often tedious and always time-consuming, the task of preparing business plans should be welcomed as a career progression opportunity par excellence.

Forecasting

Sales drive much of a business's activities; they determine cash flow, stock levels, production capacity and ultimately how profitable or otherwise a business will be, so unsurprisingly much effort goes into attempting to predict future sales. A sales forecast is not the same as a sales objective. An objective is what you want to achieve and will shape a strategy to do so. A forecast is the most likely future outcome given what has happened in the past and the momentum that provides for the business.

Any forecast is made up of three components and to get an accurate forecast you need to decompose the historic data to better understand the impact of each on the end result:

1 *Underlying trend*: the general direction – up, flat or down – over the longer term, showing the rate of change.

2 *Cyclical factors*: the short-term influences that regularly superimpose themselves on the trend. For example, in the summer months you would expect sales of swimwear, ice cream and suntan lotion to be higher than in the winter. Ski equipment would probably follow a reverse pattern.

3 *Random movements*: irregular, random spikes, up or down, caused by unusual and unexplained factors.

Using averages

The simplest forecasting method is to assume that the future will be more or less the same as the recent past. The two most common techniques that use this approach are moving average and weighted moving average.

Moving average takes a series of data from the past, say the last six months' sales, adds them up, divides by the number of months and uses that figure as being the most likely forecast of what will happen in month seven. This method works well in a static, mature market where change happens slowly, if at all.

The *weighted moving average* method gives the most recent data more significance than the earlier data since it gives a better representation of current business conditions. So before adding up the series of data each figure is weighted by multiplying it by an increasingly higher factor as you get closer to the most recent data.

Exponential smoothing and advanced forecasting techniques

Exponential smoothing is a sophisticated averaging technique that gives exponentially decreasing weights as the data get older; conversely more recent data are given relatively more weight in making the forecasting. Double and triple exponential smoothing can be used to help with different types of trend. More sophisticated still are Holt's and Brown's linear exponential smoothing and Box-Jenkins, named after those two statisticians, which applies autoregressive moving average models to find the best fit of a time series.

Fortunately all an MBA needs to know is that these and other statistical forecasting methods exist. The choice of which is the best technique to use is usually down to trial and error. Various software programs will calculate the best-fitting forecast by applying each technique to the historic data you enter. See what actually happens and use the technique that's forecast is closest to the actual outcome. Professor Hossein Arsham of the University of Baltimore (http://home.ubalt.edu/ntsbarsh/Business-stat/stat-data/forecast.htm) provides a useful tool that allows you to enter data and see how different forecasting techniques perform. Duke University's Fuqua School of Business, consistently ranked amongst the top 10 US business schools in every single functional area, provides this helpful link (www.duke.edu/~rnau/411home.htm) to all its lecture material on forecasting.

Causal relationships

Often when looking at data sets it will be apparent that there is a relationship between certain factors. Look at Figure 11.1, which is a chart showing the monthly sales of barbeques and the average temperature in the preceding month for the past eight months.

Figure 11.1 Scatter diagram example

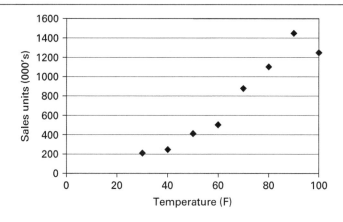

Figure 11.2   Scatter diagram – the line of best fit

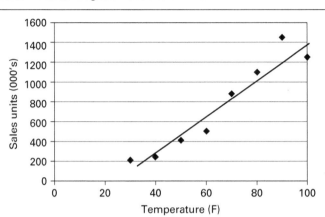

It's not too hard to see that there appears to be a relationship between temperature and sales – as we might expect. By drawing the line that most accurately represents the slope, called the line of best fit, we have a useful tool for estimating what sales might be next month, given the temperature that occurred this month; see Figure 11.2.

The example used is a simple one and the relationship obvious and strong. In real life there is likely to be much more data and it will be harder to see if there is a relationship between the 'independent variable', in this case temperature, and the 'dependent variable', sales volume. Fortunately there is an algebraic formula known as 'linear regression' that will calculate the line of best fit for you.

There are a couple of calculations then needed to test if the relationship is strong (it can be strongly positive; even if strongly negative it will still be useful for predictive purposes) and significant. The tests are known as R-Squared and Student's t-test, and all an MBA needs to know is that they exist and you can probably find the software to calculate them on your computer already. Otherwise you can use Web-Enabled Scientific Services & Applications (www.wessa.net/slr.wasp) software, which covers almost every type of statistic calculation. The software is free online and provided through a joint research project with KU Leuven Association, a network of 13 institutions of higher education in Flanders.

For help in understanding these statistical techniques, read Gerard E Dallal of Tufts' book, *The Little Handbook of Statistical Practice*, available free online (www.jerrydallal.com/LHSP/LHSP.htm). At Princeton's website (www.princeton.edu/~otorres/Regression101.pdf) you can find a tutorial and lecture notes on the subject as taught to its Master of International Business students.

Economic cycles

The current stage of the economic cycle that the business finds itself in when making forecasts will have a significant bearing on decision making. While few MBAs will be expected to have detailed knowledge of economics, they will be required to have a passing appreciation of the subject. Economies tend to follow a cyclical pattern that moves from boom, when demand is strong, to slump – the economists' term for a downturn. The death of the cycle has often been claimed as politicians believe they have become better managers of demand, but the 'this time it's different' school of thinking has been proved wrong time and time again.

The cycle itself is caused by the collective behaviour of billions of people – the unfathomable 'animal spirits' of businesses and households. John Maynard Keynes explained animal spirits this way:

> Most, probably, of our decisions to do something positive, the full consequences of which will be drawn out over many days to come, can only be taken as the result of animal spirits – a spontaneous urge to action rather than inaction, and not as the outcome of a weighted average of quantitative benefits multiplied by quantitative probabilities.

Added to the urge to act is the equally inevitable herd-like behaviour that leads to excessive optimism and pessimism. Charles Mackay (*Extraordinary Popular Delusions and the Madness of Crowds*), Joseph De La Vega (*Confusión de Confusiones*) and the more recent *Irrational Exuberance* (Robert J Shiller, 2nd edn) between them provide a comprehensive insight into the capacity for collective over-reaction. From the tulip mania in 17th-century Holland and the South Sea Bubble (1711–1720) to the internet bubble in 1999 and the collapse in US real estate in 2008 the story behind each bubble has been uncomfortably familiar. Strong market demand for some commodity (gold, copper, oil, etc), currency, property or type of share leads the general public to believe the trend cannot end. Over-optimism leads the public at large to overextend itself in acquiring the object of the mania, while lenders fall over each other to fan the flames. Finally, either the money runs out or groups of investors become cautious. Fear turns to panic selling, so creating a vicious downward spiral that can take years to recover from.

Categories of cycle

Economics is the science, in so far as it can be considered one, of the indistinctly knowable rather than the exactly predictable. Though all cycles, even the one you are in, are difficult to understand or predict with much accuracy there are discernable patterns and some distinctive characteristics.

Figure 11.3 Textbook economic cycle

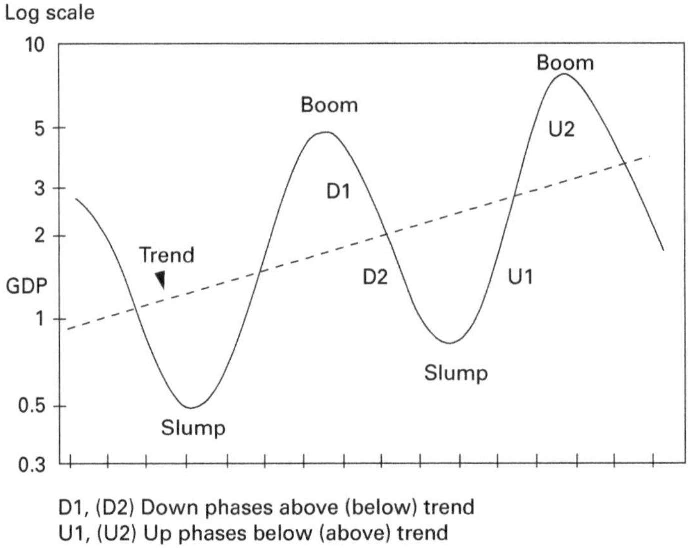

D1, (D2) Down phases above (below) trend
U1, (U2) Up phases below (above) trend

Figure 11.3 shows an elegant curve, which depicts the theoretical textbook cycle. Four phases typically occur in each textbook cycle:

U1, where demand is picking up and toeing the line of the long-term trend;

U2, where demand exceeds the long-term trend;

D1, where demand dips down to hit the long-term trend; and

D2, where demand slumps below the long-term trend.

To make things more complicated there is not one cycle but at least four that operate, each with different characteristics yet interacting one with the others.

Kondratieff's long waves

Kondratieff, a Soviet economist who fell out with Russia's Marxist leaders and died in one of Stalin's prisons, advanced the theory that the advent of capitalism had created long wave economic cycles lasting around 50 years. His theories received a boost when the Great Depression (1929–33) hit world economies and resonated in Britain in 1980–81 when factory closures, high unemployment and crippling inflation devastated the country. The idea of a long wave is supported by evidence that major technologies from the first printing press to the internet take 50 years to yield full value, before themselves being overtaken.

Kuznet's cycle

US economist Simon Kuznet, a Nobel Laureate (1971) worked in the University of Pennsylvania and made a lifelong study of economic cycles. He identified a cycle of 15–25 years duration covering the period it takes to acquire land, get the necessary permissions, build property and sell. Also known as the 'building cycle' this has credibility as so much of economic life is influenced by property and the related purchases of furniture and associated professional charges, for example for lawyers, architects and surveyors.

Juglar cycle

Clement Juglar, a French economist, studied the rise and fall in interest rates and prices in the 1860s. He observed boom and bust waves of 9 to eleven years going through four phases in each cycle – prosperity, where investors pile into new and exciting ventures; crisis, when business failures start to rise; liquidation, when investors pull out of markets; and recession, when the consequences of these failures begin to be felt in the wider economy in terms of job losses and reduced consumption.

Kitchin cycle

In 1923, Joseph Kitchin published in the Harvard University Press an article entitled 'Review of economic statistics,' outlining his discovery of a 40-month cycle resulting from a study of US and UK statistics from 1890 to 1922. He observed a natural cyclical path caused, he believed, by movements in inventories. When demand appears to be stronger than it really is, companies build and carry too much inventory, leading people to overestimate likely future growth. When that higher growth fails to materialize, inventories are reduced, often sharply, so inflicting a 'boom, bust' pressure on the economy.

Monitoring cycles

The Foundation for the Study of Cycles (https://cycles.org/), an international research and educational institution established in 1941 by Harvard economist Edward R Dewey, provides a detailed explanation of different cycles. The Growth and Business Cycle Research Group based in the School of Social Sciences, The University of Manchester (www.socialsciences.manchester.ac.uk/gbcr) provides details of current research, recent publications and downloadable discussion papers on all aspects of business cycles.

Business plans

The plan is in essence the route map from where the business is to where it wants to get and how it will go about getting there. It includes the roles and responsibilities of key players, the resources required in terms of money, people and materials, and so forth. While there is much debate about exactly what should go into the business plan and how it should be laid out, there is no doubt that it is the essential tool for ensuring that a well-thought-out strategy is executed successfully.

CASE STUDY
Boden

Johnnie Boden's first catalogue was hand-drawn by a friend and contained just eight items. That was back in 1991, and since then the business has gone from bedroom to boardroom. In an interview with Dormen (www.dormen.org.uk/2019/07/golden-titbits-kitchen-table-to/), a business mentoring organization, Boden confessed, 'I didn't have a plan for the first 5 years, it just grew around me – and this is typical of many young businesses. However, when I had one of those "perfect storm" years I was suddenly all at sea.' Having a business plan has enabled Boden to make sure the business is on track and identify any areas that are preventing him from reaching his goals.

On 6 October 2022 *The Draper*, a UK fashion magazine, reported that 'clothing and lifestyle retailer Boden reported a 7% rise in sales to £357m for the 52 weeks to 1 January 2022, driven by high demand for dresses and childrenswear'. Performance on every level was moving in the right direction. Profit before tax increased 16 per cent to £221 million, compared with £185 million in 2020, whilst the company pulled in close on 2 million customers, 6 per cent more than the previous year.

Below is the suggested general layout for a business plan as used on the MBA programme at Cranfield. From observations at international business plan competitions, it seems to be fairly universal.

Executive summary

This is the most important part of the plan and will form the heart of any presentation to the board, shareholders or prospective investors. Written last, it should be punchy, short – ideally one page but never more than two – and should enthuse any reader. Its primary purpose is to excite and inspire an audience to want to read the rest of the business plan.

Table 11.1 Executive summary – history and projections

Last year	This year	Business area	Year 1	Year 2	Year 3 etc
		Sales turnover by product/service 1. 2. etc Total sales			
		Gross profit % Operating profit % Total staff nos			
		Sales staff nos Capital employed Return on capital employed %			

The executive summary should start with a succinct table showing past performance in key areas and future objectives; see Table 11.1. This will give readers a clear view of the businesses capacity to perform as well as the scale of the task ahead.

Then the executive summary should continue with sections covering the following areas:

- What the primary products/services are and why they are better or different from what is around now.

- Which markets/customer groups will most need what you plan to offer and why.

- How close you are to being ready to sell your product/service and what if anything remains to be done.

- Why your organization has the skills and expertise to execute this strategy and, if new or additional people are required, who they are or how you will recruit them.

- Financial projections showing in summary the sales, profit, margins and cash position over the next three to five years.

- How the business will operate, sketching out the key steps from buying in any raw materials through to selling, delivering and getting paid.

- The physical resources – equipment, premises – the plan calls for.

The contents – putting flesh on the bones

Unlike the executive summary that is structured to reveal the essence of your business proposition, the plan itself should follow a logical sequence such as this:

- *Vision*: a vision's purpose is to stretch the organization's reach beyond its grasp. Generally, few people concerned with the company can now see how the vision is to be achieved, but all concerned agree that it would be great if it could be. Once your vision becomes reality it may be time for a new challenge, or perhaps even a new business.

- *Mission*: a mission statement explains concisely what you do, who you do it for and why you are better or different from others operating in your market. It should be narrow enough to give focus yet leave enough room for growth. Above all it should be believable to all concerned.

- *Objectives*: these are the big picture numbers such as market share, profit and return on investment that are to be achieved by successfully executing the chosen strategy.

- *Marketing*: this section provides information on the product/service on offer, customers and the size of the market, competitors, proposed pricing, promotion and selling method.

- *Operations*: this area covers any processes such as manufacture, assembly, purchasing, stock holding, delivery/fulfilment and website.

- *Financial projections*: detailed information on sales and cash flow for the period of the plan showing how much money is needed, for what, by when, and the most appropriate source of those funds: long- or short-term borrowings, equity, factoring or leasing finance for example.

- *Premises*: the space and equipment needed (if starting up from home, how the premises will comply with the law).

- *People*: the skills and experience you have on board that will help run this business and implement the chosen strategy; what other people you will need and where you will find them.

- *Administrative matters*: any IP (intellectual property) on your product or service; the insurance you need; the changes, if any, needed to the accounting, control and record systems.

- *Milestone timetable*: this should show the key actions you have still to take to be ready to achieve major objectives and the date these will be completed.

- *Appendices*: use these for any bulky information such as market studies, competitors' leaflets, customer endorsements, technical data, patents, CVs and the like that you refer to in your business plan.

Using business planning software

There are a number of free software packages that will help you through the process of writing a business plan. The ones listed below include some useful resources, spreadsheets and tips that may speed up the process, but are not substitutes for finding out the basic facts about your market, customers and competitors.

Business.org, an online business magazine, produces a regular review of the best business planning software. In 2022 their recommendations were:

- LivePlan: Best overall.
- BizPlanBuilder: Most user-friendly service.
- GoSmallBiz.com: Most extra features.
- PlanGuru: Best financial forecasting.
- BizPlan: Best for equity crowdfunding.
- EnLoop: Cheapest tool for startups.

Budgets and variances

Budgeting is the principal interface between the operating business units and the finance department. As a staff function the finance department or any-one with MBA skills will be expected to assist managers in preparing a detailed budget for the year ahead for every area of the organization and is in effect the first year of the business plan. MBAs are invariably expected to play a role in facilitating the process within their department. Budgets are usually reviewed at least halfway through the year and often quarterly. At that review a further quarter or half-year can be added to the budget to maintain a one-year budget horizon. This is known as a 'rolling quarterly (half-yearly) budget'.

Budget guidelines

Budgets should adhere to the following general principles:

- The budget must be based on realistic but challenging goals. Those goals are arrived at by both a top-down 'aspiration' of senior management and a bottom-up forecast of what the department concerned see as possible.
- The budget should be prepared by those responsible for delivering the results – the salespeople should prepare the sales budget and the production people the production budget. Senior managers must maintain open communication so that everyone knows what other parties are planning for.

- Agreement to the budget should be explicit. During the budgeting process, several versions of a particular budget should be discussed. For example, the boss may want a sales figure of £2 million, but the sales team's initial forecast is for £1.75 million. After some debate, £1.9 million may be the figure agreed upon. Once a figure is agreed, a virtual contract exists that declares a commitment from employees to achieve the target and commitments from the employer to be satisfied with the target and to supply resources to achieve it. It makes sense for this contract to be in writing.
- The budget needs to be finalized at least a month before the start of the year and not weeks or months into the year.
- The budget should undergo fundamental reviews periodically throughout the year to make sure all the basic assumptions that underpin it still hold good.
- Accurate information to review performance against budgets should be available seven to 10 working days before the month's end.

Variance analysis

Explaining variances is also an MBA-type task so performance needs to be carefully monitored and compared against the budget as the year proceeds, and corrective action must be taken where necessary. This has to be done on a monthly basis (or using shorter time intervals if required), showing both the company's performance during the month in question and throughout the year so far.

Looking at Table 11.2 we can see at a glance that the business is behind on sales for this month, but ahead on the yearly target. The convention is to put all unfavourable variations in brackets. Hence, a higher-than-budgeted sales figure does not have brackets, while a higher materials cost does. We can also see that while profit is running ahead of budget, the profit margin is slightly behind (–0.30 per cent). This is partly because other direct costs, such as labour and distribution in this example, are running well ahead of budget.

Flexing the budget

A budget is based on a particular set of sales goals, few of which are likely to be exactly met in practice. Table 11.2 shows a company that has used 762,000 more materials than budgeted. As more has been sold, this is hardly surprising. The way to manage this situation is to flex the budget to show what, given the sales that actually occurred, would be expected to happen to expenses. Applying the budget ratios to the actual data does this. For example, materials were planned to be 22.11 per cent of sales in the budget.

Table 11.2 The fixed budget

Heading	Month			Year to date		
	Budget	Actual	Variance	Budget	Actual	Variance
Sales	805*	753	(52)	6,358	7,314	956
Materials	627	567	60	4,942	5,704	(762)
Materials margin	178	186	8	1,416	1,610	194
Direct costs	74	79	(5)	595	689	(94)
Gross profit	104	107	3	820	921	101
Percentage	**12.92**	**14.21**	**1.29**	**12.90**	**12.60**	**(0.30)**

* Figures indicate thousands of pounds

By applying that to the actual month's sales, a materials cost of 587,000 is arrived at.

Looking at the flexed budget in Table 11.3, we can see that the company has spent £19,000 more than expected on materials, given the level of sales actually achieved, rather than the 762,000 overspend shown in the fixed budget.

The same principle holds for other direct costs, which appear to be running £94,000 over budget for the year. When we take into account the extra sales shown in the flexed budget, we can see that the company has actually spent £4,000 over budget on direct costs. While this is serious, it is not as serious as the fixed budget suggests. The flexed budget allows you to concentrate your efforts on dealing with true variances in performance.

Seasonality and trends

The figures shown for each period of the budget are not the same. For example, a sales budget of 1.2 million for the year does not translate to 100,000 a month. The exact figure depends on two factors: 1) The projected trend may forecast that, while sales at the start of the year are 80,000 a month, they will change to 120,000 a month by the end of the year; the average would be 100,000. 2) By virtue of seasonal factors, each month may also be adjusted up or down from the underlying trend. You could expect the sales of heating oil, for example, to peak in the autumn and tail off in the late spring.

Table 11.3   The flexed budget

Heading	Month			Year to date		
	Budget	Actual	Variance	Budget	Actual	Variance
Sales	753*	753	–	7,314	7,314	–
Materials	587	567	20	5,685	5,704	(19)
Materials margin	166	186	20	1,629	1,610	(19)
Direct costs	69	79	(10)	685	689	(4)
Gross profit	97	107	10	944	921	(23)
Percentage	**12.92**	**14.21**	**1.29**	**12.90**	**12.60**	**(0.30)**

* Figures indicate thousands of pounds

Online video courses and lectures

Action-driven business plan: from the 'classroom' to the world. Israel spacing is too tight here: www.coursera.org/learn/startup-entrepreneurship-capstone

Evaluating a Business Idea: This lecture at Stanford Graduate School of Business Russ Siegelman, a former vice president of Microsoft and venture capitalist at Kleiner Perkins Caufield & Byers, covers the general areas that an entrepreneur should evaluate when considering a new business idea: www.youtube.com/watch?v=y9ClKzMq3n0

Forecasting – Time series models – Simple Exponential smoothing, Prof G Srinivasan, Department of Management Studies, IIT Madras: www.youtube.com/watch?v=k9dhcfIyOFc

From Business Plan to Business Model, Alex Osterwalder talks at Aaltoes Summer of Startups Finnish start-up accelerator programme: www.youtube.com/watch?v=jMxHApgcmoU

How to Write a Business Plan: AVC's and an entrepreneur's perspective on business plans addressing the nuts and bolts detail of what is important in a plan at Berkeley-Haas: www.youtube.com/watch?v=QwlClWaR7DI

Introduction and overview of business plans. MIT Open Courseware: www.youtube.com/watch?v=ZcPNcoTbkIU

Refining and presenting your venture idea. MIT Courseware: https://ocw.mit.edu/courses/15-s21-nuts-and-bolts-of-business-plans-january-iap-2014/resources/part-2-refining-and-presenting-your-venture-idea/

Online video case studies

Boden: Live with Johnnie Boden. April 2020: www.facebook.com/ JohnnieBoden/videos/live-with-johnnie-boden/1123537997979734/

The Branson Business Plan – work hard, play hard: Richard Branson talks to Global Conversation: www.youtube.com/watch?v=g7fbe-oV-X0

Elon Musk's master plan part 3: www.youtube.com/watch?v=KoaZsH1WLV0

Facebook's new business plan: www.cbsnews.com/news/facebook-earnings-report-2021-q3-metaverse/

ImagineX group. This talk was part of the Dean's Speaker Series at Berkeley-Haas on 16 October 2014: www.youtube.com/watch?v=hUsn2tXhE14

12
Additional tools and concepts that aid understanding of financial performance

- Strategic options
- Pricing decisions
- Tools for strategic analysis
- Statistical methods

There are a range of tools and concepts that, whilst not falling directly under the umbrella of business finance, are central to understanding financial outcomes. An appreciation of these is essential to be able to play a rounded role in a management team.

Strategy and its relationship with cost

Credit for devising the most succinct and usable way to get a handle on the big picture has to be given to Michael E Porter, who trained as an economist at Princeton, taking an MBA (1971) and PhD (1973) at Harvard Business School, where he is now a professor. His book, *Competitive Strategy: Techniques for analyzing industries and competitors* (1980, Free Press, Old Tappan, New Jersey), which is in its 63rd printing and has been translated into 19 languages, sets out the now accepted methodology for devising strategy.

The three generic strategies

Porter's first observation was that two factors above all influenced a business's chances of making superior profits. First, there was the attractiveness or otherwise of the industry in which it primarily operated. Second – and in terms of an organization's sphere of influence, more importantly – was how the business positioned itself within that industry. In that respect a business could only have a cost advantage in that it could make a product or deliver a service for less than others. Or it could be different in a way that mattered to consumers, so that its offers would be unique, or at least relatively so. He added a further twist to his prescription. Businesses could follow either a cost-advantage path or a differentiation path industry wide, or they could take a third path – they could concentrate on a narrow specific segment either with cost advantage or differentiation. This he termed 'focus' strategy.

Table 12.1   Gaining competitive advantage

Market Scope	Competitive Advantage	
	Low Cost	Unique Product and or Service
Broad Whole Market	Cost Leadership	Differentiation
Narrow Specific Market Segment(s)	Focus Low Cost	Differentiation

Cost leadership

Low cost should not be confused with low price. A business with low costs may or may not pass those savings on to customers. Alternatively, it could use that position alongside tight cost controls and low margins to create an effective barrier to others considering either entering or extending their penetration of that market. Low-cost strategies are most likely to be achievable in large markets, requiring large-scale capital investment, where production or service volumes are high and economies of scale can be achieved from long runs.

Low costs are not a lucky accident; they can be achieved through these main activities:

- Operating efficiencies: new processes, methods of working or less costly ways of working. Ryanair and easyJet are examples where analysing every component of the business made it possible to strip out major elements of cost – meals, free baggage and allocated seating, for example – while leaving the essential proposition – 'We will fly you from A to B' – intact.

- Product redesign. This involves rethinking a product or service proposition fundamentally to look for more efficient ways to work or cheaper substitute materials to work with. The motor industry has adopted this approach with 'platform sharing', in which major players including Citroën, Peugeot and Toyota have rethought their entry car models to share major components. This has now become common.

- Product standardization. A wide range of product and service offers claiming to extend customer choice invariably leads to higher costs. The challenge is to be sure that proliferation gives real choice and adds value. In 2008 the UK railway network took a long, hard look at its dozens of different fare structures and scores of names, often for identical price structures, that had remained largely unchanged since the 1960s, and reduced them to three basic product propositions. Adopting this and other common standards across the rail network, it estimates, will substantially reduce the currently excessive £0.5 billion transaction cost of selling £5 billion worth of tickets.

- Economies of scale. These can be achieved only by being big or bold. The same head office, warehousing network and distribution chain can support Tesco's 3,263 stores as it could, say, the 997 that Somerfield have. The former will have a lower cost base by virtue of having more outlets to spread its costs over as well as having more purchasing power.

The experience (or learning) curve

The fact that costs declined as the output volume of a product or service increased, though well known earlier, was first developed as a usable accounting process by T P Wright, an American aeronautical engineer, in 1936. His process became known as the cumulative average model or Wright's model. Subsequently models were developed by a team of researchers at Stanford known as the unit time model or Crawford's model, and the Boston Consulting Group (BCG) popularized the process with their experience curve, showing that each time the cumulative volume of doing something – either making a product or delivering a service – doubled, the unit cost dropped by a constant and predictable amount. The reasons for the cost drop include:

- Repetition makes people more familiar with tasks and consequently faster.

- More efficient materials and equipment become available from suppliers themselves as their costs go down through the experience curve effect.
- Organization, management and control procedures improve.
- Engineering and production problems are solved.

BCG was founded in 1963 by Bruce D Henderson, a former Bible salesman and engineering graduate from Vanderbilt University, who left the Harvard Business School 90 days before graduation to work for Westinghouse Corporation. From there he went on to head Arthur D Little's management services unit before joining the Boston Safe Deposit and Trust Company to start a consulting arm for the bank. The experience curve was the strategy tool that put BCG on the path to success and has served it well ever since.

The value of the experience curve as a strategic process is that it helps a business predict future unit costs and gives a signal when costs fail to drop at the historical rate, both vital pieces of information for firms pursuing a cost leadership strategy. Every industry has a different experience curve that varies over time. You can find out more about how to calculate the curve for your industry on the Management and Accounting website (http://maaw. info/LearningCurveSummary.htm).

Figure 12.1   The experience curve

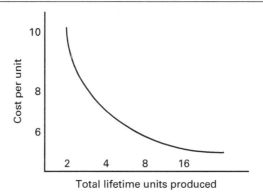

Total lifetime units produced

Differentiation

The key to differentiation is a deep understanding of what customers really want and need and more importantly what they are prepared to pay more for. Apple's opening strategy was based around a 'fun' operating system based on icons, rather than the dull MS-DOS. This belief was based on its understanding that computer users were mostly young and wanted an intuitive command system and the 'graphical user interface' delivered just that. Apple has continued its differentiation strategy, but adds design and fashion to ease of control as the ways in which it delivers extra value. Sony and

BMW are also examples of differentiators. Both have distinctive and desirable differences in their products and neither they nor Apple offer the lowest price in their respective industries; customers are willing to pay extra for the idiosyncratic and prized differences embedded in their products.

Focus

Focused strategy involves concentrating on serving a particular market or a defined geographic region. IKEA, for example, targets young white-collar workers as its prime customer segment.

Warren Buffett, the world's richest man, who knows a thing or two about focus, combined with Mars to buy US chewing gum manufacturer Wrigley for $23 billion (£11.6 billion) in May 2008. Chicago-based Wrigley, which launched its Spearmint and Juicy Fruit gums in the 1890s, has specialized in chewing gum ever since and consistently outperformed its more diversified competitors. Wrigley is the only major consumer products company to grow comfortably faster than the population in its markets and above the rate of inflation. Over the past decade or so, for example, other consumer product companies have diversified. Gillette moved into batteries, used to drive many of its products, by acquiring Duracell. Nestlé bought Ralston Purina, Dreyer's, Ice Cream Partners and Chef America. Both have trailed Wrigley's performance.

Businesses often lose their focus over time and periodically have to rediscover their core strategic purpose. Procter & Gamble (P&G) is an example of a business that had to refocus to cure weak growth. In 2000, the company was losing share in seven of its top nine categories, and had lowered earnings expectations four times in two quarters. This prompted the company to restructure and refocus on its core business: big brands, big customers and big countries. They sold off non-core businesses, establishing five global business units with a closely focused product portfolio.

First-to-market fallacy

'Gaining first-mover advantage' are words used like a mantra to justify high expenditure and a headlong rush into new strategic areas. This concept is one of the most enduring in business theory and practice. Entrepreneurs and established giants are always in a race to be first. Research from the 1980s that shows that market pioneers have enduring advantages in distribution, product-line breadth, product quality and, especially, market share underscores this principle.

Beguiling though the theory of first-mover advantage is, it is probably wrong. Gerard Tellis, of the University of Southern California, and Peter Golder, of New York University's Stern business school, argued in their book *Will and Vision: How latecomers grow to dominate markets* (2001, McGraw-Hill) and subsequent research that previous studies on the subject were deeply flawed. In the first instance, earlier studies were based on surveys of surviving companies and brands, excluding all the pioneers that failed. This helps some companies look as though they were first to market even when they were not. P&G boasts that it created America's disposable nappy (diaper) business. In fact, a company called Chux launched its product a quarter of a century before P&G entered the market in 1961.

Also, the questions used to gather much of the data in earlier research were at best ambiguous, and perhaps dangerously so. For example, the term 'one of the pioneers in first developing such products or services' was used as a proxy for 'first to market'. The authors emphasize their point by listing popular misconceptions of who were the real pioneers across the 66 markets they analysed; online book sales: Amazon (wrong), Books.com (right); copiers: Xerox (wrong), IBM (right); PCs: IBM/Apple (both wrong) – Micro Instrumentation Telemetry Systems (MITS) introduced its PC, the Altair, a $400 kit, in 1974, followed by Tandy Corporation (Radio Shack) in 1977.

In fact, the most compelling evidence from all the research was that nearly half of all firms pursuing a first-to-market strategy were fated to fail, while those following fairly close behind were three times as likely to succeed. Tellis and Golder claim the best strategy is to enter the market 19 years after pioneers, learn from their mistakes, benefit from their product and market development and be more certain about customer preferences.

Industry analysis

Aside from articulating the generic approach to business strategy, Porter's other major contribution to the field was what has become known as the Five Forces theory of industry structure. Porter postulated that the five forces that drive competition in an industry have to be understood as part of process of choosing which of the three generic strategies to pursue. The forces he identified are:

1 Threat of substitution. Can customers buy something else instead of your product? For example, Apple and to a lesser extent Sony have laptop computers that are distinctive enough to make substitution difficult. Dell, on the other hand, faces intense competition from dozens of other suppliers with near-identical products competing mostly on price alone.

2 Threat of new entrants. If it is easy to enter your market, start-up costs are low and there are no barriers to entry such as intellectual property protection, then the threat is high.

3 Supplier power. The fewer the suppliers, usually the more powerful they are. Oil is a classic example, where fewer than a dozen countries supply the whole market and consequently can set prices.

4 Buyer power. In the food market, for example, with just a few powerful supermarket buyers being supplied by thousands of much smaller businesses, these buyers are often able to dictate terms.

5 Industry competition. The number and capability of competitors are one determinant of a business's power. Few competitors with relatively less attractive products or services lower the intensity of rivalry in a sector. Often these sectors slip into oligopolistic behaviour, preferring to collude rather than compete.

Figure 12.2 Five Forces theory of industry analysis (after Porter)

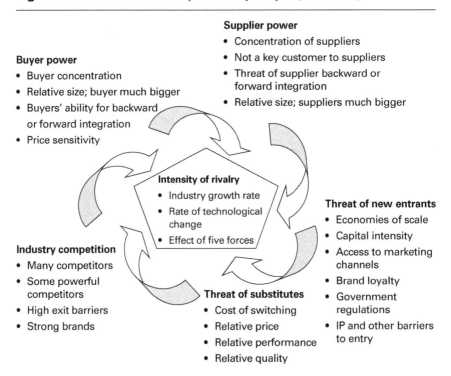

Supplier power
- Concentration of suppliers
- Not a key customer to suppliers
- Threat of supplier backward or forward integration
- Relative size; suppliers much bigger

Buyer power
- Buyer concentration
- Relative size; buyer much bigger
- Buyers' ability for backward or forward integration
- Price sensitivity

Intensity of rivalry
- Industry growth rate
- Rate of technological change
- Effect of five forces

Threat of new entrants
- Economies of scale
- Capital intensity
- Access to marketing channels
- Brand loyalty
- Government regulations
- IP and other barriers to entry

Industry competition
- Many competitors
- Some powerful competitors
- High exit barriers
- Strong brands

Threat of substitutes
- Cost of switching
- Relative price
- Relative performance
- Relative quality

You can see a video clip of Professor Porter discussing the Five Forces model on the Harvard Business School website or at: https://youtu.be/mYF2_FBCvXw.

The importance of market share

The relevant market will be shared by various competing businesses in different proportions. Typically there will be a market leader, a couple of market followers and a host of businesses trailing in their wake. The portion each competitor has of a market is its market share. You will find that marketing people are fixated on market share, perhaps even more so than on absolute sales. That may appear little more than a rational desire to beat the 'enemy' and appear higher in rankings, but it has a much more deep-seated and profound logic.

Figure 12.3   Market share of UK gluten free segment of the food market

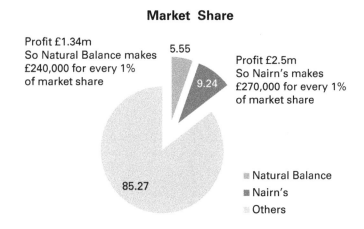

Market Share

Profit £1.34m
So Natural Balance makes
£240,000 for every 1%
of market share

5.55

9.24

Profit £2.5m
So Nairn's makes
£270,000 for every 1%
of market share

85.27

- Natural Balance
- Nairn's
- Others

Back in the 1960s a firm of American management consultants observed a consistent relationship between the cost of producing an item (or delivering a service) and the total quantity produced over the life of the product concerned. They noticed that total unit costs (labour and materials) fell by between 20 per cent and 30 per cent for every doubling of the cumulative quantity produced (see earlier in this chapter for more on the experience curve effect).

Figure 12.3 demonstrates the advantage of market share even where the shares are relatively small and the businesses are already operating successfully. Nairn's larger market share gives it an eighth more profit per percentage point of market share than its smaller rival. Natural Balance Foods, the brand behind Nakd and Trek bars, was started in Oxfordshire by Californian-born brothers Jamie and Greg Combs in 2005. Securing a contract to supply the British Athletic Association boosted its credibility. The need to grow market share explained, in part at least, why in March 2015 the company hired advisors at industry specialist Stamford Partners to find new investors to fund growth.

Pricing and management decision making

The area with which managers with responsibility for finance and all others – marketing, sales, HR, NPD et al – usually have the most contact, and not infrequently conflict, is pricing. Accountants focus on cash flow and margins, marketing have brand image in mind, and the sales team are concerned with targets and getting to a bonus threshold. So, it is essential to have an appreciation of the wider forces at work here.

The economic theory behind pricing

Figure 12.4 represents a theoretical demand curve and the principal ways that price and demand can interact. The four conditions that economists cluster analysis under are:

- Perfectly inelastic. A recent real-world example of perfectly (nearly) inelastic demand is Covid-19 vaccines. Every developed economy wanted a vaccine regardless of price, and the drug companies moved heaven and earth to meet whatever amount was demanded.

- Perfectly elastic. Commodities such corn and wheat are usually sold in a highly competitive marketplace. As long as no external event, such as occurred when Russia invaded Ukraine in 2022, affects supply then farmers can't sell for more than the going price since buyers can easily buy from their competitors. Nor will farmers will sell for a lower price, since they can sell all that they have for the going rate.

- Unit elastic. This occurs where the change in demand is directly proportional to the change in price. So if you are selling baked beans and raising the price by 10 per cent sees demand falling off by 10 per cent, you are experiencing unit elastic demand.

- Relatively elastic. This describes the most usual circumstance where price and demand are related but in a complex and changing way. Changes in price will influence demand, but not in a precise or permanent manner.

Figure 12.4   Demand curve

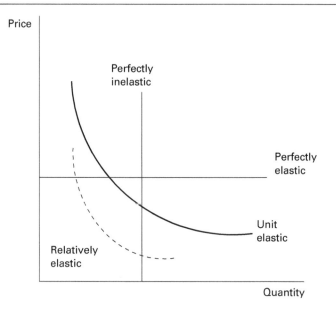

Pricing to achieve objectives

The main reasons for setting price levels are clustered under these headings, and all are aimed ultimately at increasing profit:

1 Improving customer retention. It can cost up to seven times more to win a customer than retain an old one, with a corresponding erosion of profit. So pricing to keep customers can pay.

2 Increasing sales volume. Higher volumes can result in lower unit costs and hence higher profits.

3 Enhancing brand equity. The value premium of a product with a recognizable name when compared to a generic equivalent provides opportunities for changes in pricing.

4 Competing for market share. 'Specifically, as market share increases, a business is likely to have a higher profit margin, a declining purchases-to-sales ratio, a decline in marketing costs as a percentage of sales, higher quality, and higher priced products' (R D Buzzell et al., 1975, 'Market share-a key to profitability', *Harvard Business Review*, 53 (1), 97–106.).

During the autumn of 2022 when the Russian-induced cost of living crisis hit UK consumers, Lidl and Aldi were able to increase their market share. The Waitrose brand, being stronger than Morrisons, suffered a much smaller loss in market share of 0.3 per cent compared to 0.7 per cent (see Figures 12.5 and 12.6).

Tools for strategic financial analysis

These are the important tools that, as a finance specialist, you need an appreciation of. Alongside any investment proposal, performance review or business plan you can expect to see one or more of these deployed. Indeed, you are likely to be expected to incorporate them yourself into arguments and appraisals.

Ansoff growth matrix

Igor Ansoff, while Professor of Industrial Administration in the Graduate School at Carnegie Mellon University, published his landmark book *Corporate Strategy* in 1965 in which he explained a way of categorizing strategies as an aid to understanding the nature of the risks involved. He invited his students to consider growth options as a square matrix divided into four segments (Figure 12.7). The x-axis is divided into existing and new products, and the y-axis into existing and new markets. Ansoff assigned titles and level of risk to the resulting types of strategy. You can find out more about the matrix at www.ansoffmatrix.com.

Figure 12.5 Pricing: average basket price of 47 goods, July 2022, by supermarket

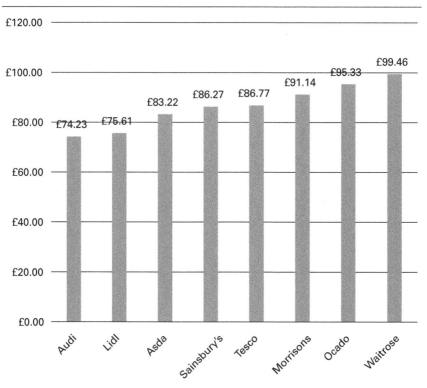

SOURCE: Which?, Which is the cheapest supermarket in 2022? www.which.co.uk/news/article/which-was-the-cheapest-supermarket-in-september-2022-aBfRG9E6JGoI

- Market penetration involves selling more of your existing products and services to existing customers – the lowest-risk strategy.
- Product/service development involves creating extensions to your existing products or new products to sell to your existing customer base. This is more risky than market penetration, but less risky than market development.
- Market development involves entering new market segments or completely new markets, either in your home country or abroad. You will face new competitors and may not understand the customers as well as you do your current ones.
- Diversification is selling new products into new markets – the most risky strategy as both are relative unknowns. Avoid this strategy unless all others have been exhausted. Diversification can be further subdivided into four categories of increasing risk profile:

Figure 12.6 Movements in supermarkets' market share, October 2022

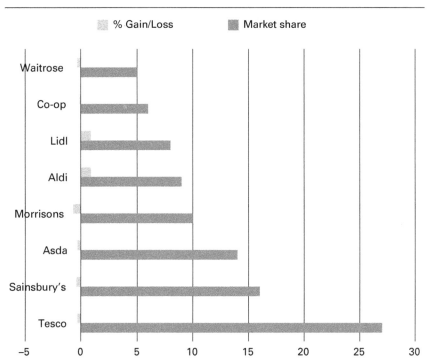

SOURCE: Kantar, www.kantarworldpanel.com/en/grocery-market-share/great-britain

- horizontal diversification: entirely new product into current market;
- vertical diversification: move backwards into firm's suppliers or forwards into customer's business;
- concentric diversification: new product closely related to current products either in terms of technology or marketing presence but in a new market;
- conglomerate diversification: completely new product into a new market.

Boston matrix

Developed in 1969 by the Boston Consulting Group, this tool can be used in conjunction with the life-cycle concept to plan a portfolio of product/service offers. The thinking behind the matrix is that a company's products and services should be classified according to their ability to either generate or consume cash against two dimensions: the market growth rate and the company's market share. Cash is used as the measure rather than profit, as that is the real resource used to invest in new offers. The objective then is to

Figure 12.7   Ansoff growth matrix

	Existing Products	New Products or Services
Existing Markets	**Market Penetration** Sell more of your existing products and services to existing customers – the lowest-risk strategy.	**Product/Service Development** Creating extensions to your existing products or new products to sell to your existing customer base.
New Markets	**Market Development** Entering new market segments or completely new markets either in your home country or abroad.	**Diversification** Selling new products into new markets; the most risky strategy as both are relative unknowns. Avoid unless all other strategies have been exhausted.

use the positive cash flow generated from 'cash cows', usually mature products that no longer need heavy marketing support budgets, to invest in 'stars', the fast-growing, usually newer products, positioned in markets in which the company already has a high market share – usually newer markets. 'Dogs' should be disinvested and 'question marks' limited in number and watched carefully to see if they are more likely to become stars or dogs (see www.bcg.com/about/overview/our-history/growth-share-matrix).

Figure 12.8   Boston matrix

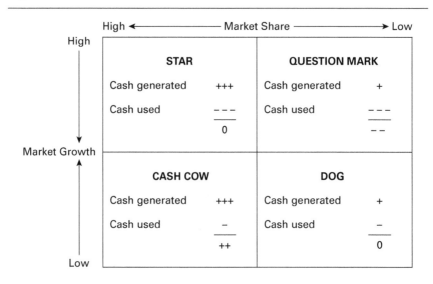

GE–McKinsey directional policy matrix

General Electric was much taken by the visual aspect of the Boston matrix and was using it to enhance its own performance while working with another consulting firm, McKinsey and Company. Between them in 1971 they came up with a variant and in some ways an improvement by substituting business strength and industry attractiveness for market share and market growth rate – the logic being that although these are subjective measures they are more accessible than market growth and share, as these are hard to establish and in any event the figures are themselves largely subjective suppositions based largely on opinions (see www.youtube.com/watch?v=j54nbyuJuU8).

Figure 12.9   GE–McKinsey directional policy matrix

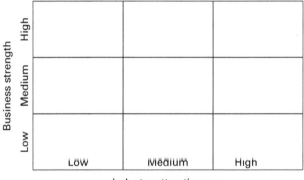

Industry attractiveness

Long-run return pyramid

Another helpful marketing planning tool is the long-run return pyramid, which is in effect a checklist of growth options. None of the options are mutually exclusive and the tool does not provide for any form of evaluation. Nevertheless, it can be a valuable *aide memoire* to ensure that no stone has been left unturned during the strategic review process. The pyramid's pedigree is unknown, but it is loosely based on DuPont's return-on-investment pyramid, used to trace all the performance ratios that influence return on investment. The pyramid in the form shown in Figure 12.10 is attributed to Robert Brown, a senior academic at Cranfield School of Management.

Balanced scorecard

The balanced scorecard (see Figure 12.11), developed by Robert Kaplan and David Norton and published in a *Harvard Business Review* article in 1992, is a management process that sets out to align business activities to the

Figure 12.10   Long-run return pyramid

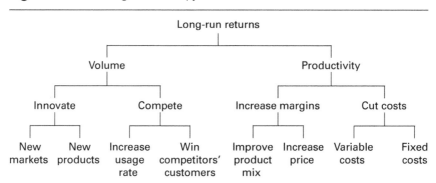

vision and strategy of the organization, improve internal and external communication and monitor organization performance against strategic goals. Its uniqueness was to add non-financial performance measures to traditional financial targets to give managers and directors a more 'balanced' view of organizational performance.

Although Kaplan and Norton are credited with coining the phrase, the idea of a balanced scorecard originated with General Electric's work on performance measurement reporting in the 1950s, and the work of French process engineers (who created the *tableau de bord* – literally, a 'dashboard' of performance measures) in the early part of the 20th century.

Four perspectives are included in the management process, which in effect extends the range of management by objectives and value-based management into areas beyond purely financial target setting. A number of objectives, measures, targets and initiatives can be set to achieve specific key performance indicators (KPIs) for each perspective:

1 Financial: These include KPIs for return on investment, cash flow, profit margins and shareholder value.

2 Customers: Here the KPIs can be for customer retention rates, satisfaction levels, referrals and complaints.

3 Internal business processes: These can include stock turn, accident rates, defects in production, reduction in the number of processes and improvements in communication.

4 Learning and growth: Employee turnover, morale levels, training and development achievements and internal promotions vs new recruits are all KPIs to use here.

The four perspectives are linked by a double feedback loop, the purpose of which is to ensure that KPIs are not in conflict with one another. For example, if customer satisfaction could be achieved by improving delivery times, achieving that by, say, increasing stock levels might conflict with a financial target of improving return on capital employed.

Figure 12.11   The balanced scorecard

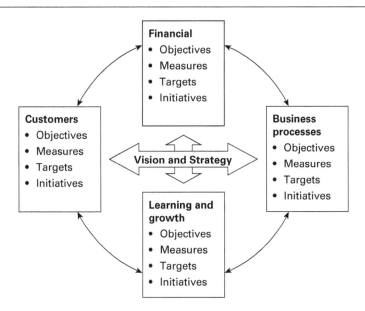

Decision trees

Decision trees are a visual as well as valuable way to organize data so as to help make a choice between several options with different chances of occurring and different results if they do occur. Trees were first used in business in the 1960s but became seriously popular from 1970 onwards when algorithms were devised to generate decision trees and automatically reduce them to a manageable size.

Making a decision tree requires these steps to be carried out initially, from which the diagram can be drawn:

• Establish all the alternatives.

• Estimate the financial consequences of each alternative.

• Assign the risk in terms of uncertainty allied with each alternative.

Figure 12.12 shows an example decision tree. The convention is that squares represent decisions and circles represent uncertain outcomes. In this example the problem being decided on is whether to launch a new product or revamp an existing one. The uncertain outcomes are whether the result of the decision will be successful (£10 million profit), just okay (£5 million profit) or poor (£1 million). In the case of launching a new product, the management's best estimate is that there is a 10 per cent (0.1 in decimals) chance of success, a 40 per cent chance it will be okay and a 50 per cent chance it will result in poor sales. Multiplying the expected profit arising

Figure 12.12 Example decision tree

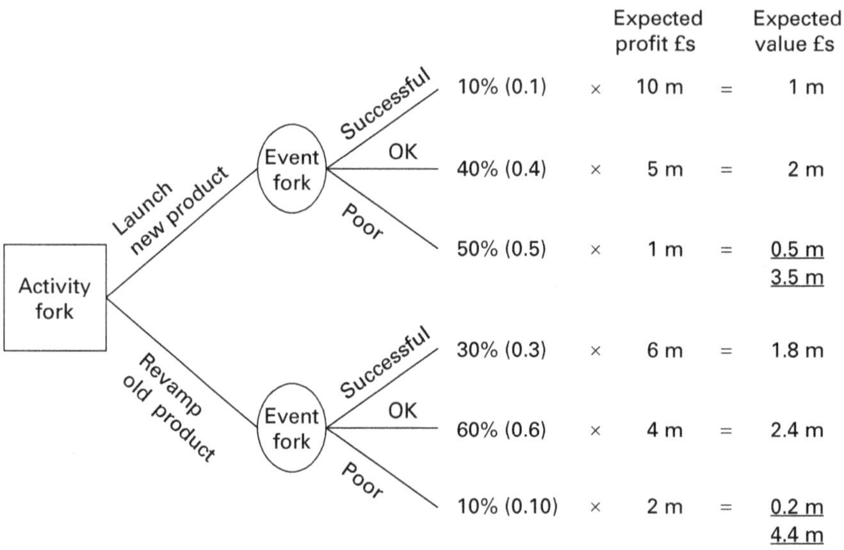

from each possible outcome by the probability of its occurring gives what is termed as an 'expected value'. Adding up the expected values of all the possible outcomes for each decision suggests in this case that revamping an old product will produce the more profit.

The example is a very simple one, and in practice decisions are much more complex. We may have intermediate decisions to make, such as whether to invest heavily and bring the new product to market quickly, or whether to spend money on test marketing. This will introduce more decisions and more uncertain outcomes represented by a growing number of 'nodes', the points at which new branches in the tree are formed.

Statistics

Statistics are the set of tools that we use to help us assess the truth or otherwise of something we observe. For example, if the last 10 phone calls a company received were all cancelling orders, does that signal that a business has a problem, or is that event within the bounds of possibility? If it is within the bounds of possibility, what are the odds that we could still be wrong and really have a problem? A further issue is that usually we can't easily examine the entire population so we have to make inferences from samples; and unless those samples are representative of the population we are interested in and of sufficient size, we could still be very wrong in our interpretation of the evidence. At the time of writing, there is much debate as to how much of a surveillance society Britain has become. The figure of 4.2 million cameras, one for every 14 people, is the accepted statistic. However, a diligent journalist tracked down the evidence to find that extrapolation of a survey of a single street in a single town was how that figure had been arrived at.

Central tendency

The most common way statistics are considered is around a single figure that purports in some way to be representative of a population at large. There are three principal ways of measuring tendency; these are the most often confused and frequently misrepresented set of numbers in the whole field of statistics.

To analyse anything in statistics you first need a 'data set', such as the following for the selling prices of a company's products:

Product 1: selling price 30

Product 2: selling price 40

Product 3: selling price 10

Product 4: selling price 15

Product 5: selling price 10

The mean (or average)

This is the most common tendency measure and is used as a rough-and ready check for many types of data. In the example above, adding up the prices – 105 – and dividing by the number of products – five – you arrive at a mean, or average, selling price of 21.

The median

The median is the value occurring at the centre of a data set. Recasting the figures above puts Product 4's selling price of 15 in that position, with two higher and two lower prices. The median comes into its own in situations where the outlying values in a data set are extreme, as they are in our example, where in fact most of the products sell for well below 21. In this case the median would be a better measure of the central tendency. You should always use the median when the distribution is skewed. You can use either the mean or the median when the population is symmetrical as they will give very similar results.

The mode

The mode is the observation in a data set that appears the most; in this example it is 10. So if we were surveying a sample of the customers of the company in this example we would expect more of them to say they were paying 10 for their products, though as we know the average price is 21.

Variability

As well as measuring how values cluster around a central value, to make full use of the data set, we need to establish how much those values could vary. The two most common methods employed are range and standard deviation from the mean.

Range

The range is calculated as the maximum figure minus the minimum figure. In the example being used here that is 40 – 10 = 30. This figure gives us an idea of how dispersed the data is and so how meaningful the average figure alone might be.

Standard deviation from the mean

This is a rather more complicated concept as you need first to grasp the central limit theorem, which states that the mean of a sample of a large population will approach 'normal' as the sample gets bigger. The most valuable feature here is that even quite small samples are normal. The bell curve, also called the Gaussian distribution – named after Johann Carl Friedrich Gauss (1777–1855), a German mathematician and scientist – shows how far values are distributed around a mean. The distribution, referred to as the standard deviation, is what makes it possible to state how accurate a sample is likely to be. When you hear the results of opinion polls predicting elections based on samples as small as 1,000, these are usually reliable within four percentage points, equivalent to 19 times out of 20, you have a measure of how important this concept is.

Figure 12.13 is a normal distribution that shows that 68.2 per cent of the observations of a normal population will be found within 1 standard deviation of the mean, 95.5 per cent within 2 standard deviations, and 99.7 per cent within 3 standard deviations. So almost 100 per cent of the observations will be observed in a span of 6 standard deviations, 3 below the mean and 3 above the mean. The standard deviation is an amount calculated from the values in the sample. (You can get free tutorials on this and other aspects of statistics at Web Interface for Statistics Education (http://wise.cgu.edu). This is a service provided by Claremont Graduate University.)

Figure 12.13   Normal distribution curve (bell) showing standard deviation

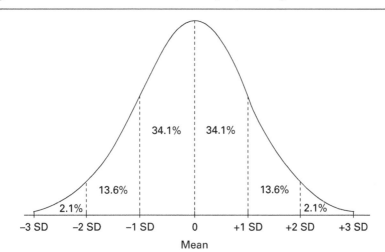

Online video courses and lectures

Business Strategy Specialization. Covering the tools you need to analyse, evaluate and recommend specific actions organizations can take to grow their value and avoid common growth pitfalls. Darden at University of Virginia: www.coursera.org/specializations/business-strategy

Create a Balanced Scorecard to Align Priorities. An online project, after which you will be able to create a balanced scorecard to communicate team goals and measure the progress made toward those goals: www.coursera.org/projects/create-balanced-scorecard-align-priorities-miro

Foundations of Strategy. Looking through the lens of Porter's Five Forces at your industry. IE Business School: www.coursera.org/learn/foundations-of-strategy-ie-business-school

Inferential and Predictive Statistics for Business. The course aims to cover statistical ideas that apply to managers' decision making. The University of Illinois at Urbana-Champaign: www.coursera.org/learn/business-statistics

International Business Environment. You'll learn about core analysis methods, including PESTLE, and Boston Box Matrices, as well as the applications of Porter's Five Forces. University of London: www.coursera.org/learn/global-business-environment

The Five Competitive Forces That Shape Strategy. An interview with Michael Porter at Harvard: www.youtube.com/watch?v=mYF2_FBCvXw

INDEX

CPSIA information can be obtained
at www.ICGtesting.com
Printed in the USA
JSHW041741160523
PP12598800001B/4